D0927999

Race and Meaning

Race and Meaning

The African American Experience in Missouri

Gary R. Kremer

UNIVERSITY OF MISSOURI PRESS

COLUMBIA

Cataloging-in-Publication data available from the Library of Congress.
ISBN 978-0-8262-2043-1

∞™ This paper meets the requirements of the
American National Standard for Permanence of Paper
for Printed Library Materials, Z39.48, 1984.

Typesetter: K. Lee Design & Graphics
Typeface: Minion

Contents

Acknowledgments   ix

Prologue
Race and Meaning in Missouri History: A Personal Journey   1

Chapter 1
Some Aspects of Black Education in Reconstruction
Missouri: An Address by Richard B. Foster   17

Chapter 2
Pennytown: A Freedmen's Hamlet, 1871–1945   28

Chapter 3
"Yours for the Race": The Life and Work of
Josephine Silone Yates   41

Chapter 4
The World of Make-Believe: James Milton Turner
and Black Masonry   54

Chapter 5
George Washington Carver's Missouri   68

Chapter 6
Nathaniel C. Bruce, Black Education, and the
"Tuskegee of the Midwest"   82

Chapter 7
"The Black People Did the Work": African American
Life in Arrow Rock, Missouri, 1850–1960   95

Chapter 8
"Just like the Garden of Eden": African American
Community Life in Kansas City's Leeds   113

Chapter 9
The Whitley Sisters Remember: Living with
Segregation in Kansas City, Missouri   130

Chapter 10
The Missouri Industrial Home for Negro Girls: The 1930s   142

Chapter 11
Black Culture Mecca of the Midwest: Lincoln University,
1921–1955   158

Chapter 12
Lake Placid: "A Recreational Center for Colored
People" in the Missouri Ozarks   171

Chapter 13
William J. Thompkins: African American Physician,
Politician, and Publisher   185

Chapter 14
The Abraham Lincoln Legacy in Missouri   200

Epilogue
New Sources and Directions for Research on the
African American Experience in Missouri   213

Notes   225

Index   261

For Lorenzo Johnston Greene,
mentor and friend,
with deepest appreciation

Acknowledgments

I have incurred many debts over the past four decades doing research for and writing the essays included in this anthology. I apologize in advance for my inevitable failure to remember all of those individuals who have assisted me through the years.

I want to begin by thanking University of Missouri Press Editor-in-Chief and Associate Director Clair Willcox. This book was his idea. I am grateful to him for encouraging me to pull together these essays and for offering helpful critical advice along the way. I am also indebted to two anonymous readers for the Press whose suggestions helped me to produce a final product that is much improved over my initial effort. I also appreciate the help of Press staff members Jane Lago, Mary Conley, Greg Haefner, Kristi Henson, and especially managing editor Sara Davis and my editor, Pippa Letsky.

Through the years, countless individuals have invited me in to their homes so that I could listen to their stories about Missouri's rich African American heritage. I am especially indebted to the Whitley Sisters (Irene Whitley Marcus, Geneva Whitley Carple, and Gertrude Whitley Bardwell). Likewise, sisters Vivienne Starks Smith and Yvonne Starks Wilson were unfailingly generous with their time. Leonard Pryor and Mamie Hughes also made themselves and their rich collections of photographs and documents available.

I have taught thousands of students since I first stepped into a Lincoln University classroom as an instructor in 1972. Often, those students proved an important sounding board for me as I talked about whichever research project I was engaged in at the time. Many of those students asked questions and offered suggestions that helped to inform and shape my research and writing. In a few instances, some of them engaged directly in research with and for me. I am grateful to all who helped in any way, especially students and colleagues who co-authored some of the essays contained in this collection: Lynn Morrow, Linda Rea Gibbens, Trina Philpot, Cindy M. Mackey, Antonio F. Holland, Evan P. Orr, and Patrick J. Huber. Likewise, during my teaching career at William Woods University, that school's president, Dr. Jahnae H. Barnett, went out of her way to encourage my research and writing. I am grateful to her for her support.

Beginning in 1978, and off and on for some two decades, the State Historic Preservation Office (SHPO) supported my effort to undertake cultural resource surveys of African American historic sites in Missouri. I appreciate the SHPO's assistance. I also received support from the Missouri Humanities Council via their Scholar-in-Residence grants. That support was critical to the work I did on the African American community of Arrow Rock, in particular.

For a number of years during the 1990s, the Missouri State Museum based its Black History Month exhibits on my work in the state's African American communities. That effort enhanced my ability to collect oral histories, photographs and documents. I appreciate the museum's support of that effort. I am especially indebted to Missouri State Museum historian John Viessman who worked with me on those projects.

Through the years, librarians and archivists have patiently answered my research questions and helped me find answers, even when answers were not easily obtainable. I am especially indebted to Ithaca Bryant and the staff of the Inman E. Page Library at Lincoln University, the staffs of Dulany Library at William Woods University, the Missouri State Archives, the Missouri History Museum, the Kansas City Public Library, the St. Louis Public Library, and the State Historical Society of Missouri. Missouri State Archives Local Records Director Lynn Morrow and his successor John Korasick and local records archivists Rebecca Weber Bowen and Mike Everman were especially helpful in bringing to my attention newly available public record groups.

All of the essays in this collection have appeared in one form or another in other publications. I appreciate the permission to reprint those essays from the following institutions: the State Historical Society of Missouri, ABC-CLIO/Greenwood Press, Department of American Studies at the University of Kansas, Department of African and Afro-American Studies Program at Washington University, Kansas City Regional History Institute at the University of Missouri–Kansas City, and the Missouri Folklore Society.

I could not have completed this book without the help of a number of my co-workers at the State Historical Society. Gerald Hirsch and Kristen Bland Anderson led the effort to scan, OCR and correct the original essays that formed the basis of the book. Kristen likely spent more time on this book than I did, and she was unfailingly cheery, even when I asked more than I had a right to of her. She was assisted by Christina George and Katherine Fallon. Anne Cox worked her usual magic on the photographs in the book. Lynn Wolf Gentzler, John Brenner and Laura Jolley read the book's "Prologue" and offered helpful suggestions for improvement. Jeneva Pace helped to keep me on task so that the book could be completed in a timely manner. The Executive Committee of the Board of Trustees of the State Historical Society of Missouri, and especially President Stephen N. Limbaugh Jr., has been unfailingly supportive of my research and writing. To all of my SHSMO colleagues, thank you very much.

Finally, I am indebted to my family for allowing me the time and freedom to pursue my research interests over the course of more than four decades. I wish to thank my wife, Lisa, son Randy and his wife Michaela, daughter Sharon and her husband Travis Bax, and daughter Rebecca and her husband Jeffrey Dazey. I am also grateful to grandchildren Dustin, Brooke and Bladen Kremer, Logan, Kaden, Saylor and Halston Bax, and Brennan Dazey for inspiring me to try to shape their future by discovering and preserving our collective past.

Any deficiencies that remain in this book can be blamed on my own inadequacies rather than the quality of all of the good help I have received.

Gary R. Kremer

Race and Meaning

Prologue

Race and Meaning in Missouri History

A Personal Journey

"The problem of the twentieth century is the problem of the
color-line, the relation of the darker to the lighter races of men"

W. E. B. DuBois, *The Souls of Black Folk* (1903)

I have been deeply interested in "the color line" for most of my life. Like
W. E. B. DuBois, I think that the dominant "problem" of the twentieth
century, certainly for Americans, has been race. For nearly half a century,
I have devoted the bulk of my professional life to studying, researching,
and writing about race in Missouri history. That is an improbable journey
for someone who grew up during the 1950s in one of the most homog-
enous all-white communities in the state. I knew one African American
as a child, a middle-aged man named Oscar "Toad" Anthony, a World
War II veteran who lived in the small mid-Missouri town of Chamois in
northeastern Osage County. Although I did not know it at the time, Toad
was the last member of what had once been a thriving African American
community of hundreds of persons in and near Chamois that dated to the
antebellum days of slavery.

I had no African American schoolmates or playmates. Once, when I
was twelve and playing baseball on a team of similarly aged boys from
the nearby town of Linn, I came face-to-face for the first time with some
African American boys, also my age, from Jefferson City. I had never encountered a black person my own age. A group of us, white and black,
stood making small talk around the pitcher's mound of a baseball field,
while all the time I tried to muster the courage to reach out and shake

the hand of the boy nearest me and tell him that I thought black people and white people could and should get along and that I wanted to be his friend. But the gesture was not made, the thought remained unspoken, and the opportunity was lost.

Despite my lack of personal exposure to African Americans, I developed a deep interest in racial justice at a very early age. In hindsight, I think there were multiple reasons for this. One was that the Catholic nuns who taught in my elementary school took seriously Archbishop Joseph Ritter's call during the late 1940s for racially integrated Catholic education and racial justice in the St. Louis archdiocese, which included the community of my childhood.[1] The nuns' exhortations about racial equality were reinforced by my exposure by means of television to the battles of the civil rights movement of the 1950s and 1960s. I was quietly offended and even outraged by what I saw happening in Selma and Birmingham and other places in the Deep South during the early to mid-1960s. I may have been a child, but even I knew who "Bull" Connor was, and I could tell that what was happening to African Americans in the South was wrong. That exposure, combined with an early reading of Michael Harrington's influential book on poverty in the United States, *The Other America* (1962), led me to want to be a social worker, which is the career path I envisioned for myself when I enrolled as a sociology major at Lincoln University in Jefferson City, during the fall of 1966.

I attended Lincoln University because it was only thirty miles from my home and because it was the most affordable public institution of higher education in the state at the time. I was unaware of the school's rich history as Missouri's university for African Americans prior to racial integration during the 1950s. Nor did I know when I enrolled there in 1966 that its student population was roughly equally divided between African Americans and whites.

Destiny intervened and altered my plan to be a social worker. I enrolled in a History of Western Civilization course, taught by Dr. Lorenzo Johnston Greene. I did not know that he was considered an expert on the African American experience. I thought that he surely must have been a Greek or Roman scholar, because he knew so much about the ancient world.

I discovered his true expertise when I enrolled in his two-semester course on African American history, called Negro History then. I took his course because of my desire to gain a deeper understanding of the origins of the civil rights movement. I got hooked on history, and I transferred my interest in social work among marginalized Americans into an interest in the study of those same people's history.

Dr. Lorenzo J. Greene
(courtesy of the State
Historical Society of
Missouri)

I was trained as a conventional historian by Dr. Greene, one of the masters of the profession. Educated at Howard University and Columbia University, Dr. Greene had served as a research assistant to Dr. Carter G. Woodson, the father of Black History, during the late 1920s and early 1930s. I was privileged to become Greene's research assistant during the late 1960s and early 1970s.

A significant part of my apprenticeship with Dr. Greene consisted of listening to stories about Dr. Woodson and his pioneering effort to promote African American history during the first half of the twentieth century. Greene enjoyed talking about Woodson's single-minded purpose, about what a harsh taskmaster Woodson had been, and about how Woodson insisted that his research assistants focus all of their energies on Woodson's Association for the Study of Negro Life and History. More than once Dr. Greene told me how angry Woodson had become with him when he discovered that Greene had gone out to a movie with a date on a Friday night. In a stroke of bad luck, Greene and his date happened to run into Dr. Woodson, who was taking his evening "constitutional." "Mr. Greene," Woodson thundered, "we scholars do not have time for such frivolity." There followed a lengthy period that extended into weeks, during which Woodson refused to speak to Greene. Woodson was not one to entertain "frivolity." He rarely sought entertainment; he never married. According to Greene, when asked why he had not married, Woodson would reply, "I have a mistress. She is history, and she is jealous."

These were more than mere stories. They were also exhortations to take seriously the career path I had chosen. Dr. Greene wanted me to understand the difficulties and challenges under which Woodson had operated, and the intensity of Woodson's commitment—and by extension, his own—to the study of African American history. He also wanted me to embrace the notion that researching and writing about African American history was more than a job, it was a calling. At least once he read to me from a diary he had kept during his years of working for Woodson. The diary entry was dated Monday, February 10, 1930, and it began: "This has been an unforgettable day." In the entry Greene went on to describe two "Negro History Week" events he had attended, including a huge gathering that evening. The highlight of the evening event, attended by approximately five thousand people, was a speech by former African American congressman John R. Lynch of Mississippi. Reflecting on the day's activities, and especially Congressman Lynch's speech, Greene penned these words: "Tonight's involvement makes me a confirmed and dedicated associate of Dr. Woodson. Negro History henceforth shall be my life's work. . . . It is my cause and shall transcend everything else."[2]

Dr. Greene wanted me to have that same level of commitment and to regard what I was doing as a "cause." He took every opportunity to encourage me to attend annual meetings of Woodson's organization, the Association for the Study of Negro Life and History (now known as the Association for the Study of African American Life and History). When circumstances allowed, he introduced me to Woodson's contemporaries, scholars such as Charles Wesley, Dorothy Porter Wesley, and Rayford Logan, all of whose writings he had required me to read, and he invited them to share their stories about Woodson with me as well. He introduced me to John Hope Franklin, a man whose father, Buck Colbert Franklin, had known the African American attorney James Milton Turner, a subject of my early interest. In introducing me to these pioneering scholars, Dr. Greene made clear to me that he was preparing me to continue the work that they and he had begun. It was, indeed, an awesome responsibility, one he would not allow me to take lightly.

Despite my exhilaration over the opportunity to work closely with someone of Dr. Greene's stature, however, I was often reminded of the pervasive impact race has had on American society. Once, when I was still a graduate student, a distinguished scholar of African American history, who happened to be black, startled me with a transparently hostile question: "What in the hell is a white boy like you doing studying black history?" Sadly, that was a question I was destined to hear countless additional times over the course of my career, although rarely with the same level of virulence. Dr. Greene sensed that I would be vulnerable to this sort of criticism and challenge. In an effort to help me deal with it, he introduced me to the works of two white scholars of African American history whom he had befriended and helped through the years. One was August Meier, who was forever grateful to Dr. Greene for publishing one of the earliest essays he wrote in the *Midwest Journal*, which Greene edited during the late 1940s and early 1950s. The other was Herbert Aptheker, who also published in the *Midwest Journal*.[3]

With Dr. Greene's encouragement, and that of people such as Meier and Aptheker, I learned to embrace the criticism of those who questioned whether a white person could write African American history, and I used it to hone my skills as a researcher and writer. As a young professor at Lincoln University during the mid-1970s, for example, I found myself teaching an Afro-American History class to twenty-five Missouri State Penitentiary inmates, many of whom were followers of Elijah Muhammad and, thus, saw whites such as me in very negative terms. They certainly regarded me with wariness and suspicion, at least in the beginning. Their mistrust forced me to look ever more deeply for authentic African American voices in the history I studied and taught, lest I be accused of "seeing" history through the prism of white cultural bias.[4]

This desire to identify authentic African American voices in history led me, during the late 1970s, to look for new approaches to the study of black history. I found a "new" way in the form of the "cultural resource survey" in 1978. Influenced by the writings of Constance M. Greiff and others, I had been troubled for some time by the disappearance of large numbers of buildings that were tied to the African American past. As Greiff wrote in 1972, "properties associated with [ethnic minorities] were often working class homes and shops, construction frequently was not substantial and is subject to rapid deterioration. Urban structures in particular have been prey to freeways and clean-scape renewal programs."[5]

In 1978 I launched the Lincoln University Black Historic Sites Project, funded through the Office of Historic Preservation housed in the Missouri Department of Natural Resources. This was the first effort to identify systematically "Black Historic Sites" throughout the state of Missouri.[6] Over the next several years and with the help of a number of Lincoln University colleagues and students, I began the attempt to identify buildings that had relevance to the African American experience in the state, and which might be eligible for nomination to the National Register of Historic Places.

This focus on the built environment caused me to ask new questions. Why did African Americans build the kinds of structures that they built? What folk traditions influenced not only this process but, more generally, how they lived? I began to read secondary sources beyond the kinds of sources that conventionally trained historians such as myself were used to consulting. I found especially helpful and thought-provoking works by John Michael Vlach, starting with his seminal essay "The Shotgun House: An African Architectural Legacy," which appeared in 1976 in back-to-back issues of *Pioneer America*.[7]

In the course of working on this project, I also discovered the value of collecting oral histories and studying oral traditions within the state's African American communities. I found especially helpful in this regard William Lynwood Montell's book *The Saga of Coe Ridge: A Study in Oral History*.[8] By emphasizing what could be learned from a community's oral traditions, Montell's book opened an entirely new research horizon for me and gave me another vehicle through which I could hear authentic African American voices.

Much has changed in the kinds of research materials available to scholars of the African American experience, as well as the ways in which scholars have used that material, since I began to focus my academic interest on that topic. To a great extent, the essays in this collection illustrate the changes in African American historiography, a point to which I shall later return. In addition, I have included an Epilogue to this collection, which identifies major sources for writing about black history in Missouri as well as some suggestions for future research topics.

What has not changed, however, is the fact that race is relevant—that it matters—in Missouri history. It always has. Perhaps it always will, although Dr. Greene never failed to mention in his lectures that he longed for the day when there would be no need for African American or Black History as a separate field of inquiry. He wanted the African American experience to be incorporated into the general history of the United States so that the role and contributions of African Americans would be told as part of the broader story of American history.

My starting point for writing about race has always been that race impacts people's histories as well as their interpretations of those histories. To put it quite simply, our personal histories have often caused African Americans and whites to see the world in fundamentally different ways. This being the case, it behooves all of us to study and understand the different frames of reference that race provides us. This was a principal tenet of virtually every lecture Lorenzo Greene gave on history. He often employed the metaphor of a tapestry: "History is like a beautiful tapestry," he would say, "made beautiful by the multi-colored threads from which it is composed. If you begin to pull different colored threads out of the tapestry, you reduce its beauty, as well as its strength."

Every essay in this collection was influenced by Professor Greene. The first essay, "Some Aspects of Black Education in Reconstruction Missouri: An Address by Richard B. Foster," is really an annotated document, which reflects Greene's interest in teaching with documents and relying on primary sources to interpret history. This particular document is one that my Lincoln University colleague Professor Antonio F. Holland and I ran across when we were assisting Dr. Greene with the writing of an essay titled "The Role of the Negro in Missouri History, 1790-1970," published in the 1973-1974 edition of the *Official Manual: State of Missouri.*

Richard B. Foster was a white second lieutenant in the US Army's Sixty-second Colored Infantry, composed of former Missouri slaves. He was the man they entrusted their money to in 1866, when they charged him with the responsibility of establishing a school for Missouri freedmen. The "Address" captures the chaos of the immediate post–Civil War era in Missouri as well as the difficulty of establishing schools for Missouri blacks during that period. If I was reworking that essay today (nearly four decades later), I would probably provide greater evidence of this difficulty by quoting from county superintendents' reports such as this one from the man in charge of the Mississippi County schools in 1871: "The breed of negroes of this latitude are returning to their primeval state. . . . To attempt to educate them is folly."[9] I would also be inclined to comment on Foster's patronizing if well-meaning attitude toward African Americans, as well as his call for reparations for former slaves.

This collection contains a number of biographical sketches, including an essay about James Milton Turner. Lorenzo Greene was a strong advocate of biography, especially of biography that brings to light the contributions of previously unknown "heroes" of history. I discovered Turner under the tutelage of Greene in my search to uncover "unsung" African American heroes of Missouri history whose stories had not been adequately told. This was the focus of much of the writing about African American history during the early days of the "Black History" movement. During the late 1960s and 1970s, historians such as Greene placed much emphasis on "firsts," such as James Milton Turner's being the "first" significant African American political power broker in Missouri and the "first" African American US foreign minister to the West African country of Liberia.

My essay "The World of Make-Believe: James Milton Turner and Black Masonry," however, illustrates how the writers of African American history began to move away from a kind of writing that some argued bordered on hagiography rather than history and move toward a more critical analysis of the role played by these African American historical figures in the times in which they lived. The Turner essay that appears in this collection, first published in 1979, is more analytical, and probably more critical, of Turner's life than it likely would have been had it been written a decade or more earlier.[10]

During the early 1980s, as part of my effort to identify African American historic sites throughout the state, I discovered a complex of buildings in Chariton County that had once housed the Dalton Vocational School. This was an institution established during the late nineteenth century by a former Tuskegee Institute student who had known and worked with both Booker T. Washington and George Washington Carver. An African American named Nathaniel C. Bruce, that former student, came to Missouri to create what he sometimes referred to as the "Tuskegee of the Midwest." Bruce ran head-on into the complexity of race relations in Missouri. In 1917 he wrote to his former Tuskegee Institute professor George Washington Carver: "Under our Missouri conditions, what I am working hardest on is food—two sorts of food, in fact—material food and mental food." Elaborating, he added, "I find that the Missouri Negro is far behind in the matter of general intelligence; so he needs mental food as well as material food."[11]

Although racial integration led to the closure of the Dalton Vocational School during the late 1950s, a number of the buildings from the campus were still standing in the 1980s, including the school's main classroom. The buildings' owner, a hog and tobacco farmer named Roland Hughes, was a great source of information about the school's history. The story is told in the essay "Nathaniel C. Bruce, Black Education, and the 'Tuskegee of the Midwest,'" coauthored with Patrick Huber, then a graduate student at the University of Missouri.

Similarly, through my colleague and friend Lynn Morrow, who was then doing cultural resource survey work in Saline County, I discovered an African American church that was the only surviving building from what had once been a thriving black community known as Pennytown. Lynn introduced me to Josephine Lawrence, who was one of the last residents of the community, which had ceased to exist in about 1960. Conversations with Mrs. Lawrence supplemented our archival research and led to publication of the essay "Pennytown: A Freedmen's Hamlet, 1871-1945," which I coauthored with Lynn in the 1989-1990 issue of the *Missouri Folklore Society Journal*. That essay, by the way, was heavily influenced by Leon F. Litwack's magisterial book, *Been in the Storm So Long: The Aftermath of Slavery*, which focused attention on the ways in which African Americans responded to freedom and tried to carve out lives for themselves during the generation after the ending of the Civil War.[12] If I were to revise that essay today, I would include richly textured information that could be gleaned from the federal census returns of 1920, 1930, and 1940, none of which was available when the essay was first written.

My interest in and writing about George Washington Carver may have been the most serendipitous of all my research projects over the past four decades. As I have written elsewhere, Carver's life and work were of relatively little interest to me and many other students of African American history during the late 1960s and through the 1970s.[13] Many of us thought that he was too much of an accommodationist, much like his Tuskegee Institute boss, Booker T. Washington. Indeed, one Carver biographer from that era accused Carver of "out Bookering Booker."[14]

During the early 1980s, however, I was asked by officials from the George Washington Carver National Monument in Diamond, Missouri, to catalogue scores of pieces of correspondence to and from Carver that were held by the monument. At the time, I saw this project as nothing more than an acceptable alternative to teaching summer school! I did not anticipate what was to happen subsequently, namely, that I was to become utterly intrigued by the complexity of Carver's personality and relationships. Ultimately, I produced two books about Carver and have developed an enduring relationship with the staffs of the Carver National Monument and the Tuskegee Institute Archives. The Carver essay in this anthology first appeared as a paper that I delivered at a George Washington Carver Symposium at Missouri State University in Springfield in 2010. That paper was subsequently revised and was published as a chapter in my 2011 biography of Carver.[15] The essay makes a case for assessing Carver's accomplishments while at Tuskegee against the background of his early years in Missouri.

My discovery during the 1970s of the cultural resource survey as a new way of doing African American history paralleled another expansion of my research interests during this period, this one into the area of women's history. Curiously, my interest in women and gender studies derived from my witnessing a rather unusual confrontation between one of my professors and a fellow graduate student in a seminar at the American University in Washington, DC. The professor praised the female student for what he referred to as a brilliant review she had written of a book authored by the professor's friend. The professor read aloud to our class a letter he had penned to the author about the review. The confrontation occurred when the professor got to the point in the letter where he identified the student as one of the brightest and prettiest members of his class. The student, a National Organization of Women (NOW) officer and women's rights activist, took exception to this reference to her physical appearance and pointed out the obvious gender bias in the professor's comment.

That conflict between a graduate student and a professor jolted me into an awareness of gender bias in the historical profession and led to an ongoing conversation with the graduate student about the ways in which historians had neglected to address the topics of women and gender in their studies. This experience, and the graduate student's encouragement, led me to discover the writings of a long list of women historians, including classic works by Hallie Q. Brown, Elizabeth L. Davis, and Ida Wells-Barnett. Later works by (among others) Nell Irvin Painter, Darlene Clark Hine, Elsa Barkley Brown, Elizabeth Clark-Lewis, and Evelyn Higginbotham added an entirely new dimension to my own inquiry into the rich complexity of the African American experience.

During the late 1970s, I began to teach the first women's history course at Lincoln University and to search for a research topic that combined my long-standing interest in race with my emerging interest in gender. I found that topic in Missouri State Archives records when I discovered material that documented the story of the Missouri Industrial Home for Negro Girls, a "reform" school located near the Moniteau County town of Tipton.

The Missouri Industrial Home for Negro Girls opened in 1916 after a controversial effort to place it elsewhere in the state. Missourians, at the time, did not want young black female offenders housed with young white female offenders at the Missouri Industrial Home for Girls in Chillicothe. Indeed, many white Missourians did not want this correctional facility in their community. Nowhere was this sentiment expressed more bluntly and harshly than in the *Mansfield Press*. An article titled "Don't Like Niggers," which was reproduced in the *Wright County Republican*, commented on "the proposition to locate a young nigger-wench reform school" near the county line separating Wright and Douglas Counties. The newspaper reported that "any attempt on the part of the state to locate a nigger reform school within the boundaries of Wright or Douglas counties will meet with fiery opposition from the residents."[16]

The young girls who ended up at the Missouri Industrial Home for Negro Girls were doubly disadvantaged: they were victims of both racial and gender bias. The essay in this collection, coauthored with my then-colleague at Lincoln University, Linda Rea Gibbens (Warner), describes how the African American matron of the facility, Ethel "Mother" Bowles, tried not only to lift these girls morally but also to train them to be self-sufficient once they returned to their often troubled homes.

The next essay in this collection, coauthored with a William Woods University student, Cindy M. Mackey, is titled "'Yours for the Race': The Life and Work of Josephine Silone Yates." This essay continued my exploration of African American women's history in Missouri. It tells the story of a young African American woman from New York who traveled to Jefferson City in 1881 to teach at the all-black Lincoln Institute. Yates quickly grasped the challenge facing African American women in post–Civil War Missouri: they often outnumbered black men in outstate Missouri, and they could often get jobs more easily than black men could. As a result, Yates tried to shape the curriculum at Lincoln Institute in a way that would prepare black women to become "assistant breadwinners," who could provide for themselves in the event that their husbands could not find jobs or if they had to fend for themselves because they had no male partner.

This collection also contains an essay directly focused on my alma mater, Lincoln University, during its "golden years" (1920s–1950s), when it was sometimes referred to as "The Black Harvard of the Midwest." The context for the "golden years" was that the Missouri legislature changed Lincoln Institute's name to "Lincoln University" in 1921, the consequence of legislation sponsored by Missouri's first African American legislator, Walthall Moore, elected from St. Louis in 1920. In part, white legislators effected this name change to discourage African Americans from seeking admission to the all-white University of Missouri. The name change was accompanied by a significant increase in financial support from the state, which allowed Lincoln University president Nathan B. Young to raise faculty salaries so that he could attract African American scholars with graduate degrees from prestigious institutions such as Harvard, Cornell, and Columbia Universities. Many of these scholars—including my mentor, Lorenzo J. Greene, a Columbia University graduate—remained at Lincoln University for decades. During that period, they created a "Black Culture Mecca of the Midwest," a designation that also serves as the title of an essay in this collection. That essay was first presented as a paper at a conference on the "Black Heartland," hosted by Washington University during the early 1990s. The conference organizer, Washington University professor Gerald Early, subsequently compiled papers presented at the conference into a small book titled *Black Heartland: African American Life, the Middle West, and the Meaning of American Regionalism.*

During the mid-1990s, I became interested in the African American roots of what by that time had become an almost all-white town, Arrow Rock, located in eastern Saline County along the Missouri River. My focus on Arrow Rock stemmed from the donation of two historic properties associated with the town's black history to the Friends of Arrow Rock. The donors, Ted and Virginia Fisher, and the executive director of the Friends group, Kathy Borgman, sought the help of the executive director of the State Historical Society, Dr. James W. Goodrich, in documenting the history of those two buildings, as a prelude to restoring them.

Dr. Goodrich asked my assistance in this effort. Subsequently, with the help of a "Scholar-in-Residence" grant from the Missouri Humanities Council, I began working with the Friends to uncover the rich African American heritage of this town whose population had once been nearly half black.

Although much archival research went into the process of discovery of Arrow Rock's African American heritage, we also relied heavily on oral history, interviewing dozens of blacks and whites who had once called Arrow Rock home. One of the most striking themes that ran through these interviews was the recollection of the strength of African American institutions through the oppressive racism that characterized the Jim Crow era, from the last quarter of the nineteenth century through the middle of the twentieth. The black school and its teachers, the black churches and their preachers, and the black fraternal and sisterhood organizations—including the Ancient Free and Accepted Masons, the United Brothers of Friendship, the Odd Fellows, and their female affiliates, including the Daughters of Jericho—gave African Americans vehicles by which they could control and shape their own lives, away and apart from white influence and control.

There were a number of secondary sources that informed my interpretation of black Arrow Rock's history, including the work of Elizabeth Clark-Lewis, whose history of domestic servants in Washington, DC, documented the significance of their ability to "live out" of white households rather than "living in."[17] Additionally, works by Andrew Billingsley and Ira Berlin also shaped my thinking.[18] Had my essay not already been near the maximum number of words allowed by the *Missouri Historical Review*'s editorial policy, I would have included information on diet and everyday life literally dug up by archaeologist Timothy E. Baumann and documented in his 2001 dissertation, "Because That's Where My Roots Are."[19] In the future, I anticipate that more and more historians will consult the work of anthropologists and archaeologists as they write about everyday life among African Americans.

The focus on what other historians have called "agency" or control over their own lives among African Americans is taken up in other essays in this collection, particularly during the period of the so-called Great Migration, which extended from the era of World War I down through the mid-1940s. In writing about this period, I have found especially helpful the scholarship of Robin D. G. Kelley and his emphasis on writing "history from below."[20]

"The Whitley Sisters Remember: Living with Segregation in Kansas City, Missouri," traces the 1920 journey of one black family from Wright County deep in the Missouri Ozarks to Kansas City where Frank Whitley, the husband and father of the family, hoped to find work. Tragedy soon struck the family, however, when Whitley's wife died from double pneumonia and he was unable to find work. He departed Kansas City for California and left behind his three daughters, all of whom were under the age of five. These "Whitley Sisters" were subsequently raised by their maternal grandparents in an all-black community, where they attended all-black schools and an all-black church and patronized a whole host of all-black businesses and other services located within their racially segregated community. Indeed, "The Whitley Sisters Remember" is largely the story of African American resilience, creativity, and mutual support among a group of people who for generations were systematically denied their full social, political, and economic rights.

Similarly, "'Just like the Garden of Eden': African American Community Life in Kansas City's Leeds" also takes up the topic of the Great Migration. Whereas the Whitley sisters lived in the heart of Kansas City, the community of Leeds emerged on its periphery, at the eastern edge of the city's corporate limits. African Americans who settled in Leeds were largely World War I–era migrants from the South, in search of economic opportunity. They were attracted to Leeds by the low cost of property and the opportunity to pay for their house and/or real estate on installments, over time. Although the streets of Leeds were unpaved and water and sewer lines were often blocks away or nonexistent, the area's remoteness from the urban center allowed African Americans to replicate their southern lifestyle by raising their own gardens and livestock and hunting and fishing in nearby woods and streams. In short, just like the Whitley sisters, the residents of Leeds overcame the negative impact of segregation and took control over their own lives. Working on the history of Leeds, by the way, gave me one of the most rewarding experiences I have had as a researcher over the course of the past five decades. In August 2000, I attended a "homecoming" celebration of present and former Leeds residents in the community's Liberty Park. Speaking to hundreds of African Americans who had gathered to enjoy the homecoming then-Missouri senator Yvonne Wilson, who grew up in the community, encouraged those present to talk to me and my colleague John Viessman, a Missouri State Parks employee. Standing on the back of a large trailer, Senator Wilson pointed to John and me and assured her listeners that "you can trust them with your story." It was a statement that evidenced the absence of racial mistrust.[21]

"Lake Placid: 'A Recreational Center for Colored People,' in the Missouri Ozarks", coauthored with William Woods student Evan Orr, continues a discussion of the same theme of self-reliance but with an emphasis on the creation of a recreational facility for African Americans who were denied the use of "white" facilities such as the Lake of the Ozarks or were

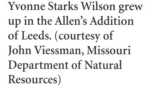

Yvonne Starks Wilson grew up in the Allen's Addition of Leeds. (courtesy of John Viessman, Missouri Department of Natural Resources)

relegated to "black" sections of white facilities, such as "Watermelon Hill" in Kansas City's Swope Park.

Dr. Percy C. Turner, superintendent of General Hospital Number Two, Kansas City's all-black publicly supported hospital, wanted a place to hunt, fish, and relax in the Missouri Ozarks. He discovered and purchased a hilly, forested area near the borders of Morgan and Benton Counties from a Depression-era white farmer in the region who was down on his luck. Turner's desire to have a lake on the property coincided with Kansas City political boss Tom Pendergast's effort to solicit the black vote for the Democratic Party, in an era when African Americans in Missouri and throughout the nation were beginning to abandon their traditional loyalty to Republicans. Working through Pendergast's lieutenant, Matthew Murray, Dr. Turner was able to secure a federal Works Progress Administration (WPA) grant to build a dam that allowed for the creation of a fifteen-acre lake. Turner's use of federal funds to build a private lake was allowed because he agreed to open the lake to the public in the event of a drought!

Dr. Turner's creation, "Lake Placid," soon became a recreational destination point for other middle-class Kansas City African Americans including doctors, lawyers, preachers, and teachers. The lake's popularity spread until it became a retreat place for African Americans from not only Kansas City but also St. Louis, Columbia, and Jefferson City. It even attracted vacationers from centers of black population in Kansas and Iowa. The presence of black professionals, especially physicians, in a remote area of the Ozarks where few African Americans lived made for interesting interactions between urban black vacationers and local white residents.

Dr. William J. Thompkins, a predecessor to Dr. Turner as superintendent of General Hospital Number Two, is the subject of an essay titled "William J. Thompkins: African American Physician, Politician, and Publisher." A native of Jefferson City and a graduate of that city's Lincoln Institute, Thompkins attended medical school at Howard University in Washington, DC, before returning to practice medicine in Missouri. As a physician and later administrator of Kansas City's segregated public hospital for African Americans from 1914 to 1916 and again from 1918 to 1922, Thompkins quickly learned he needed to find favor with Boss Pendergast. Thompkins aided Pendergast in his effort to attract African American voters to the Democratic cause. With Pendergast's help, Thompkins published a black newspaper, the *Kansas City American*, whose purpose was to serve as a counterbalance to the black Republican newspaper, *The Call*, published by Chester Franklin. Thompkins's actions in support of Democrats not only made him an important figure on the Missouri political scene but also made him a regional and even national player. Thompkins's efforts on behalf of Democratic presidential candidate Franklin D. Roosevelt led the latter to appoint the doctor to the coveted position of Recorder of Deeds for the District of Columbia. This position, once held by the great nineteenth-century African American leader Frederick Douglass, was among the most influential patronage positions in the federal government available to blacks. Thompkins moved to Washington, DC, in 1933 and remained there until his death in 1945.

The final essay in this collection, "The Abraham Lincoln Legacy in Missouri," explores the ways in which Missouri's African Americans sought to honor the Great Emancipator during the years after the Civil War ended, especially by naming African American schools for him. "Lincoln Schools" emerged in all parts of Missouri: from St. Joseph and Excelsior Springs to Sikeston and Charleston; from Joplin and Neosho to Bowling Green and Louisiana; and even in the so-called Little Dixie counties of the Missouri River Valley. This essay, influenced by historian David Blight's work, also takes up other ways in which Missouri's African Americans celebrated the memory of emancipation, including through annual "Emancipation Day" picnics, often held on or near August 4.[22]

Taken together, then, the essays that comprise this book cover a significant portion of Missouri history and the ways in which Missourians have struggled to deal with the issues of race and race relations over the course of more than a century. These essays acknowledge, at least implicitly, that Missouri is a border state, neither completely Northern nor Southern. Although many antebellum Missourians traced their ancestry to states that would subsequently make up the Confederacy, Missouri escaped much of the rigid, legal segregation that characterized the post–Civil War South. This does not mean that Missourians were any less racist; it does mean that the racism was often more subtle and disguised and that understanding its many nuances requires greater sensitivity and exploration.

The question of race and how to deal with it is, as W. E. B. DuBois indicated in 1903, an ongoing challenge, one that is worthy of our continued conversation. I have been privileged to have had a part in the discussion.

Chapter 1

Some Aspects of Black Education in Reconstruction Missouri

An Address by Richard B. Foster

**Richard B. Foster (courtesy of the State Historical
Society of Missouri, 009790)**

In 1933 Carter G. Woodson, writing on the educational problems
confronted by black Americans, charged that whites "had thoroughly
demonstrated" they were no longer willing to serve a useful function
in the educational life of blacks.[1] "They have not," he said, "the spirit of

their predecessors and do not measure up to the requirements of educators desired in accredited colleges." That, Woodson suggested, was unfortunate. For there had been a time, shortly after the Civil War, when a number of sincere Northern whites had gone South "and established schools and churches to lay the foundation" for black colleges. There was, in Woodson's view, little doubt about the moral soundness of those men's motives. Indeed, in his words: "Anathema be upon him who would utter a word derogatory to the record of these heroes and heroines."[2]

Some thirty-four years later, Henry Bullock, another historian of black education in the South, also extolled the qualities of whites who founded Southern black schools during the early years of Reconstruction. These people, whom he categorized as coming mainly from the religious groups of the North: "were in the main devout Christians. . . . They were largely trained in New England colleges and universities and were probably some of the best prepared of the nation's small supply of common school teachers. They had interpreted the Emancipation Proclamation in terms of what it was supposed to mean—the freedom of Negroes to care for themselves and participate in a free society like other people."[3]

Richard B. Foster, a founder of Lincoln University of Missouri, was one such man. Foster was born and raised in Hanover, New Hampshire, and was graduated from Dartmouth College, well steeped in the Congregationalist tradition. He was the descendant of an old New England family which had emigrated from Ipswich, England, before the Revolution. He taught school in Illinois and Indiana prior to the outbreak of the Civil War. Foster demonstrated his abolitionist sentiments as early as 1856 by taking part in the John Brown raid upon Fort Titus, Kansas. In 1862 he entered the service of the Union Army as a private in the First Nebraska Regiment. When Abraham Lincoln authorized the formation of black regiments, Foster immediately volunteered to join the Sixty-second United States Colored Infantry, later rising to the rank of lieutenant. He was in command of the rear guard at the battle of Palmetto Ranch, Texas, May 25, 1865.[4]

At the end of the war, Foster was asked by the men of the Sixty-second and Sixty-fifth colored regiments to act as their agent in the establishment of a school for blacks in Missouri. Foster accepted this expression of confidence and left the next year for Missouri, carrying with him more than $6,000.00 in cash and pledges raised by the members of the Sixty-second and Sixty-fifth. In 1866 he founded Lincoln Institute in Jefferson City, Missouri, and there served the cause of black education as principal of the school for the next six years.

The following document, an address delivered before the State Teachers' Association in St. Louis in 1869, offers some insight into the problems he faced in Jefferson City, and the problems black education, in general, faced in Reconstruction Missouri. Foster's address was published in the Jefferson City weekly *Missouri State Times*, May 21, 1869.

Address Upon Colored Schools
Delivered Before the State Teachers' Association
at St. Louis, Mo., May 17th, 1869
By R. B. Foster, of Jefferson City

The State Superintendent reports in this State thirty-four thousand colored children "of educable age." As it is at last discovered that they are educable, it becomes an interesting question what provision is made that their possibilities of educableness may be realized.

A summary of the reports of County Superintendents shows fifty-nine public colored schools in the state, and an attendance of 2,000 pupils. One-seventeenth! This showing must be erroneous. There must be more than 2,000, there must be more than one-seventeenth of the colored children of the State in school. There are many subscription schools, some of them quite small, and some taught by indifferent teachers, but still doing something. There are many schools supported by benevolent societies in the North, whose teachers are thoroughly qualified, and endued with self-denying missionary spirit. [Many of these have not been][5] reported by indifferent superintendents.

All this is so. The office of the Freedmen's Bureau in this City has reports of seventeen schools, with sixteen hundred pupils, some of whom are and [some are] not, included in the other list. I estimate that there are about five thousand colored children in the State attending school.

On the other hand, the same indifference that fails to report all the schools, also fails to report all the children. I shall not be thought unreasonable if I estimate fifty thousand as the number of this class for whom schools should be provided; certainly not if a small allowance be made for adults.

So, instead of the number two thousand, and the ratio one-seventeenth, we may claim the number of five thousand, and the ratio one-tenth, as actually provided with schools. Is this a showing to be proud of? Can we point to those figures with exultation?[6] But perhaps the character of such schools as the colored people enjoy is so high as to atone in part for the paucity of their numbers. Would it were so! But is it reasonable to expect this? By what test or tests shall we judge? By the respect given to the teacher? By the money paid them? By the cost of the school-houses? By the value of the furniture and apparatus provided? Alas! by all these tests, the colored schools are inferior.

It is undeniable that as a general rule, the teachers of colored schools are held in less estimation, and are in less danger of becoming rich than the teachers of the white schools.[7] Understand, it is not the teachers but the schools, whose cause I am pleading. If there is any teacher of a colored school, who cannot make a living at that, let him do something else or starve. Better that an incompetent should starve than go into the school-room as a teacher, even of Negroes!

But as to school-houses. How many *good* school-houses in this State have dusky faces for occupants? Houses that would be satisfactory to the white children of the locality? Where are they? Where is one? In St. Joseph the colored school-house is a frame building—all rest are brick.[8] Are there any forty thousand dollar school-houses in St. Louis for the five thousand colored children?[9]

In Jefferson City, has been partly bought and partly built, within a year and a half, a comfortable brick for the white children, containing four [large] rooms and a recitation room, and furnished with good desks—at a cost of about ten thousand dollars.Not too much certainly, no, not half enough for one thousand children. But the colored school is provided with a frame twenty-two feet wide, built for a school-house in the antediluvian ages, and for years considered worthless, resuscitated by an outlay of five hundred dollars, and furnished with the home-made desks thrown out of the white school-house. How is that single room for three hundred and fifty children? [10]

Number of colored children one-fourth the whole, cost of their school-house one-twentieth! Would St. Louis, would the state show a nearer approximation to equal justice than that? I imagine not. I suppose the majority of colored schools in this state are taught in cabins and in churches. In the rural districts in cabins never meant for school-houses, and in towns in churches never fit for a school-house. For though a church may well go into a school-house, a school should never go into a church.[11]

In fact, I presume that my school-house, the one just referred to, that cost five hundred dollars to revive it—is much better than the average house occupied by my kind of school. I have a room six feet too narrow, but of good length; with an entry, in an airy, beautiful situation; with good windows and good roof; not quite a good floor; wall and ceiling plastered; walnut desks, made by a mechanic who was a good workman, but who did not know how a desk should be made for the comfort and health of the pupil; and a good, large black-board, and three small ones. In that room—not always as good as now—I have taught nearly three years. Will you bear with me while I describe the scene of my first entrance on my labor there as memory recalls it?

The rain is pouring in torrents. As I approached the school-house, I am stopped by a creek, the bridge over which has been swept away—usually fordable, but now impassable by reasons of the flood. A half hour's detour, and the scrambling of several fences brings me to the sanctuary of learning. What a sanctuary! The rains pour through the roof scarcely less than outside. I could throw a dog through the side in twenty places. There is no sign of a window, bench, desk, chair or table. In this temple of the muses I meet two pupils. On the next day the same scene is repeated. The third day the rain has ceased, the creek has become fordable, and seventeen pupils are enrolled; and for more than six weeks, new names are added to the register every day. I will not weary you with details of gradual improvement since. I have taught one hundred and thirty pupils in that house at one time, without assistance. But since last January, half my scholars have been sent to an assistant, half whose wages are paid by the school board, who teaches in a church with her brother, the principal of Lincoln Institute, and I have been comparatively happy.[12]

I have not troubled you with these details as supposing they have any value of themselves, but they illustrate the difficulties under which colored schools have been established in this State. And I was not the pioneer. It deserves to be recorded that the two ladies who first taught a colored school in Jefferson City were stoned in the street, and owed their safety to the protection of Governor [Thomas] Fletcher. Yet I think our circumstances were and are not worse but better than the average. Still less are you to suppose that I have taken this covert means to complain of the board of education. Far from it. Their treatment of me has been generous, and they have gone to the extreme limit of their means in providing for my school.[13]

But we may as well accept that the colored schools of this State are mostly in poor condition; too few in number, little thought of, little cared for. As a state we are not doing our duty for the education of the colored people, and probably not doing half so much as most of us, in our self-complacency, think we are.

It is comparatively of less consequence that the teachers of white schools should be fit for their post. For, mark you, the colored children have no other means of education than the school room. They have no intelligent parents, no refined homes supplied with books and papers, to supplement the deficiencies and correct the mistakes of the teacher. Let him have provincialisms of speech, antiquated and false methods of instruction, and his pupils receive it all as law and gospel. Soon the older pupils will be taking little subscription schools in the rural district, and will at least perpetuate and propagate all the falsehoods they have learned.[14]

Therefore, I say emphatically the colored schools need the best of teachers. How shall they be obtained? There are not competent teachers for the white schools in the State. Have any of you known a surplus of thoroughly competent teachers, unable to find situations in any community in the State? But, as I have intimated, the white schools usually give better pay in money and social position than the colored; and teachers would be more than human if they did not seek the best places. There are needed today in this State one thousand first class teachers for colored schools, and there are not one hundred whose qualifications rank as fair. I know of only one way to [get] colored teachers. We can draw some from the North and East; we must educate the most at home.

There are but few occupations fairly open to the colored people that are both honorable and lucrative. Next to farming, which is the most honorable of all, the rightly pursued, the most lucrative, for it pays health, quiet, peace of mind, communion with God and nature—the highest, purest, sweetest life is that of him who sucks the breast of mother earth, next to farming is teaching. That profession has received a special honor in taking a Prof. [Ebenezer Don Carlos] Bassett from his school-room in Philadelphia—and mark you, he had a good school-house—to be Minister to Hayti.[15] Missouri has a colored teacher, J. Milton Turner of Boonville, who, if he did not receive the mission to Liberia, was at least worthy of it. He, instead of myself, ought to have delivered this address to you.[16]

In encouraging colored teachers I would not discourage white teachers from taking colored schools. I am no friend to the dogma that colored people must keep to themselves in school and church. I am the sworn enemy of caste in all its forms. But here is an inviting field which fit persons ought to enter, the need can not be otherwise supplied, and in some cases, not being themselves entirely free from that caste spirit that has been and is such a bitter enemy to them, they prefer teachers of their own color.

They are an imitative race, and imitation, like love and justice is blind. It seizes alike on virtue and vice. And they have derived from us something of that spirit of caste which we so faithfully cherish.

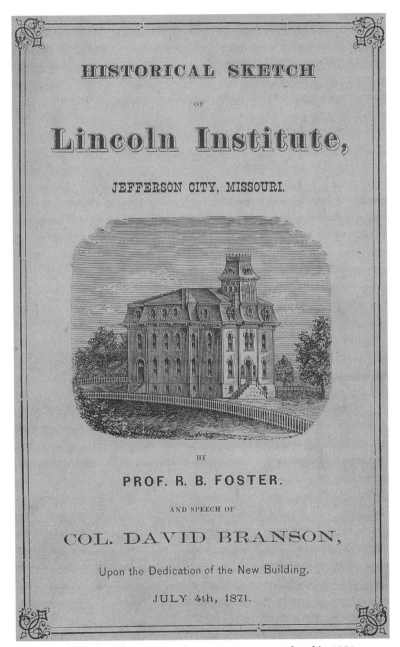

HISTORICAL SKETCH

OF

Lincoln Institute,

JEFFERSON CITY, MISSOURI.

BY

PROF. R. B. FOSTER.

AND SPEECH OF

COL. DAVID BRANSON,

Upon the Dedication of the New Building,

JULY 4th, 1871.

The first structure at Lincoln Institute was completed in 1871. (courtesy of the State Historical Society of Missouri, 024272

While no white church in the land would accept the ministrations of a colored pastor, though he were another Athanasius or Augustine; while no white regiment would consent to be led into battle by a colored colonel, though he were a worthy successor to Hannibal and Toussaint L'Ouverture, let us not blame *them* too severely if they sometimes prefer teachers of their own class, especially as some white men and women have thought themselves good enough to teach schools, who were confessedly not fit to teach white children.

We must then have colored teachers. Whence? How? We must draw what we can from outside. Immigration has been the salvation of Missouri. A few carpet-baggers of the right kind would help the colored people amazingly. [But] we can not count much upon them. The supply of suitable material is too limited; and other fields, where the blacks are stronger, an educated man might get to Congress, are more attractive. Then we must educate them at home. How? In the scattered, irregular, inferior schools, and poor school-houses they now have? How many teachers of colored schools are there today in Missouri who are graduates of some good normal school, up with the progress of the age and the science of teaching, and thoroughly competent to train teachers? If there is one, it is beyond my knowledge. Then we must have a normal school to train colored teachers.

That's what we want. A normal school in a suitable location, provided with good buildings and a good corps of instructors, and with tuition free. There are large numbers who would seek its advantages, who, in two years, would make second class teachers, and in four years would become first class.

Some of the pupils would, in one year, be better qualified than three-fourths of those now in the field. The buildings for such a school ought to be erected this summer, and the school to open with two hundred pupils next September. Is it possible to do that? Ten thousand dollars added to what is now ready for that purpose would put up the buildings. Let me explain what I refer to as now ready for the purpose.

In January, 1866, I was in Texas, a Lieutenant in the Sixty-second regiment United States Colored Infantry. I was about to be mustered out on a consolidation of the regiment into four companies. A sort of spontaneous movement arose to raise a subscription to establish a school in Missouri—ours was a Missouri regiment—of which I should take charge. The primary idea was for the benefit of colored soldiers. I did not suggest the undertaking, but accepted it as an indication of providence as to my field of duty. The immediate results, were five thousand dollars from our regiment, thirteen hundred and twenty-five from the [S]ixty-fifth, and two thousand dollars from the Freedmen's Bureau; the organization of a legal board of trustees under the name of Lincoln Institute; and the opening of the school in September, 1866, in the manner I have before referred to.

The results to this time have been that [the school has been established and] is now taught in a church by a colored man, Mr. W. H. Payne, a graduate of Adrian College, and his sister; an agent, a colored man, Rev. C. R. Beal, is at work in the East, and rather more than keeps the school going by his labors; and there is a permanent endowment, above expenses for three years, of seven thousand dollars, mostly invested in land near Jefferson City.[17] The trustees are anxious first of all to preserve the funds committed to them, safe from all abuse and chance of loss. Counsels of the utmost prudence have prevailed. They will not build or spend more than is necessary to keep the school alive till the way is clear. They have asked the Legislature for a small share of the three hundred and thirty thousand acres of Agricultural College land given by Congress to this State, and in two successive sessions a bill has passed the Senate embracing that feature. Once it failed in the House to receive a constitutional majority, though there were ten more votes cast for it than against it, and last winter its consideration was postponed till the adjourned session. So far as I know, opposition to the bill was confined to other features, viz. The proposed disposal of the principal part of the grant! so that it may be assumed that this provision is likely to become law, and a fund thereby realized at some future time, the product of say thirty thousand acres of land.[18] According to the standard of North Carolina this would come to fifteen thousand dollars. According to the standard of Minnesota to one hundred and fifty thousand. But in either case this is uncertain, except as to the fact that it will not be available for years; and an agriculture college is not a normal school.[19] But if the colored people of this State are to have good common schools supplied with competent teachers; if they are to have the opportunity of a higher education in agriculture, the mechanic art, law, medicine, theology, science and art, without going out of the State for it, and without waiting for the slow process of such correction of public sentiment as will open our high schools and colleges to them—a process much hindered by their ignorance—it is simply a necessity of the case that all the means available should be concentrated in one institution, strong enough to be respectable and useful, and with elasticity to develope each department of a complete university as it may be needed.

It is not a necessity that this institution be called Lincoln Institute, that it be located at Jefferson City, or that the individuals who now constitute the board of trustees of Lincoln Institute have control of it. But there are seven thousand dollars and an actual beginning of a school; and while I speak for myself alone, without authority of the board, [I] think I am safe in saying that that sum can be joined to any other funds that may be raised to establish such a school as is needed, in any location and under any name that may be most advisable.

The normal school should be the first department open. That is the most pressing necessity. I ask the State [Teachers'] Association to adopt [a resolution] urging the Legislature to [act] without delay [and requesting] a generous and philanthropic public not to wait for the legislature, but to contribute enough to inaugurate the work.

It will be said that teachers are not the only need. Our reply, they are the greatest. I know of schools waiting for teachers; schools that have applied to me for teachers, and I could not send them. Other schools have applied to the State Superintendent for teachers and he could not supply them.

Here I desire to call attention to a very effective provision of our school law: that namely which makes it the duty of the State Superintendent to establish colored schools where the local board fails to do so. It is within my knowledge that the mere fact of that law on the Statute book, coupled with a firm impression that the Superintendent would obey it, has caused [sic] number of schools to be established where other means had failed. If in any community where the local board neglects to provide a school, the colored people have one intelligent friend, he can do them no other service so great, as by assisting them to make out a case for the Superintendent. He can only act "upon satisfactory proof."

It appears by the last biennial report of the State Auditor, that during two years 6,000 dollars had been appropriated from the State Treasury to the Military Institute at Lexington; $10,000.00 to build the president's house at Columbia; and $29,259.23 out of "seminary moneys" [sic] to the State University—in all $45,259.23 to seminaries of learning above the grade of the common school. No colored student is ever seen in either of those institutions. No Statute law forbids their presence, but it is prohibited by a law whose edicts are more certain to be obeyed than those of the Legislature—the law of public opinion. I demand that the next biennial report of the State Auditor shall show disbursements to an institution of learning above the grade of the common school that shall be open to colored students.[20]

But there are those who will say to this class, "Now you ought to be content with what you have obtained. Your masters have lost a great deal of money by your liberation. You are now as free as anybody. Equal civil rights are guaranteed to you by the laws. We expect some of you want to learn to read and [write and we will give you a chance,] but you must not expect that the people, (have you ever noticed, how in talking about the people, it is almost universally assumed that Negroes are no part of the people?) but the people won't stand a tax to build you fine school-houses and hire as good teachers as the white schools have. Niggers are impudent and forward anyhow." I say language substantially like that expresses the view of a great many honest and well-intentioned persons. But I do not agree that that view is essentially sound. I think it is essentially wrong. With due deference to those who differ from me, I advance the following:

The natural rights of all classes are alike. If there is any difference in their claims, it is the result of fortuitous circumstances. Long continued deprivation of just rights does not constitute a valid reason to perpetuate that deprivation. From the first settlement of this State down to 1865, the Negroes were deprived of liberty and incidentally of education. During that period their unremunerated labor created a vast amount of the material wealth of the State. To give them now the widest possible opportunity for education, to let them have the fullest chance to find out what capacities God has given them, is perhaps to lessen the obligation but it is not to cancel it. The debt is one which from its nature and from its magnitude can never be payed. It is true they have not much property to pay taxes on; but let society restore to them the earnings of which they were feloniously deprived and they will need no help. A particular case will put this in a clearer light than a general statement. My friend and neighbor Cyrus Trigg, was 68 years old when freedom came. For 50 years, with stout muscles and vigorous health he had done a man's work and received a slave's wages.[21] Now, considering that money was formerly worth more than its present value, reckon his work at $100.00 a year more than such food and clothing, as he received, and interest averaging 25 years at only 4% and not compounded, and we have $5,000.00 principle, and as much more for interest that we owe him. I say we, for his master is not specially to blame. The responsibility lies on the State of Missouri, the State of Virginia, and the American nation, North and South. The United States owes him. How much it owes him in the nature of damages, for the repression and subjugation of his manhood, for false imprisonment, for tearing from him all his twelve children, ten of whom have never been recovered—I will not undertake to say, but I will say that we owe to him and his class that the number of colored schools in this State be increased ten-fold, the value of the houses for such schools one-hundred fold, and the character of their teachers raised to the highest possible rank.

Chapter 2

Pennytown

A Freedmen's Hamlet, 1871–1945

Rayford W. Logan, in his now-classic book *The Betrayal of the Negro: From Rutherford B. Hayes to Woodrow Wilson,* described the period from 1877 to 1918 as the "nadir" or low point of black life in post-slavery America.[1] Emphasizing the crystallization of the "separate but equal" doctrine, Logan catalogued the indignities and outrages suffered by blacks at the hands of whites during that period. Logan found fault particularly with the federal government for its failure to protect and enhance black rights. Among other things, he wrote, the federal government should have done more to guarantee economic equality for the ex-slaves by helping them to become property owners in the land of their birth.

There can be little doubt that much, if not all, that Logan wrote about white racism and its many manifestations was true. But focusing attention almost entirely on white misdeeds directs the attention of students of the past *away* from an analysis of how creatively and successfully some blacks coped with the harsh realities of life in post–Civil War America.

This essay offers one example of a community of Missouri blacks that struggled during Logan's period of the "nadir." Indeed, ironically and paradoxically, this community in south-central Saline County, known as Pennytown, reached the height of its success during that period and started to decline in the mid-1920s, precisely at the time when Logan began to see slow but steady improvement. Moreover, this community achieved stability without the federal assistance deemed to be so crucial by Logan.

Pennytown functioned as one of Missouri's freedmen's hamlets settled by emancipated slaves, who bought small parcels of land in fee simple from white landowners. The purchases eliminated postwar feelings of confusion and helped blacks in reconstruction Missouri to look optimistically toward a future. The hamlet persisted as a vigorous provincial culture with a legal, territorial home unknown in the participants' collective past. Pennytowners created a revolution of identity.

Pennytown had its origins in the black desire to own and control property. Such a goal was pervasive among ex-slaves. As Leon Litwack has written, "With the acquisition of land, the ex-slave viewed himself entering the mainstream of American life, cultivating his own farm and raising the crops with which to sustain himself and his family. That was the way to respectability in an agricultural society, and the freedman insisted that a plot of land was all he required to lift himself up."[2]

Presumably, that is what brought Joseph Penny, a middle-aged freedman from Kentucky, to Saline County, Missouri, in the late 1860s. Penny's arrival coincided with great social and economic transitions taking place throughout the South and West. Saline County's former plantations were becoming decentralized. New priorities in national marketing of crops

Members of the Pennytown community. Joseph Penny is in the center; Pennytown is in the background. (courtesy of the State Historical Society of Missouri)

(such as wheat instead of hemp) and of livestock had changed the face of agricultural lands. Although large landholdings were significantly reduced, tenantry dramatically increased and so did the number of smaller yeoman farms.

Penny started out as a tenant farmer, but by March 1871 he had accumulated enough money to buy eight acres of land from John Haggin for $160.[3] Those eight acres formed the nucleus of what later became Pennytown. Pennytown oral tradition holds that "white people laughed at the sale of land to Penny; they only sold it to him so that the law would know where to find him." Penny's purchase lay precisely along an ecological transition zone—it was on the edge of Saline's great rolling prairie and within the timbered breaks of Blackwater River drainage; to the north and the west were large landholders. The upper reaches of a hollow leading to Blackwater River soon became the primary "road" that Pennytown residents used to get to the river and later to their local school.

Penny's purchase was the first of eleven during the 1870s in the emerging hamlet. Seven other enterprising blacks bought tracts of land from John Haggin. Penny himself held his land for only two years and sold it in March 1873 to his step-daughter Evaline Butler, but the Penny family continued to live in the same house together. The event that served as a catalyst for the concentration of black families at the new freedmen's hamlet was the purchase by Edward Railey and Daniel Lewis of twenty acres in 1875. The average parcel purchased was six and one-half acres, and the tracts ranged from one and one-fourth to twenty acres.

By 1879 this communal group of settlers owned almost 64 acres of the 160 acres in section 24 of the county. Surnames of these "first families" settled at Pennytown—Brown, Jackson, Lewis, Montgomery, Washington, and others—remained familiar in the locale into the mid-twentieth century.[4] Among Saline County's historic black hamlets (Union Hill, Cow Creek, Elk Hill, Salt Pond, and Dresden), Pennytown became the largest.[5] The Saline County Atlas, 1876, reported only one instance of a freedmen's hamlet, that of "J. Railey & others Co. [colored]," including seven houses within a forty-acre plot.

By 1880 Joe Penny and others had organized a discrete neighborhood and had accomplished what J. B. Jackson calls "a reorganization of the southern cultural landscape" in Saline County.[6] In the local historical process, nucleated plantation villages had disappeared in favor of freedmen's hamlets. Pennytown's residences, labor services, field systems, traditional health care, subsistence economies, and more accounted for a new viable subculture in Saline County.

In 1880 there were twenty-six all-black households in Salt Fork Township, while twelve white households maintained black occupants. This ratio remained relatively constant for another generation: the 1900 census reported thirty-five black households, with nineteen white households including black occupants. The occupational divisions of labor in 1880 were listed as farmer, farm laborer, and servant. In addition, three hucksters and one blacksmith worked in the community.

The black heads of household listed in the 1880 Salt Fork Township agricultural census were practically all associated by residence with Pennytown at one time or another.[7] Most blacks in the township lived at or near Pennytown in the western part of Salt Fork, while some lived in the east near Napton. The agricultural census suggests division of labor and sharing within the black settlement. Of eleven landowners, three had some machinery, eight had a horse or two, six had milk cows (though only four produced butter), seven had swine, three raised wheat, seven raised corn, two raised tobacco, three raised Irish potatoes, three raised apple trees, six cultivated peach trees, apparently all had poultry and eggs, six produced molasses, seven cut cordwood, and three had built some fencing. Dick Green, long remembered as an expert sorghum maker, produced eighty gallons of molasses, the highest number in that category. Owners managed a median of seven acres; their land was valued at forty dollars per farm. These figures and oral tradition help define a domestic environment of communal living in part-time gardening, farming, hunting, fishing, and working out for neighboring white commercial agriculturalists.

By the turn of the century, Pennytown blacks had matured demographically and socially. The black township population remained around two hundred, but by 1900 the age cohorts were all older than in 1880, and those older than forty comprised one-fifth of the population.

	1880	1900
0–19	62%	49%
20–39	25%	31%
40–up	13%	20%

The only black in 1900 who had been born out of the southern uplands was one resident who had moved to Pennytown from Kansas.

In viewing the black family through the census years of 1870, 1880, and 1900, one must conclude that blacks made a strong commitment to dual-head households.[8] Most children in all-black households lived with two parents, and the incidence of single-parent households was minimal. As seen in the table below, a venture like Pennytown helped to consolidate the black community spatially, as a lower percentage of white households after 1880 boarded black occupants.

	all-black households	black single parent	white households with black occupants
Blackwater Twp. 1870	38	1	35
Salt Fork Twp. 1880	26	2	12
Salt Fork Twp. 1900	35	3	19

These figures complement the general findings of Herbert Gutman's *The Black Family in Slavery and Freedom, 1750–1925*.[9] Like those in Gutman's inquiry into urban blacks in 1880–1925, Pennytown families established two-parent households as the norm. The black family tended to function as an institutional constant and became the normal channel for the transmission of a folk heritage from one generation to another.

The occupational designations in the 1880 and 1900 census records for Pennytown remained virtually the same, except for more specific designations of washerwoman, cook, woodchopper, and gardener. Of three dozen heads of household, fully one-half (eighteen) owned their property free of mortgage, while four others still paid on a mortgage; another fourteen heads rented land. All but two households ranged in members from one to seven; two families, those of William E. Lewis and James Jackson, housed eleven and twelve respectively.

Throughout Pennytown's history, the hamlet functioned as a labor village for regional commercial farms. Most blacks had experience only in agricultural work, and few were qualified for jobs in town. Pennytown tradition relates that white landowners disliked the early development of the hamlet because it removed black tenants from their former masters' land. Nevertheless, blacks continued in agricultural labor. C. L. Lawrence Sr. in later years remembered all the balloon tires that went flat, the clogged gas lines from the summer's dust, and the humming telephone lines he listened to when stranded on the road as he traveled by car to jobs on nearby farms and in Marshall. Lawrence said, "We never finished a lot of trips we started or we arrived extremely late."[10]

Pennytowners practiced communal cooperation in getting their work accomplished. Each family kept a "hog killing book" that had the dates and number of swine each family intended to kill that fall. As the proper time approached, Pennytowners gathered at each family's hog killing. Afterward, dogs guarded the meat in smokehouses from intrusions of opossums and other varmints. Throughout the year families accumulated woodpiles near their homes. During Christmas week the men of the hamlet traveled from house to house with axes, breaking up each woodpile into stove wood for the winter. The Pennytown sorority, Sisters of Mysterious Ten, gathered weekly at the lodge for a mission social. They crafted quilts and rugs and made pies and cakes. At an appointed time they raffled their products at the Baptist church and placed the proceeds in a church treasury, so a community fund would be available as health insurance for the sick.[11]

Most women worked out of the home for neighboring farmers' wives. Daughters above the age of twelve or fourteen accompanied their mothers. Sons of the same age assisted in their fathers' work in the timber, trailed a mule and plow in the fields, and tended the truck-patch gardens. Apples, peaches, molasses, eggs, and chickens became exports to Marshall grocery stores. Women who found time at home quilted while listening to a used battery-operated radio that broadcast soap operas.

White landowners, including the Kings, Perrys, Shannons, Steeles, and others, worked with blacks on sharecropping arrangements, loaned them money, and allowed blacks to plant small parcels for their own use. The latter agreement by whites was in part an effort to retain the reliable labor pool offered by Pennytown men. Other blacks, such as William Brown, sold stove wood and cordwood in Marshall, sold rails and white oak posts to farmers, manufactured folk remedies to treat ailing livestock, and planted trees along Marshall's beautiful Eastwood Street.

The daily absence of so many adult women required a sharing of responsibilities in raising the children, a task usually adopted by the elderly and those not quite old enough to work out. Children also played a crucial role by feeding and caring for livestock and chickens, and they chased birds and rodents away from fruits and vegetables that lay drying on rooftops.[12]

Inside the Pennytown homes a few pictures hung on the walls—Abraham Lincoln (whom Pennytowners honored with Republican voting), family portraits, and pictures cut from magazines. Most houses during the twentieth century were single- and double-pen arrangements, enlarged as each family could afford secondhand materials. Tin roofs, helpful in water conservation, and metal siding were common. For house repairs residents procured a few boards from a sawmill in a nearby forest known as Shannon's Woods, and they sprinkled the mill's sawdust on the ground for walkways. The loose construction of many of the houses required sealing around the windows with mud and papers, using rags for insulation, and blocking drafts in the eaves. Most houses had iron beds, folding beds, and cots for sleeping. There were no closets; possessions hung on nails, rested in dressers, or were covered by sheets and quilts. No one had indoor plumbing at Pennytown, and the only refrigerator was owned in the 1960s by Francis and Willa Spears, the last representatives of Pennytown's self-conscious pioneers.

Residents built a community icehouse, which they filled by hauling winter ice from Blackwater River. After this was gone, they drove wagons to Marshall to purchase ice, covering it with blankets until they arrived home with what had not melted. In warm weather, women spent a great deal of time hauling water. Women did laundry in the Davis hole of Blackwater River, using limbs of trees in Pennytown as clotheslines. Others filled water cans for home bathing and for watering the chickens. Although there were a few hand-dug wells, a small spring, and catchment-barrel cisterns that stored rainwater from the roofs of houses, the water supply never lasted into hot weather, and its volume never totally met the needs of people and animals.

Men hunted and trapped small game; they used muzzle-loading shotguns, twenty-two caliber rifles, and most commonly, clubs and dogs. Large game had long since disappeared but squirrel, rabbit, raccoon, opossum, and groundhogs provided meat for their families. The pelts were sold in Marshall. Fishing at Blackwater River, and occasionally at Salt Fork River, proved a regular duty and pastime. Men fished mostly at night since they had time then, using seines for larger harvests. They fished often, as they lacked refrigeration to keep the harvest; occasionally someone canned fish. Fishing continued year-round.

Pennytowners, like southern mountain whites, became expert gatherers. In season they collected large numbers of gooseberries, walnuts, hazelnuts, and hickory nuts. The Shannon Woods provided mushrooms and wild greens—lamb's-quarter, carpenter's square, wild tomato, lettuce, mustard, poke, dandelion, narrow dock, thistle, and more. Women stored dried fruit in paper bags and in stone jars; they protected some food in small cellars for long-term storage. Although everyone raised chickens, the more prosperous added ducks, geese, turkeys, and guinea fowl. Men traded work to white farmers in exchange for runt pigs. Some bartered for males, others for females. After raising them to maturity, neighbors bred the swine and later divided the brood.

Over the years it became increasingly common for blacks to travel to Marshall looking for work, and two "Pennytown corners" developed there, one at the southeast corner and one near the northwest corner of the square, where blacks stood in the morning waiting for whites to pick them up for work. In the evening they congregated there hoping for rides south toward Pennytown. Some blacks began to patronize Marshall doctors including Dr. S. P. Simmons, Dr. W. H. Madison, and Dr. Webb, but since transportation was slow and unpredictable, many persons continued to depend upon age-old folk remedies to combat sickness.

The flu epidemic of World War I exacted a heavy toll among the blacks, and tuberculosis, dropsy, and especially scarlet fever plagued the hamlet. During outbreaks of scarlet fever, they installed quarantine signs on the roads approaching Pennytown. The folk-medicine remedies extracted from weeds, trees, and animals constituted a major part of a successful semi-subsistence economy. Everyone wore asafetida bags, hung around the neck in the fashion of an amulet to ward off germs.[13] Youngsters normally removed the asafetida bag in summer but adopted its use again in the fall. Practitioners mixed skunk grease and quinine for colds and pneumonia; they combined skunk grease and goose grease for croup; and they imbibed sheep-nanny tea for kidney infections. A favorite recitation in the folk tradition came from an Old Testament verse, Ezekiel 16:6, uttered three times: "And when I passed by thee, and saw thee polluted in thine own blood, I said unto thee when thou wast in thy blood, Live; yea, I said unto thee when thou wast in thy blood, Live."

All children were born at home. Dr. Tom Hall delivered many, but women often desired the services of midwife Mrs. Mary Ann Adams, who was widely respected as a folk doctor and known for her special herbal treatments. The last child born in Pennytown was in 1944.

One of the critical cohesive forces in Pennytown was a Baptist church. In 1886, after fifteen years of holding worship services in their homes and in brush arbors, Pennytown residents acquired permission from David Merry, a white landowner, to build a frame house on his land to be used as a church. Perhaps, in the Pennytowners' building tradition, a former white church or school was dismantled and refashioned into the new Baptist church. Dismantled churches, schools, and barns commonly provided materials for new dwellings and "add-ons" in Pennytown from the 1870s into the mid-twentieth century. In 1894 a new owner of the land, Elias D. Shannon, sold one-half acre to the trustees of the Free Will Baptist Church of Pennyville.[14]

At the zenith of Pennytown's development, the frame Free Will Baptist Church burned. Its structural demise in 1924 was only one in a long list throughout Pennytown's history of buildings destroyed by fire. At about the same time, Green Valley Methodist Church at Pennytown discontinued regular services. The community faced for the first time in forty years the prospect of no institutional center; industrious churchwomen launched a drive to build a new one.

Church members bought tile blocks at the Daniels' lumberyard in Marshall. At the time thousands of tile-block buildings were making their appearance on the north and central Missouri landscape due to the economical tile block produced by the Missouri clay industries. Pennytown's block may have come from one of the largest regional producers, two counties north in Chillicothe. Ladies sponsored dinners, held shoebox auctions, and promoted numerous fund-raisers to get the hard-to-come-by cash and materials. Finally, Marshall carpenter Percy Watson and local workmen completed the new church in 1926.

Earlier in the mid-1890s, south Saline County blacks had formed another institution—a fraternal brother- and sisterhood group. Perhaps through association with other Missouri River freemasonry groups, local leaders established a Blackwater Lodge of the United Brothers of Friendship at Napton. By 1905 the C. W. Wright Lodge #166 became the official representative of Pennytown and Napton blacks, and five years later, in March 1910, trustees for the United Brothers of Friendship bought land in Pennytown to build a lodge facility for C. W. Wright Lodge #29.[15]

The United Brothers of Friendship (UBF) and the accompanying Sisters of Mysterious Ten (SMT) had their origins in mid-nineteenth-century Louisville, Kentucky. The organization is known for its membership being drawn from diverse social classes and for its inclusion of males and females.[16] The establishment of this lodge—combined with the institutions of the home, church, and school—gave stability to this growing freedmen's hamlet. It is also important to mention that this lodge, like its Anglo and German American counterparts, enlisted ministers and upwardly mobile blacks for its leadership. In 1924 Rev. Richard Lewis, serving in a long career of leadership, had become "Worshipful Master." William Brown, whose wife was one of the few Pennytown women who never worked out of the home, had become secretary. Twenty-nine members belonged to the UBF and twenty-seven to SMT. Nearly everyone who belonged to the lodge also belonged to the churches.

Dr. Tom Hall, a patron of area blacks, donated money for a small parcel of ground south of the Baptist Church that became known as the "Hall Ground." Dr. Hall regularly housed several blacks as servants and laborers, and he traded his services for Pennytown labor. Pennytown citizens built a foundation and floor as a recreational center to hold picnics, fish fries, and card games. Revelers listened to a hand-cranked Victrola and men pitched horseshoes. Children gathered to play marbles, mumbly-peg, and London Bridge. Unfortunately, not enough money could be raised to construct a building on the floor.

East of the Hall Ground in the Shannon Woods, a bootleg still operated. Saline County whites often met there to purchase the local brew and drink it with Pennytowners. The owner of the Woods allowed Pennytown people to select groves from which they cut their firewood. Occasionally, stray livestock found in the woods provided unexpected sustenance.

The 1920s was a perilous time in American agriculture, and dropping prices and reduced markets resulted in limited work. Pennytown men began staying several days at commercial farms that hired them. Soon they began to move to other parts of Saline and Pettis Counties in order to eliminate costly and time-consuming travel. Stanley Lawrence bought the Green Valley Church and moved it to Marshall, where he refashioned it into a house. Pennytown's population suffered a precipitous decline. In the 1930s men normally made fifty cents a day; some earned a dollar a day in harvest time. Women made fifty cents a day for two or three days and worked the rest of the week for food and milk. A few men worked in regional quarries to supply WPA construction projects, but only a couple of men enlisted in a CCC camp. A select few worked as horse trainers.

The Pennytown folks continued to buy land during the Great Depression. In 1933 Nellie Jackson and Ada Wheeler of Marshall executed a contract for the sale of two acres. Jackson was to pay fifty dollars in monthly installments of three dollars.[17] Five years later, Mrs. J. B. Finley sold a plot of land to Francis Spears for one hundred dollars, payable in regular installments. Indicative of difficult economic times and of both parties' desire to see the real estate deal through, the contract included this clause: "In case this deal falls through Francis Spears promises to pay rent of $10 per year. And if payments have been made to take from ([the] original) amount for settlement of same."[18] Spears, in irregular payments over three years, managed to secure his land.

Within District 93 of Saline County's 112 rural school districts, Pennytown youngsters attended Thomlea School.[19] The community located it in the Bottom—that is, in "lower Pennytown," down the draw leading to Blackwater River. It was a struggle to keep a teacher employed and the school open. In the late 1930s teacher Frank Brown issued a formal complaint to Missouri's attorney general reporting a two-hundred-dollar shortage of Thomlea School's annual allotment. Brown wrote Nellie Jackson, secretary for Pennytown's Patrons Community Association: "If you folks will set in the saddle and ride, the old ship will land us, even tho it costs me my job. I am willing to lose it, right will win so I am not uneasy."[20]

As Brown predicted, he did lose his job, and he, like other Pennytowners, migrated to Kansas City, where he continued to teach school and pastored in the Free Will Baptist Church; he later returned to Saline County to pastor a church in Slater, organize a short-lived boys' ranch near Pennytown, and become a local leader, involving the National Association for the Advancement of Colored People (NAACP) in labor disputes in Marshall. In Saline County the Marceline chapter of the NAACP, organized on the eve of World War II, owes its origin to Brown, a man admired by Pennytown families for his many talents.

Frank Brown also organized Pennytown school exhibits at the Missouri State Fair in Sedalia. Blacks viewed the exhibits while honoring "Black Folks Day," a tradition of fair attendance involving a large network of black families throughout Missouri. The designation, originating in the early twentieth century, appointed Thursday as the day when all blacks, rural or urban, who wanted to and could attend the fair would go to Sedalia to meet friends and relatives. The phrase "Black Folks Day" is still used among those who remember the tradition when visiting friends in contemporary Missouri.

After the 1942–1943 school year Thomlea School disbanded. A half dozen children remained in the last classes that teachers taught, through the ninth grade. The remaining households also soon left, moving to Marshall, except for the elderly who died at Pennytown. Reverend Alexander did not wish to give up regular church services at the Free Will Baptist Church; during the 1960s he often held service without any congregation, meditating alone. As Pennytowners took up residence elsewhere in order to have better jobs, to have a larger society from which their children could choose mates, and to put an end to the incessant hauling of water, they also sought to maintain a connection with the past—an event to ward off "the fear that the comforts of the past may be vanishing before their eyes" and to convince descendants "that the past is present."[21]

At the end of World War II, Penelope Lewis, born among the Pennytown settlers, founded an annual homecoming.[22] It is still held on the first Sunday in August, always near August 4, the traditional black Independence Day.[23] The homecoming is normally well attended and traditionally includes members and descendants of Pennytown's Green Valley Methodist Church. Homecoming convenes at the last building still owned by Pennytown people, the Free Will Baptist Church; in fact, this is the only known institutional building in Missouri that survives at the location of a freedmen's hamlet.[24] Revivalists from St. Louis, Kansas City, Sedalia, and elsewhere once held two- or three-week services at Pennytown; today's celebrants gather for one day a year. They have given donations for the periodic maintenance of the building, but no work has been conducted for about ten years.

An ever-present danger to American life ways is the vulnerability of landscapes developed by ethnic immigrants, a particularly pressing issue for supporters of historic preservation. Buildings that reflect the vernacular architecture of America's ethnic groups often succumb to the vagaries

Pennytown Baptist Church(courtesy of the State Historical Society of Missouri)

of "progress" and the expansion of modern developments.[25] Even at Pennytown the Missouri Farmers Association has for years tried to purchase or condemn the site in order to bulldoze the building and incorporate another one-half acre into its contiguous research farm.

Each August, echoes of 1870s freedmen's voices are heard as former Pennytowners gather on the front lawn of the church to sing "Amazing Grace," "In the Sweet Bye and Bye," "When He Calls Me I Will Answer," and more. The 1986 homecoming included a community dinner at the Mt. Olive Missionary Baptist Church in Marshall. The fellowship remembered their origins, continuing to illuminate the past for the younger generation. A large banner on the wall proudly proclaimed that the "Spirit of Pennytown Lives on 1871–1986."

Chapter 3

"Yours for the Race"

The Life and Work of Josephine Silone Yates

Josephine Silone Yates (courtesy of the Lincoln
Collection, Inman E. Page Library, Lincoln University)

Recent scholarship has drawn historians' attention to the lives and work of a relatively small number of elite African American women who devoted themselves to the fight against racial and gendered prejudice during the first and second generations after slavery.[1] Working through such organizations as the Baptist Church, the Colored Women's League, the National Federation of Afro-American Women, and the National Association of Colored Women, leaders such as Mary Church Terrell, Josephine St. Pierre Ruffin, Ida B. Wells-Barnett, and a host of others sought to uplift the entire race, even as they climbed to lift themselves above the degradation and disadvantage of racial oppression.[2]

One of the many interesting things about these women is that, while they protested against white racism in all its virulent forms during the late nineteenth century, they spent an equal, if not greater, proportion of their time and energy encouraging blacks to live lives that were above reproach. Class mattered to these women. They understood that all blacks, themselves included, would be judged by the actions of the lower class, and they sought to change those actions, to uplift those persons, at all costs. As historian Willard Gatewood has written, "From the perspective of upper-class black women, it was imperative that they assist in lifting the submerged masses, else they ran the risk of being dragged backward into the lower-class ranks."[3]

Josephine Silone, a longtime teacher at Jefferson City's Lincoln Institute and a writer whose passionate pleas for racial uplift appeared in such periodicals as the *Southern Workman*, *The Voice of the Negro*, the *Woman's Era*, *The (Indianapolis) Freeman*, and the *Kansas City Rising Son*, provided the most distinctive mid-American voice in this struggle. Born in 1859 in Mattituck, New York, she was the youngest daughter of Alexander and Parthenia Reeve Silone. Her father was "descended from the dark-brown Silone family of Long Island." According to family legend the Silones traced their ancestry from refugees of a slave ship that wrecked off the coast of New England. Those aboard gained their freedom nearly a century earlier than slaves of the South.[4] Whether or not this account is historically accurate or merely apocryphal, its retelling by family members is consistent with the experiences of many African Americans during the post–Civil War period. Free blacks often wanted to differentiate and even dissociate themselves from "freedmen" and emphasized their free lineage, often by tracing their ancestry to African nobility.[5]

One of Silone's earliest and fondest memories was that of being taught to read from the Bible while snuggled on her mother's lap, her mother "requiring her to call the words as she pointed them out." As a result of this early training, Josephine entered a local district school and was at once admitted to a class of higher standing. She was well advanced in the subjects of reading, writing, and mathematics.[6]

At the age of nine, Josephine wrote and submitted a story for publication to a New York weekly magazine. Although the periodical rejected her manuscript, the girl received a letter of encouragement that "only served to increase rather than diminish her ambition."[7]

Two years later Silone went to Philadelphia to live with a maternal uncle, the Reverend John Bunyan Reeve, so that she could attend the Institute for Colored Youth, a famous black school directed by Fannie Jackson Coppin. Founded by the Society of Friends in 1837, the institute served as a classical high school. It included a preparatory department, a teacher-training course, boys' and girls' high school departments, and later, an industrial curriculum offering courses in carpentry, shoemaking, printing, bricklaying, dressmaking, cooking, and plastering.[8]

At age fourteen Silone accepted the invitation of a maternal aunt to live with her in Newport, Rhode Island, and attend Rogers High School. Silone completed the four-year course in three years and graduated valedictorian of the class of 1877. Next, she studied at the Rhode Island State Normal School, graduating with honors in 1879. Prior to graduation she took the teachers' examination and earned the highest mark recorded in Newport to that date. She was the first African American certified to teach in the schools of Rhode Island.[9]

Silone's early life and education differed from that of the vast majority of African Americans living in the southern and border states during the first generation after the Civil War. Indeed, no evidence indicates that she had even traveled to a former slave state prior to her accepting a job at Missouri's Lincoln Institute in 1881. Silone, only twenty-three years old, arrived at Lincoln fifteen years after the school had been established as a black subscription school, eleven years after it had been designated Missouri's black normal school, and just two years after the state took over its operation. It was also near the end of the first year of Inman E. Page's presidency.

Born a slave in Virginia in 1852, Page was freed when his hardworking father purchased the freedom of Inman, his mother, and his sister. The family moved to Washington, DC, where Inman attended a private school before entering Howard University. During the early 1870s, he attended Brown University in Rhode Island. Graduating in 1877, the same year that Silone graduated from high school in the same state, Page took a teaching job at Natchez Seminary in Natchez, Mississippi. He came to

Lincoln in 1878 as an assistant to the principal, Henry M. Smith. As W. Sherman Savage, the historian of Lincoln University, points out, "Page was the only Negro on a faculty completely manned by white teachers."[10] Page subsequently became the first African American to head the school.

Bowing to the commonly held notion that black parents and students preferred black teachers, one of President Page's first priorities was to replace all the white faculty with black teachers. Josephine A. Silone was among the first persons that he hired. Still a very small school when Silone arrived in the summer of 1881, Lincoln had a faculty consisting of four persons besides herself: the principal, Page, who earned an annual salary of $1,500; a male assistant, who received $600 a year; and two other female assistants who, like Silone, made $500 a year. Enrollment totaled 148 students, most of them in the normal department.[11] Exactly what Silone taught in her first few years at Lincoln is unclear: the 1881 board of regents minutes list her simply as a "female assistant." The 1885 minutes identify her as a teacher of "Chemistry, Elocution and English Literature."[12]

While few details are known about Silone's life as a teacher at Lincoln Institute between 1881 and 1889, there are a few points that can be stated with certainty about the school during this time period. In the 1880s and for decades thereafter, Lincoln was a highly regimented and patriarchal institution. Like Booker T. Washington's Tuskegee Institute, Inman Page's Lincoln was a place where "the management of the school was to be directly under the control of the president."[13] Faculty members not only lived on campus (as did virtually all the students, most of whom were drawn from the working class), they also lived in the same dormitories as the students, providing the teachers with a ready opportunity to exercise direct control over their students. The faculty voted on the disciplinary action to be taken against students who violated the institute's strict code of behavior. For example, during Silone's first year at Lincoln, Charles L. Robinson, a student accused of theft, was expelled from school by a unanimous vote of the faculty.[14] Silone's attitude toward teaching can be gleaned from a 1904 essay entitled "The Equipment of the Teacher," which she published under her married name, Josephine Silone Yates, in *The Voice of the Negro*.[15]

Although she wrote in this essay that "the aim of all true education is to give to body and soul all the beauty, strength and perfection of which they are capable, to fit the individual for complete living," much of the article dealt with less grandiose, more practical matters. Recognizing that her audience was predominately if not entirely African American, Yates assumed that the primary task of the teacher was to encourage and teach behavior that would help to diminish negative racial stereotypes. She considered personal example the best way to accomplish this. Indeed, she asserted, "Some of the most effective functions of the teacher are really performed when he least seems to be teaching, for the very important reason that the power of the teacher's own personal character is constantly creating ideals in a way not laid down in any book."[16]

Well aware of the charge that blacks were less than attentive to personal hygiene, Yates argued, "The teacher should be able to stand before the scholar, before the world, as an illustrious example of what proper attention to the laws of hygiene will do for a man, or a woman." She even asserted, "That educational institution is at fault which sends forth a teacher without this necessary knowledge of hygienic principles."[17]

Aware also of the charge that black teachers were too often unprepared or less prepared than whites, Yates urged black teachers to be ready for their awesome responsibilities. Teaching, she wrote, must be "raised to the dignity of a profession," and it must call forth dedicated men and women willing to devote their lives to its cause. Teachers must be well read and well traveled; they must have "a well disciplined mind, a breadth of vision, a scope of horizon, that comes only with a liberal education, and from personal contact with the affairs of life." To fail as a teacher was more than a personal failure: it was a betrayal of the race.[18]

Silone's success as a teacher during the 1880s attracted the attention of Booker T. Washington. In 1886 he offered her the position of "lady-principal" at Tuskegee Institute if she would leave Lincoln. She declined the offer. Silone did leave Lincoln Institute in 1889 to become the wife of William W. Yates, the Kentucky-born principal of the black Wendell Phillips School in Kansas City. Exactly how or when Silone and Yates met is unclear, but as early as 1885 the two of them appeared on the same program at an annual meeting of the state teachers' association.[19] Silone's abandonment of her teaching career, at least temporarily, in the wake of her marriage to Yates is somewhat surprising considering her later criticism of women who approached teaching as a vocation to be undertaken only until a proper suitor came along.[20]

Although her activities over the next few years remain largely unknown, she gave birth to two children in the 1890s: a daughter born in August 1890, whom the proud mother named Josephine Silone Yates, Jr., and a son, born in August 1895. The son was named William Blyden Yates and called Blyden, presumably in honor of the famed pan-Africanist Edward W. Blyden.[21] She may also have taught in a Kansas City black school. According to some sources, she pursued a career as a writer "mainly for newspaper publication, on a variety of subjects, including such wide-ranging topics as economics and Russian literature." She spent part of her time tutoring those who could not attend the public schools.[22]

In 1893 Yates served as the leading force behind and the first president of the Women's League of Kansas City, an organization of African American women. Among the first projects of the league was the establishment of "an industrial home and school for teaching cooking, sewing and other useful employments." The organization also started a kindergarten and later purchased a six-room house at 1625 Cottage Street as a "Home for Working Girls."[23] No doubt, Yates and other league members were aware of the employment situation for black women in Missouri. According to the 1900 federal census, blacks made up only 5.1 percent of Missouri's total population, yet black women comprised nearly 14 percent of the female labor force in the state. In 1900 there were 21,272 black women participating in the state's paid labor force; 92 percent of them worked in domestic and personal service, most as servants, waitresses, and laundresses.[24]

The Women's League of Kansas City was one of the many black women's clubs that emerged during the last decade of the nineteenth century. Like white women's clubs of the same era, these clubs attracted women with a "similarity of tastes, abilities and character." The clubs provided opportunities for game playing and social interaction, but they also offered much more. Indeed, as Gatewood argues, "By the turn of the century, the club life of upper-class black women had undergone considerable alteration. The emphasis had shifted from domestic concerns and self-culture to an interest in civic reforms and racial uplift efforts."[25]

During 1894–1895, Yates served as the Kansas City Women's League's correspondent to the *Woman's Era,* the first monthly magazine published by black women in this country. Established by the Boston Woman's Era Club in March of 1894, its initial purpose was to inform subscribers "about fashion, health, family life, and legislation."[26] Later issues reflected the club movement's shift to racial uplift efforts and a new emphasis on cohesiveness among clubs. This desire for interaction with like-minded women is evident in Yates's August 1894 correspondence to the periodical: "The possession of such a magazine as the *Era* will give force to the movement and contribute largely toward welding the various organizations into one complete whole, thus rendering work for the race more effective. . . . We look forward with pleasure to the August *Era,* believing that new ideas are gained and possible difficulties avoided by this 'personal contact' as it were with our co-laborers." The letter is signed "Yours for the race, J. Silone Yates."[27]

The growing number of black women's clubs in the 1890s led to the 1896 establishment of a federation of many such clubs into an organization called the National Association of Colored Women (NACW). According to historian Dorothy Salem, "The catalyst for calling a national convention was a slanderous letter sent by a southern journalist to a British reformer. The British reformer sent the letter to Josephine Ruffin, editor of the *Woman's Era*, who included a copy in a Communication to subscribers." The "southern journalist" referred to by Salem was Missouri Press Association president John W. Jacks, who wrote, "The Negroes of this country were wholly devoid of morality, the women were prostitutes and were natural thieves and liars." The NACW formed to refute such sentiments. Mary Church Terrell was elected as the organization's first president.[28]

In her first address to the NACW, Terrell offered this explanation for the organization's scope and membership:

> We have become National because from the Atlantic to the Pacific, from Maine to the Gulf, we wish to set in motion influences that shall stop the ravages made by practices that sap our strength, and preclude the possibility of advancement. . . . We call ourselves an Association to signify that we have joined hands one with the other, to work together in a common cause. We proclaim to the world that the women of our race have become partners in the great firm of progress and reform. . . . We refer to the fact that this is an association of colored women, because our peculiar status in this country . . . seems to demand that we stand by ourselves. . . . Our association is composed of women . . . because the work which we hope to accomplish can be done better . . . by the mothers, wives, daughters, and sisters of the race.[29]

Josephine Silone Yates apparently involved herself in NACW affairs from the beginning. She was elected fourth vice president at the first biennial meeting held in Nashville in September of 1897.[30] W. E. B. DuBois reported that Yates presented an outstanding paper at the organization's 1899 biennial meeting held in Chicago. DuBois asserted that "the women assembled at Chicago . . . were rather above the average of their race, and represented the aristocracy among the Negroes." He praised Yates: "Perhaps the finest specimen of Negro womanhood present . . . a dark-brown matron, with a quiet air of dignity and earnestness." DuBois listed Yates's paper on "An Equal Moral Standard for Men and Women" as among "the best papers of the meeting." The title of the paper suggests a gender consciousness characteristic of elite black women of this period.[31]

At the NACW annual meeting held on July 9–12, 1901, in Buffalo, New York, the election for the office of president deeply divided the membership. The two leading candidates for the position were Margaret Murray Washington, wife of the Tuskegee founder, and Josephine Bruce, spouse of former US senator Blanche K. Bruce. During the convention, however, Washington and Bruce offended many convention delegates by attending a white club meeting instead of a candidates' reception hosted by the all-black Phyllis Wheatley Club of Buffalo. Angered by this apparent act of effrontery, delegates shunned Washington and Bruce and elected Josephine Silone Yates as their president.[32]

This incident may have affected Yates's response to a situation that arose during a stopover in Chicago on a trip to the East later that summer. Ida B. Wells-Barnett, the famous anti-lynching activist, hosted a luncheon, attended by both black and white clubwomen, in Yates's honor. An invitation was extended to Yates to meet with a group of white clubwomen on her return trip through Chicago. "In the meantime," Wells-Barnett later recalled, "an article appeared in one of the daily papers which stated that members of the Chicago Women's Club were being approached to find out if they would accept an invitation to meet a colored woman president of colored women's clubs." Friends sent Yates the article, and she promptly informed Wells-Barnett that she would not meet with any members of the Chicago club. Wells-Barnett encouraged Yates to attend, telling her that the whole thing had been a misunderstanding and urging her to remember "that she must not forget that white women who try to be our friends risked friendships and social prestige by so doing and that we ought not to add to their burdens by taking a narrow viewpoint ourselves." Ultimately, Yates agreed to attend the luncheon and also later attended a meeting of the Social Economics Club where, according to Wells-Barnett, "she delivered a very forceful address and gave that group of white women an opportunity to see and hear one of the ablest black women of the country."[33]

During Yates's presidency, the NACW's membership rose to unprecedented numbers. According to Yates, by 1904 the organization boasted fifteen thousand members spread among twenty-six states and the Indian Territory. Annual meetings were held in each of those states, and "papers on questions of the day [were] read, discussed, and the usual business of a State Federation carefully conducted."[34] As president of the NACW,

Yates continued to urge African Americans to live exemplary lives. In her address at the organization's 1904 convention in St. Louis, she spoke of how slavery had led to "soul debasement" among black people and how, "because of this soul debasement, the Negro, on emancipation, not less than the South, needed to be reconstructed." Much "reconstruction," she argued, had been accomplished, but much remained to be done "before [the Negro's] evolution can be considered complete." Women of the race, Yates stated in a defining comment, had a special responsibility: "It is the position of the women of a race that forms, perhaps, the surest index of its real advancement; of its moral and spiritual growth, as well as of its physical and intellectual advancement." The work and progress of NACW women, she argued, was "one of the best demonstrations or object lessons of the achievements of the race in forty years of freedom." Yates urged her audience to continue toward even greater progress: "These are the years of pioneering; let's hurl a challenge to the women of the country to lift our status higher as we climb."[35]

Years later, in response to an invitation from DuBois to write a section on "Women's Clubs" for one of his Atlanta University Publications series, Yates noted, "Organization is the first step in nation-making, and . . . a nation can rise . . . no higher than its womanhood." She praised the NACW for being a "notable exception" among women's clubs in that it was "an organization founded and controlled entirely by women." That Yates had a dramatic effect on the African American women's club movement, especially in Missouri, is evidenced by the fact that many clubs honored her by naming their organizations for her, including the Josephine Silone Yates Art Club of Sedalia, the Josephine Silone Yates Club of Clayton, and the Yates Literary and Art Club of Louisiana, Missouri.[36]

Yates's role as the NACW president provided her with numerous opportunities to speak and write on racial uplift. She availed herself of those opportunities. In a 1902 letter to Margaret Murray Washington, for example, Yates wrote of speaking trips to Illinois, Iowa, Kansas, and Michigan. In 1903 she was invited to deliver addresses at Atlanta University and at Wilberforce University.[37] Yates also wrote widely. In a 1904 essay published in *The Voice of the Negro*, she encouraged blacks to engage in "the study of high class music" because she believed "that music in the Negro is a heaven-born gift that should be cultivated to its highest extent." She loved classical music of the type performed by violinist Joseph Douglass, grandson of the great Frederick Douglass, at a 1903 Lincoln Institute concert. "The entire character of the concert," Yates wrote, "was such as to raise the Anglo Saxon concept of the Negro's advancement and capacity for the highest degree of culture as well as to increase the latter's respect for the genius of his race." She worried that this gift "should never be allowed to degenerate into a low and unseemly amusement, calculated to degrade rather than to uplift the race." No doubt, ragtime, which had been growing in popularity since the publication of Scott Joplin's *Maple Leaf Rag* in 1899, especially concerned her. Aristocrats of color such as Yates thought ragtime was low-class music and associated it with the un-seemly behavior that they presumed occurred in honky-tonks and dives. The editor of *The (Indianapolis) Freeman*, a newspaper for which Yates periodically wrote, called ragtime tunes "semi-barbaric productions."[38]

Yates also warned against intemperance, calling it "one of the great-est foes to the progress and development of the Negro." She urged black women to develop marketable skills because "the Negro woman has been, and for some time must continue to be . . . 'an assistant' bread-winner if the finances of the race are to be improved." Developing breadwinning skills would help African Americans to become "self-sustaining, indepen-dent, self-reliant," attributes that "the race as a unit" needed to develop "above all else."[39]

Josephine Yates returned to Lincoln Institute to teach for the 1902–1903 school year. The college had grown considerably during the decade she was gone; enrollment numbered more than 250 students. In a 1905 essay entitled "Educational Work at Lincoln Institute," Yates praised those students who were "making heroic struggles to acquire education." She held them up as a model to those "who are daily wasting golden oppor-tunities, and meanwhile are helping to increase the number of criminal Negroes."[40]

Yates's return to the institute coincided with the rise of Benjamin F. Allen to the school's presidency. Born in Savannah, Georgia, in 1872, Allen graduated from Atlanta University. He taught English and pedagogy at Lincoln Institute from 1896 until 1901, took a teaching job at Georgia State College for the 1901–1902 school year, and was elected to the Lincoln presidency on June 12, 1902.[41]

Allen's presidency witnessed a heavy emphasis on vocational training. As Savage has written, "While its special mission was to train teachers for the Negro public schools of the state, the industrial features were stressed, including instruction given in farming, gardening, carpentry, woodworking, blacksmithing, mechanics, shoemaking, sewing, cooking and laundering."[42]

During these years, Yates frequently wrote columns for the *Kansas City Rising Son* and *The (Indianapolis) Freeman* in which she praised Allen and highlighted what she thought were some of the great strides being made at the school under his direction. On one occasion she wrote approvingly of an address President Allen had given. "He spoke of the necessity of building up excellent communities in various parts of the state; of putting brain into one's work; and emphasizing the fact that the Negro must learn to have something that other people need if he hopes to demand proper respect from the world at large."[43] In September 1904, Yates praised the annual Farmers' Convention instituted by Allen. She warned her readers, "If the Negro fails to be land-wise in his day and generation, he will eventually awaken to find himself not only disfranchised, but also minus that other strong, right arm of liberty—the ownership of land." Thus Yates, despite her urban northeastern roots, seemed to understand the great value that landownership held for the former slaves. She argued, "Unless [the Negro] develops much more satisfactorily along other industrial, or professional lines, he must be content to be pushed closer and closer to the wall."[44]

In addition to teaching English and drawing, Yates also served as the advisor of women at Lincoln.[45] One of her responsibilities included advising the women of the Olive Branch, "a musical and literary society composed of the young ladies of the senior and junior classes." In October 1904, Yates wrote that the organization celebrated President Allen's return from a trip "by tendering him a complimentary banquet." She

Cooking Class (courtesy of the State Historical Society of Missouri, 1995-0112)

noted that the Olive Branch held membership in the NACW and reported, "Its members are pledged to go forth into their various communities and ta[k]e up some form of community work for race elevation."[46]

Among the many interesting relationships Yates established during her relatively short life, none was more intriguing than her friendship with Anna Julia Cooper, the author of *A Voice from the South by a Black Woman of the South*. Written in 1892, this book has been referred to by Henry Louis Gates, Jr., as "one of the founding texts of the black feminist movement."[47] Cooper and Yates may have first met in 1893 when Cooper was among a trio of black women invited to speak at the Women's Congress in Chicago. They certainly knew each other by 1899 when they both appeared on the program for the annual meeting of the Afro-American Council, held at the Bethel Church in Chicago. On the second day of the conference, Cooper participated in a panel discussion on the topic "Best System of Education Needed for the Race." On the same day, Yates served as a panelist for a discussion on "Moral Training—Its Needs and Methods."[48] In 1902 Cooper accepted a teaching job at the famous M Street High School (later Dunbar High) in Washington, DC. She was fired from this job in a dispute with the board in 1906. Soon thereafter, and presumably at the instigation of Yates, Cooper became the chair of languages at Lincoln Institute.[49]

For the next several years, Yates and Cooper lived in the same dormitory, a building later named for Yates. In 1910 Cooper went back to teach at the M Street School, and Yates moved to Kansas City following the death of her husband. She continued to teach, this time at the Lincoln High School.

Josephine Silone Yates died abruptly in Kansas City on September 3, 1912, after a two-day illness; she was only fifty-three years old.[50] *The (Indianapolis) Freeman*, which had once carried Yates's articles, eulogized her as a person "who was especially concerned . . . for the betterment of colored women, and for the betterment of the race generally." The *Freeman* bemoaned not only the loss of Yates, but the decline in the number of women who would write clearly and forcefully on the race issue as she had once done. "It looks," the *Freeman* suggested, "as if the mantle of Josephine Yates is interred with her. . . . A few women of Mrs. Yates' ability are yet among us . . . [but] the new people are not playing their part. . . . We deplore the loss of the woman who had such a large share in the colored women's work of racial uplift."[51]

Yates combined the mind of the intellectual with the pragmatism of the politician and the zeal of the missionary. She understood that African American northern migration and urbanization would force black women into the labor force in disproportionate numbers. She sought to prepare those women for their roles as "assistant breadwinners." Understanding the irrationality of white racism and the propensity of racists to judge all blacks by the worst actions of the lowest class, she sought to encourage working-class blacks to live respectable, even impeccable, lives. One could not live only for oneself, she reasoned, especially as a person of color in America. Instead, one must live for the race, and lift even as one climbed.

Chapter 4

The World of Make-Believe

James Milton Turner and Black Masonry

James Milton Turner (courtesy of the State Historical
Society of Missouri)

In 1916 Charleton H. Tandy, a powerful leader of the Missouri black community in his own right, testified before a St. Louis circuit court hearing arguments in the disposition of the recently deceased James Milton Turner's estate.[1] The eighty-one-year-old Tandy had lived in St. Louis since 1857, the year he first met Turner. The court asked the "Old Captain" to confirm the judgment that Turner "was a very prominent man in the country." He responded that Turner was "very prominent; [he was] one of the foremost leading negroes in the State of Missouri."[2]

Tandy's judgment appears accurate, especially if the adjectives "noticeable" and "conspicuous" are considered synonymous for "prominent." And yet, for much of his seventy-six-year life, which began in 1839, Turner was a leader without a constituency. The explanation for his ineffectiveness as a leader involves a somewhat long and complicated story, the ins and outs of which are detailed elsewhere.[3]

The essence of Turner's problem, however, was that his education and socialization as an antebellum free black in Missouri and at Oberlin College in Ohio oriented him toward a set of values quite different from the values of the black masses who emerged from slavery in the 1860s.[4] Well-steeped in white middle-class standards, Turner measured success, both his and the black masses', by those standards. After some brilliant successes as a leader of the Missouri black community, especially in the 1870 election, Turner lost his following because he condescendingly snubbed the way of life of the former slaves and because he appeared to be too opportunistic. Likewise, white racism precluded his acceptance into white society.

This rejection by both the black masses and whites caused Turner to seek membership in an elite black fraternal organization—Prince Hall Freemasonry. This organization institutionalized the very type of white bourgeois values and behavior with which Turner was comfortable.[5] Consequently, Masonry provided him with an island of familiarity and friendliness in a sea of hostility and hate. Masonry, as the well-known black sociologist E. Franklin Frazier wrote, offered one method of retreating into "the world of make-believe."[6]

William A. Muraskin's conclusions about black Freemasonry generally, outlined in his book entitled *Middle-Class Blacks in a White Society: Prince Hall Freemasonry in America*, seem to apply to Turner.[7] Muraskin argues that, among other things, Prince Hall Masonry performed significant psychological and social functions for its members. It allowed the black victim of white racism to respond creatively to the limitations placed upon him. It permitted the black person to

> create an integrated self-image for . . . [himself] as an upstanding
> American citizen; it . . . helped psychologically bind the black Ma-
> son to white society by enabling him to identify with the Caucasian
> middle class; it . . . created a haven within the larger black society
> where bourgeois Negroes have received protection from the life
> style of the nonbourgeois blacks who surround[ed] them; and while
> having helped to create a positive sense of community among its
> middle-class adherents, it . . . served to estrange them from the mass
> of black people.[8]

Those functions proved important to Turner. He always had been different from the masses of black people and he cherished the difference.
He grew up in St. Louis, the son of a free black horse doctor, whose life
bore little resemblance to that of the black masses. His family sought to
perpetuate and even heighten that differentiation in his own life by sending him to the best schools available. His education, in violation of Missouri law, in white and black Christian schools oriented him toward the
bourgeois values best summed up in E. Franklin Frazier's phrase, "piety,
thrift, and respectability."[9] Later, as a young adolescent, he attended that
hotbed of Christian abolitionism, Oberlin College in Ohio. Subsequently,
as a post–Civil War educator, he tried to pass on to the freedmen those
same virtues, thereby hoping to alter the value system of the black folk
culture that he thought they had inherited from slavery days.[10]

In the late 1860s, Turner emerged as the most important black educator in the state. The exposure he gained in his work on behalf of black
education made him a natural choice for the Radical Union party when
it searched for a leader who could coalesce a potentially powerful black
vote. By 1870 the Radicals experienced political problems. They needed
the black vote and prepared to recruit it through extensive efforts. The
motives of the Republicans who aligned themselves with blacks exempli-
fied utilitarianism and short-sightedness. Their support of black causes
reflected more the precariousness of Missouri politics than a genuine
manifestation of concern for black people.[11]

Both the Radicals and Turner stood to gain from this alignment. Unable to separate his own progress from that of the general population of
black freedmen, Turner interpreted the Radicals' overtures as evidence of
their commitment to equal opportunity for all blacks. Consequently, he
viewed the Republican party as an effective vehicle for the advancement

of all black people, including himself, into the world of the white middle class. So convinced, he actively campaigned for the Radical political candidates in 1870, delivering, according to one contemporary account, twenty thousand black votes to their cause. Throughout that campaign, he exhorted the freedmen to adopt the values of industry and frugality so that they could accumulate wealth, which he labeled as the source of all power.[12]

His almost fanatical commitment to the Radical party, however, had mixed results. On the one hand, the Radicals rewarded his unfailing support by facilitating his appointment to the position of Minister Resident and Consul General to Liberia. On the other hand, a wave of suspicion swelled up around him, raising questions about the purity of his motives.[13]

Turner carried his bourgeois value system with him to Liberia. He was proud of his position, largely because it gave him status and recognition; in short, it differentiated him from the black masses. He, in turn, continued to identify middle-class values as the keys to success. Indeed, because he found the native African lifestyle so inconsistent with those values, he searched for ways to uplift what he continuously referred to as a barbaric civilization. He earnestly desired to become an instrument for progress and Christianization on the west coast of Africa.[14]

Ultimately he had little success in the achievement of that goal, and in 1878 he returned to St. Louis, hopeful of going on to bigger and better things. Unfortunately, his extremely optimistic expectations proved a far cry from the social reality he faced upon his return. Post-Reconstruction America was unconcerned about black civil rights.[15]

Turner tried, in 1878, to reestablish a black political coalition that would allow him to regain power and influence. However, racist Republicans rejected his bid for public office in that year. Moreover, after he had some initial success with the black masses, many of them began to see his politicking as transparently opportunistic. Hence, he became a focal point of controversy in the late 1870s and early 1880s when he tried to established an agency to facilitate the movement of southern blacks to the "promised lands" of Kansas and Oklahoma.[16]

This effort also failed. Turner, however, discovered another cause to which he could apply his many talents: in 1883, he struck off to right wrongs, and get rich, in the Oklahoma Territory. Having long before become convinced that wealth could buy power and status, he sought to make money. But because he also saw his own destiny inextricably bound to the advancement of black people, he welcomed an opportunity "to do well by doing good." In Oklahoma he engaged in complicated but potentially profitable legal maneuverings on behalf of black freedmen who had been the slaves of Indians in antebellum days.[17]

Turner worked as an attorney for the freedmen regularly from 1883 until his death in 1915. Throughout the first decade of that thirty-two-year period he made repeatedly unsuccessful efforts to reestablish the kind of political power that had earned him the Liberian ministership in 1871. He was unable to obtain a following, however, largely because the constituency he courted saw his motives as being self-serving.[18]

These non-Masonic aspects of Turner's career must be understood if one is to come to grips with one of the most important points about Turner as a Mason: he did not turn to Masonry until he had virtually given up on retrieving his lost status, in both the white and the black communities. Turner left behind no explanations about why he waited until 1890, fifty-one years after his birth, to become a Mason. Clearly, although he did not become a Mason until 1890, he had repeated and prolonged contact with Masons for thirty years or more. Masons made up a large part of the leadership of the Missouri Equal Rights League, which came into existence in 1865 and which Turner served as secretary. Despite the presence of Masons in Monrovia, Liberia, the small West African city in which Turner lived from 1871 to 1878, no extant evidence indicates that he became a member. For instance, in 1879 a committee of St. Louis Masons investigated the status of Masonry in Liberia. Turner had just returned from that country the year before. Certainly he could have been expected to provide information if he had been a Mason. Apparently he was not contacted, for his name is not mentioned in the committee's report.[19]

Turner's failure to associate with the Masons during the years of the 1860s through the 1880s corresponds with his optimism during much of that period of being accepted into the mainstream of white society. Lodges were separate and, consequently, inferior to white society; Turner refused to accept an inferior position in life because of his race. Not, at least, until the frustrations of the 1880s had sufficiently dulled his expectations did Turner seek status and solace elsewhere.

Prince Hall Freemasonry appeared the logical place for Turner to turn. Institutionally, Freemasonry accepted and endorsed the same bourgeois standards of respectability and morality that Turner had made part of his value system in antebellum Missouri. Endorsement of those values meant, by extension, a good deal of emphasis on differentiating Masonic behavior from the behavior of the black masses, a cleavage that Turner had always tried to effect in his own life.[20]

Turner entered the mysterious world of Masonry slowly, simply being listed as one of eighty-two members in Widow's Son Lodge of St. Louis in 1890. He did not attend the Annual Communication that year.[21] By 1893, however, he had risen to the level of second-ranking officer in Widow's Son Lodge.[22] At last he had found a forum for political activity in which he could act out all the roles he had longed to play in the mainstream culture. That, Muraskin argues, was one of the vital functions performed by Masonry. "Free Masonry allows its adherents to act as if they were first-class American citizens," he writes. "If one wishes to be an active participant in the democratic political process and carry out civic responsibilities, one can."[23]

In 1894, Turner rose to the leadership of Widow's Son. As its Worshipful Master, he represented his lodge at the Twenty-eighth Annual Communication, held at Moberly.[24] He actively participated in the election of officers for the Communication, obviously relishing the reality of his ability to once again influence votes and persuade people. He also took particular interest in two measures designed to preserve the history of black Masonry in Missouri.[25]

According to William Muraskin, the Masonic sense of history proves crucial to an understanding of the organization. By tracing its foundation to Prince Hall, a free black of the eighteenth century, the fraternity "has erased from the mind of the black Mason his actual descent from slaves." In the process, also, it has given him a new heritage; or, as Muraskin writes, it has allowed the black man, as the inheritor of the Masonic past, to cease "to be a poor, insignificant member of an oppressed group and . . . become a member of the most important and idealistic institution the world has ever seen!"[26] Little wonder, then, that Turner, who had so often been maligned and unappreciated, moved to keep the same thing from happening to others in that 1894 meeting. On the first day of the convention an address was delivered by "Bro. W. P. Brooks, one of the oldest Masons in Missouri." Brooks remained the only living charter member of the Grand Lodge of Missouri. He recounted in an "impressive and interesting" fashion the early days of the organization. At the conclusion of Brooks's remarks, G. W. Guy and Turner offered a resolution. Subsequently adopted by the convention, the resolution called for Brooks to furnish a synopsis of the lodge's early history for publication in the *Official Proceedings*.[27]

Another resolution followed, offered by Joe E. Herriford, G. W. Guy, and Milton Turner. It recalled "with pride" the record of Missouri's Most Worshipful Grand Lodge and pointed out the necessity of maintaining a historical record of that proud past. Additionally, it proposed to collect the proceedings of each of the previous twenty-eight Annual Communications, bind them, and place them under the care of the Grand Secretary. Turner offered an amendment to the resolution, calling for a copy of each of the *Proceedings* to be sent to the Missouri Historical Society in St. Louis and for W. P. Brooks to be a member of the committee formed to carry out that task.[28]

Elected Worshipful Master of Widow's Son Lodge again in 1895, Turner represented his lodge at the Annual Communication in Lexington.[29] He continued to participate actively in the routine business of the convention and offered a special resolution for consideration by the entire body.[30]

The resolution proposed "to establish a Masonic Home for indigent Master Masons, their widows and orphans."[31] The Grand Master appointed a committee to carry out the resolution. Perhaps assigning the task to a committee temporarily destroyed it, for the Masonic Home did not come to fruition for another decade.

Turner's advocacy of the Masonic Home, nevertheless, can be seen as symbolically significant in two ways. First of all, it came at a time when his disillusionment with white America had reached its height. Convinced that blacks could no longer look to whites for help, he endorsed a plan by which they could take care of their own. That same logic compelled him to support the resolutions offered by the Committee on Masonic Relief, on which he also served. The committee had the responsibility of approving payments to indigent Masons.[32]

The Masonic Home and the Relief Committee performed another, perhaps more important, function. William Muraskin has indicated that one of the basic goals of orphanages was that "the children in the home were raised to be model citizens, embodying as much as possible all the middle-class virtues in which Masons placed so much faith." In short, the Masonic Home provided Masons with the opportunity to be frugal, save their money, and invest in a project that would ultimately contribute to the advancement of the race. It gave them complete control, and it became "an arena for the realization of the ideals of self-help, thrift, hard work, and cleanliness." In the process, it also served as a mechanism for differentiating the behavior of black Masons from the black masses.[33] This appeared an important distinction to Turner.

The Thirtieth Annual Communication occurred in Jefferson City in 1896, the scene of many of Turner's political triumphs more than a quarter of a century before. He attended the meeting, although he no longer served as Worshipful Master of Widow's Son.[34] On the second day of the proceedings, Turner, whose status had been enhanced by an appointment to the rank of "Grand Orator," proposed that the lodge appropriate money to buy land for a Masonic Orphans' Home.[35] The Committee on Masonic Relief subsequently endorsed Turner's proposal and created a committee "to devise ways and means of founding and maintaining said home." As a matter of procedure, however, the proposal had to be submitted to all the lodges throughout the state.[36]

On the third day of the Communication, meetings were temporarily suspended so that the lodge could accept Capital City Lodge No. 9's invitation "to take a drive to the principal points of interest in the city." Grand Master J. H. Pelham placed the lodge in the hands of Special Grand Marshal, J. Milton Turner.

The 250 lodge members gathered in the driveway encircling the Capitol, where carriages awaited them. The caravan crossed "the great new steel bridge [spanning the Missouri River] connecting North Missouri with South Missouri." It continued on to the prison, then to Lincoln Institute, then to "other points of interest." The institute offered the greatest attraction. The cortege gathered to hear speeches in the institute's newly erected forty-thousand-dollar building, Memorial Hall, at which point Grand Master Pelham urged "the Brethren" to send their children "to this great institution of learning."[37] The tour over and the lodge back in session, Turner offered a resolution of pride in "Lincoln Institute and its management." He called attention to the institute as "the magnificent gift of the old soldiers and the generous State of Missouri to the cause of education." Ever consistent in his belief in education as the key to black upward mobility, Turner included in his resolution the assertion that the institute held "great promise for the Negroes of the State of Missouri." He added, "we commend it to the hearty support of the Negro Masons of the State."[38]

Turner represented Widow's Son Lodge at the 1897 annual meeting and served on three regular committees: "Rules and Order of Business," "Jurisprudence," and "Grand Master and Grand Lecturer's Address." The Grand Master devoted much of his address to an endorsement of the proposed Masonic Home. He commended his listeners on Masonic progress over the past decade, reporting to them that their efforts had made it possible for sixty thousand dollars to be paid to widows and orphans during that period. However, he warned against too much self-adulation. "If it shall transpire," he said, "after all our grand pretentious and phenomenal success, we permit a Negro Mason to die in destitution or in the alms house of the State we shall be disgraced." He urged his fellow Masons to "take immediate steps . . . to provide for the wants of our poor and destitute Masons." That, he argued, was the real purpose of Masonry. "As I comprehend its symbols," he said, "*this* is its teaching, and as I believe in its principles *this* is its design."[39]

Inspired by the speech, Turner called for its submission to the *St. Louis Globe-Democrat* for publication.[40] Later, his Committee on the Address "heartily" endorsed the Grand Master's suggestion "with reference to the subject of Masonic Relief" and resolved "to entirely adopt the language of his address, and to request the M. W. Grand Lodge to set apart a day for a sermon, to be universally preached throughout this Jurisdiction upon the subject of Masonic Relief and Charity." The resolution went on to recommend that the Committee on the Masonic Home be "empowered during the ensuing Masonic year, for a reasonable rental or lease to secure premises for such few indigent Masons, their widows and orphans as may be within the financial power of this M. W. Grand Lodge to care for."[41]

Although a member of Widow's Son Lodge in 1898 and 1899, Turner did not attend the Communication those years. In addition, no further mention of the proposed Masonic Home appeared in either the 1898 or 1899 Annual Communications.[42] Perhaps Turner's work among the Cherokee freedmen and a short-lived farm-implement business, begun in St. Louis in 1898, kept him too busy during that time.[43]

No *Official Proceedings* are available for the years 1900 and 1901, to reveal whether Turner returned as an active Mason during those years. He did attend the annual meeting held on August 19-21, 1902, at Cape Girardeau. Still a member of Widow's Son, Turner was nominated for the post of Junior Grand Warden. Curiously, he asked that he not be considered for the post.[44]

The 1902 gathering also witnessed a pathetic, but unexplained, display of self-pity by Turner that apparently moved the entire convention. For whatever reason, Turner obviously sought recognition. Perhaps his status in the Missouri Masonic community was less than he thought it should be. He might have expected to be named to the Worshipful Grand Mastership rather than to the lesser position of Junior Grand Warden. At any rate, Turner arose ostentatiously during the middle of the convention and asked permission to bid the members of the Grand Lodge good-bye, "because imperative duties called him away." In his leave-taking, he asked that a special record be made of his desire "that Bros. Chinn, Pelham, Ricketts and Kenner [all high-ranking Masons] be selected to pronounce the Masonic eulogy over his lifeless remains" should "death call him hence before the next session." According to the *Official Proceedings*, Turner then said good-bye, "with an impressiveness that lent solemnity to the scene . . . amid the tearful silence of numbers deeply affected."[45]

Whatever the explanation for the strange leave-taking, death did not call Turner before the next meeting, and he returned for the Thirty-seventh Annual Communication, held at Richmond in 1903.[46] Whether the result of his impromptu speech of the year before or not, the 1903 gathering conferred upon him an honor reserved for only a select few. For the first time, Turner's photograph appeared in the *Official Proceedings*, the same uncommon honor that he had recommended for W. P. Brooks nine years earlier.[47] In addition, Turner resurfaced as an active participant in the routine business of the lodge and served on several committees.[48]

One of those committees assessed the current condition of black people in the country. The committee's report thus offers insight into Turner's view of the status of blacks as of 1903. The report asserted that the conditions confronting black people were "ominous and threatening." It emphasized that the United States was the home of American blacks, recalling Frederick Douglass's statement, "now that he [the black man] is a free man [he] demands that he be allowed to rest beneath the protecting folds of the stars and stripes."[49] Turner had expressed a similar sentiment nearly thirty years before when he adamantly opposed Liberian emigration schemes. In 1877 he wrote that the American black man was "as much a foreigner as any other people" to Africa.[50]

The committee also emphasized that American blacks had been loyal to their government. It recalled how "the pages of history records no more brilliant achievements" than the role played by black men who bore arms in defense of their country from the American Revolution through the Spanish American War. Black literacy rates, the committee emphasized, had risen from 22 percent in 1880 to 46 percent in 1890 and 64 percent in 1900. In keeping with its bourgeois orientation, the Masonic committee singled out Booker T. Washington as an exemplar of industry and virtue and identified Tuskegee as "a magnificent testimonial to the capability and genius of the greatest Negro educator of the age."[51]

The committee acknowledged that the country had been prosperous during the previous six years. Blacks, it stated, had clearly contributed to and benefited from that prosperity. Despite the efforts and successes of black people, however, the fact remained that "the humiliating conditions attempted to be forced upon the Negro have become more accentuated than at any time since the Negro was clothed with the panoply of American citizenship." The most appalling example of that "humiliating condition" related to the increase of "the atrocious and indefensible crime of lynching."[52]

Not all of the problems afflicting blacks, the committee acknowledged, emanated from white racism. In words reminiscent of Turner's long-standing criticism of the black masses, it noted that the "moral condition" of blacks needed to be "decidedly improved," adding that "it behooves every Negro [who] desires the prevalence of a better condition of affairs, to bend their whole energies to instill in the masses higher ideals and more wholesome surroundings." The committee's report on the "State of the Country" concluded with an appeal to all American citizens "to rally to the standard of fair play and equal opportunity."[53]

The topic of a Masonic Home was finally revived at the 1905 Annual Communication, after being ignored for nearly ten years. Turner led discussion on the topic, serving as chairman of the Special Committee on the Masonic Home. His report to the Communication argued that Masonic charity remained one of the fundamental principles upon which the Masonic order rested. The best way to demonstrate a firm belief in

Masonic Home near Hannibal (courtesy of the State Historical Society of Missouri, 001746)

the importance of "this great human principle" was to create a fund, "for the purchase of a Masonic Home for poor and indigent . . . Masons, their widows and orphans." This could be done, he explained, by assessing each Mason five cents per month. Those present accepted Turner's proposal and authorized the Grand Master and Grand Secretary to select a site. A Masonic Home was in operation near Hannibal by the next annual meeting.[54]

Turner's name appeared on the Widow's Son Lodge roster in 1905. He played an active role at the meeting that year. The Communication was held in Boonville, the site of one of Turner's early teaching positions nearly forty years before. The Boonville mayor greeted the convention-eers with an opening address, to which Turner was asked to respond. He stated that his long acquaintance with the town's residents allowed him to acknowledge "gladly" their "genuine character." He hinted that he wanted to become the Most Worshipful Grand Master of the organization when he pointed out that the last three Grand Masters had been persons identi-fied with the educational interests of Boonville. He went on to assure the mayor and his listeners that "Boonville was the Masonic Mecca, dear to the hearts of all those who aspired to that position," an obvious statement about his own aspirations.[55]

Brother Turner also served as a cochairman of the Committee on Complaints and Grievances in 1905.[56] This committee acted as an ap-peals court for Masons dissatisfied with the justice handed out to them by local lodges. It also helped the Masons police themselves and enforce the higher moral standards called for by Turner's committee in its 1903 "State of the Country" message. The importance of outward behavior to the Masons demanded that brushes with the civil authorities be treated harshly. In 1905, for example, Turner's committee sustained a judgment by William Henry Lodge No. 45 of Platte City, expelling William Pearson for criminal conviction by the Missouri courts. Likewise, it sustained a similar ruling by True Blue Lodge of St. Louis against Thomas Sanders. It also recommended the indefinite suspension of W. S. Carrion who was found guilty by Wilkerson Lodge "of shooting with intent to kill . . . J. R. A. Crossland."[57]

Masonic records for the years 1906 and 1907 cannot be found. In 1908, however, Turner again participated actively in Masonic affairs when members assembled at Hannibal for the Forty-third Annual Communi-cation. His photograph appeared in the publication of that year, along with the following notation: "Bro. Turner is a national character. He has held many responsible positions as representative of his people. He is deservingly popular with the craft for his suave manner and unselfish devotion to the elevation of his fellow man."[58]

Appropriately enough, there also appeared in the 1908 *Proceedings* a photograph of the new Masonic Home that Turner had been instrumental in establishing.[59] The Grand Master, in his annual address, said that "the purchase of property and the establishment of a home for the old and decrepit members of this Jurisdiction" was "the most creditable thing [we] have ever done." He congratulated those present, offering them an invitation to visit the home, a short distance from the convention site.[60]

Turner participated in other ways as well in 1908. Early in the convention he addressed the entire body, recalling the importance of Masonic history, speaking "eloquently of the sacrifices of the Masonic pioneers with whom he was acquainted." He emphasized "that we owe to those heroes a debt of gratitude which we should be ever ready to pay."[61] Again he participated in the election process, seconding Brother Ricketts's nomination to the office of Grand Master.[62] Brother Ricketts, in turn, named Turner as Grand Marshal for the "public parade."[63] In addition to those activities, Turner also served again on the Committee on Complaints and Grievances.[64]

Turner appears to have become quite inactive after that 1908 meeting, although the evidence is inconclusive. *Official Proceedings* for the period 1909 through 1915 are not available, except for 1910. The record of the annual gathering at Hannibal in that year includes Turner's name as a member of Phoenix Lodge No. 78 in St. Louis. He did not, however, attend the annual meeting.[65] Likewise, Turner's will, written only a few weeks before his death on November 1, 1915, hints that he had ceased Masonic activities several years prior to 1915.[66]

Why Turner's Masonic career ended so abruptly cannot be ascertained. Perhaps he had been hopeful of rising to the leadership of the Missouri Masons, as his speech of 1905 suggests, and simply gave up on that hope by 1910. If so, holding the position of Grand Marshal and having his photograph published in the *Official Proceedings* were insufficient recognition when measured against his expectations. Likewise, perhaps status in a segregated organization no longer seemed desirable to him. Whatever the reason for his withdrawal, Turner obviously came to feel less eager about being involved in Masonic activities. When he died in Oklahoma in 1915 as a result of injuries suffered in a tank car explosion, the *Official Proceedings* included a brief obituary, noting his membership in Phoenix Lodge. Significantly, it spoke of Turner as a hero out of the somewhat distant past, identifying him as "for many years Grand Marshal of the Grand

Lodge." His name had been a household word among blacks in the early 1880s, it said, implying that he had been much less known, if not forgotten, after that, and concluded by noting that he was "as an orator . . . gifted as few men this race and country have ever known."[67]

Turner's name appeared in the *Official Proceedings* for the last time in 1917. George L. Vaughn, attorney for the Most Worshipful Grand Lodge of Missouri, reported that the lodge had become a litigant in the disposition of Turner's estate. His will had been contested by "persons alleging themselves to be his heirs." Turner had willed one thousand dollars to the Masonic Home at Hannibal.[68]

That deed provided a fitting end to Turner's relationship with black Missouri Masonry. By 1909 or 1910, Turner virtually had given up on ever receiving what he regarded as his just due, either in white or black society. Not even the Masonic world of make-believe could completely insulate him from what he considered to be racist whites and unappreciative blacks. However, he had not given up his belief that the values he had internalized early in his life still held the key for the advancement of the black masses. Hence, his support of the Masonic Home, both in life and in death, was a measure of his commitment to passing that orientation on to a new generation of particularly vulnerable blacks. His growing estrangement from Masonic activities after that time period and his penchant for isolating himself from the political and social activism of his earlier years were acts of submissive resignation: he knew that, at least for himself, it no longer mattered.

Chapter 5

George Washington Carver's Missouri

On March 31, 1888, the *Ness County News,* published in Ness City, Kansas, carried a brief biographical sketch of George Washington Carver's life.[1] At the time Carver was a young, twenty-something, would-be sodbuster, still far removed from the fame he would gain as a scientist a generation or more later. He had not yet enrolled at Simpson College in Iowa; he had not yet attended Iowa State College at Ames; he had not yet gone to work at Tuskegee Institute in Alabama. Indeed, one wonders if at that early date he had even heard of Tuskegee or its famous founder, Booker T. Washington.

One wonders, in fact, what he had really accomplished by 1888 that prompted the newspaper biographer to take note of him. Like virtually all of the Carver biographies since, the story in the *Ness County News* emphasized Carver's rise from slavery and measured the progress of his life against the obstacles he faced. Already by 1888, the biographer noted:

> [Carver's] knowledge of geology, botany and kindred sciences is remarkable, and marks him as a man of more than ordinary ability.... [He] has gathered a collection of about five hundred plants in a neat conservatory adjoining the residence of his employer, besides having a large geological collection in and around the place. He is a pleasant and intelligent man to talk with, and were it not for his dusky skin—no fault of his—he might occupy a different sphere to which his ability would otherwise entitle him.

I want to explore this notion of Carver "as a man of more than ordinary ability," something that was recognized by a *Ness County News* writer even before Carver's career as a scientist began. And I want to look back into George Washington Carver's early life, and into Carver's Missouri, to try to understand at least a little more about him and why he stood out from the crowd.

Any account of the Missouri years of the distinguished African American scientist George Washington Carver must begin with an explanation of the challenging circumstances surrounding his birth and early life. It would be difficult to imagine how he could have been born at a more dangerous time, in a more threatening place, under more challenging circumstances.

The exact date of Carver's birth has been disputed for more than a century. Even he remained unsure of his birth date. In a memoir written in "1897 or thereabouts," he reported, "[a]s nearly as I can trace my history I was about 2 weeks old when the [Civil] war closed."[2] That would place his birth date in the early spring of 1865, perhaps in late March or early April. In a second reminiscence, written some twenty-five years later, Carver reported that "I was born in Diamond Grove, Mo., about the close of the great Civil War."[3] Both Linda McMurry and I accepted the 1865 birth date for Carver in our books; if that date is, in fact, right, George Washington Carver was never a slave, since slavery officially ended in Missouri on January 11, 1865.

Still later in his life, Carver often reported his birth year as 1864, although he offered no evidence to support that date. His uncertainty about exactly when he was born, his inability to establish a definitive date, and the fact that his birth was such an inauspicious event that no one recorded or remembered its occurrence were factors that could have scarred and stifled him for life. He was, after all, one of more than a hundred thousand African Americans living in Missouri, a state where for decades blacks were regarded as property before the law and as inferior to even the lowest class of whites.

Carver's mother was a slave named Mary, owned by an Ohio-born couple, Moses and Susan Carver, who moved to Newton County, Missouri, during the late 1830s, making them among the earliest white settlers in the area. The Carvers acquired Mary in 1855, their alleged hostility toward the institution of slavery overridden by their need for help in a land where free labor was scarce and expensive. The 1860 federal slave schedule for Newton County suggests that Mary was twenty years old in that year and that she was the mother of an infant son, George's older brother, James. She was one of 426 slaves in a county whose population numbered more than 9,000 people.[4]

Carver's father, he later learned, "was the property of Mr. Grant, who owned the adjoining plantation," by which, no doubt, he meant "farm."[5] There were no Old South–like plantations in Newton County. The "Mr. Grant" to whom Carver referred was likely James Grant, a North Carolina native who was seventy-five years old in 1860 and the owner of two male slaves, one forty-six years old in 1860, the other Mary's age in the same year. While either of those men, or even Moses Carver, could have been George's father, it seems likely, at least to me, that the younger man would have served that role. George's father, whose name he apparently never knew, was killed in an accident before the future scientist was even born.

Moses and Susan Carver, the white couple who owned the black Carvers, were forty-seven and forty-six years old, respectively, in 1860. Living in their household in that year, in addition to Mary and James, was a twenty-two-year-old Missouri-born white male named Jackson Carroll, who worked on the farm as a laborer. As such, he was the principal assistant to Moses Carver on the southwest Missouri prairie land farm that consisted of 220 acres of unimproved land and 100 acres of improved land. The 1860 agricultural census suggests that the Carver family subsisted on the farm's produce, with relatively little being raised for a market economy. In 1860 the Carvers owned eleven horses, at least some of which, according to local lore, were "race horses," four "milch" cows that produced two hundred pounds of butter, and eleven head of "other" cattle. The farm's major crop was Indian corn; Carver raised a thousand bushels of it, most if not all of which would have been consumed by his livestock. He also raised two hundred bushels of oats. Eleven sheep produced twenty-four pounds of wool, and bees owned by the Carvers produced two hundred pounds of honey. Moses Carver slaughtered his own meat, including one or more of his fifteen head of swine. The farm was, indeed, a relatively small operation, and it would have been a place where Carver would have learned firsthand the lessons of frugality, conservation, and making do.

The Civil War, which officially began with the Confederates' firing on Fort Sumter in South Carolina, on April 12, 1861, was an especially fratricidal conflict in deeply divided Missouri. The state's governor, Governor Claiborne Fox Jackson, one of Saline County's largest slave owners, sought to move the state into the Confederacy in the wake of President Abraham Lincoln's election in the fall of 1860. Lincoln, the candidate who opposed the expansion of slavery, garnered only twenty-two votes in Newton County, out of nearly fourteen hundred votes cast. The secessionist candidate, John C. Breckenridge of Kentucky, received more than ten times the number of votes that Lincoln earned. Union Democrat Stephen A. Douglas of Illinois carried both the state and the county, although in Newton County more voters cast votes for his three opponents than for him.

When a state convention held in St. Louis in January 1861 refused to allow the state to secede from the Union, Governor Jackson tried to effect the state's secession on his own. Driven from the capital city by Union soldiers under the command of General Nathaniel Lyon in June 1861, Governor Jackson tried some months later to set up a rump government in the Newton County seat of Neosho, where Confederate General Sterling Price occupied the town for a time, before moving on to Arkansas and later Texas. Jackson died in exile in 1862, still convinced he was Missouri's legitimate governor.

Many Missourians, although certainly not a majority, continued to support the Confederate cause throughout the war years, even though Missouri remained officially in the Union. Bloodshed, violence, and mayhem reigned in Missouri throughout the four-year conflict and beyond.

Much violence and destruction occurred in Newton County, where Carver was born, during the Civil War as well. After all, nearly 3,000 of Newton County's 8,895 residents in 1860 were born in the Southern states of Tennessee, Kentucky, North Carolina, or Virginia. The county was the location of a hard-fought contest between Union and Confederate sympathizers in September of 1862. The Battle of Newtonia, as it was called, was a decisive Confederate victory, a battle in which at least fifty Union soldiers were killed and eighty or more captured. But that battle was only the most pronounced and visible of the conflicts that occurred in the county during the war. Guerilla violence by supporters of both sides was common during the war, and some county residents, like Missourians elsewhere, used the war to settle old scores, real or imagined. People were robbed and killed and property stolen. Private and public buildings, including the county courthouse, were destroyed. The economy was left in shambles.[6]

Missouri's Union Provost Marshal reviewed 178 cases in Newton County alone during the war, an average of nearly one per week during the four years of fighting. Many of these cases had to do with questions about loyalty to the Union. Others dealt with charges of violence against Newton County residents and/or the destruction of property. Early in the war, a series of cases documented a fight over control of a lead-smelting operation at Granby, and in late 1863, the Provost Marshal addressed the charge that a marauding band of uncertain allegiance had robbed a smallpox hospital near Newtonia, taking food and clothing and small arms from a nearby house.

The Battle of Newtonia occurred less than thirty miles from the Moses Carver farm in Newton County. The war came directly to the Carver household on multiple occasions, the first apparently in 1862, when Moses Carver was accosted by marauders who strung him up by his thumbs in an attempt to force him to tell where he had allegedly buried a cache of gold. This incident remained an important part of Carver family lore long after its occurrence.

Still later in the war, not long after George's birth, another band of armed men attacked the Carver household. This time, instead of trying to steal money they stole two of Carver's slaves, the young woman named Mary and her infant child, George. Moses Carver apparently had time to hide George's older brother, James. According to an account of the event written by Carver in 1922, he reported that the thieves, "carried my mother and myself down into Arkansas, and sold my mother." Moses Carver hired someone to try to retrieve mother and son, but the man was able only to return the infant George to his master. Carver's account of the story, presumably as told to him by either Moses or Susan Carver, was that his return to the Carver farm cost Mr. Carver a prized race horse worth three hundred dollars.[7] The retelling of this story, confirming as it did the lack of regard for the humanity of an infant slave, could simply have nurtured Carver's harsh understanding that he had once been regarded as property rather than as a person. Instead, however, Carver seems to have taken pride in the notion that his master bothered to retrieve him and that Moses Carver was willing to do so at the cost of a valuable horse at a time when the state of Missouri had either already abolished slavery or was getting ready to do so.

Young George tried for years to find his mother and suffered her loss throughout his life. Late into his life, he regarded as his most prized possessions the bill of sale that made his mother the property of the Carvers and a spinning wheel that had belonged to her. Perhaps it was George's longing for his lost mother that seemed to make him always more comfortable around women than men.

Not only did George no longer have his mother to care for him, but he was returned to the Carver household near death, suffering from whooping cough. Although he survived that bout of illness, he remained sickly throughout his childhood. One of his contemporaries, Forbes Brown, recalled in late life that Carver was so frail as a child that he always assumed

This photograph was taken at about the time that Carver left to attend school in Neosho. (courtesy of the George Washington Carver National Monument)

that George simply did not get enough to eat. George remembered that he was small for his age as a child and that "my body was very feble [*sic*] and it was a constant warfare between life and death to see who would gain the mastery."[8]

What must George's life have been like, growing up in the household of a late-middle-aged white couple, in a township that contained only sixteen African Americans in 1870, among a total population of 1,166 residents? Carver rarely spoke or wrote in detail about his childhood.

James Carver (courtesy of the George Washington Carver
National Monument)

Late in life, when pressed to do so by biographer Rackham Holt, he responded simply that "It will be very difficult indeed" to recall his early
life in detail, "as there are so many things that naturally I erased from
my mind." "There are some things that an orphan child does not want to
remember," he added.[9]

This reluctance to remember, however, should not be taken to mean
that George and his brother, Jim, were necessarily mistreated by the
Carvers or that the boys bore hostility toward them. There are a number of indications that the white Carvers regarded their former slaves as
surrogate children and that they treated them with kindness and even
affection. A professional portrait of George as a young boy and another

of George and Jim together in their youth, likely paid for by Moses and Susan, suggest parental pride that transcended a purely economic relationship. Like many other former slaves in Missouri, Jim stayed with the Carver family for more than a decade after slavery ended and retained the Carver surname into adulthood. George returned to Newton County on multiple occasions to visit his former masters.

Further evidence of George Carver's relative contentment as a child comes in his correspondence during the 1920s with Eva Goodwin, a Newton County native who was the daughter of one of Moses Carver's grand-nephews, a man who had been George's boyhood playmate. In a letter to Mrs. Goodwin, George told her that her recent correspondence "causes tears to come to my eyes as I recall childhood's happy days." He also told Mrs. Goodwin that he loved her father "as I did my own brother." Later, in another letter, he told her, "I would love to get with your Father and talk over old times at home," adding, "you really are my home folks."[10]

Carver's childhood fragility and frequent illnesses precluded his ability to work outdoors on the Carver farm—that responsibility was assigned to his older brother, James. The Carver farm seems, in fact, to have declined in productivity and prosperity during the Civil War decade, perhaps a predictable development. By 1870, the aging Moses Carver had fewer horses, milch cows and other cattle than he had ten years earlier. He did have more sheep (thirty-five) and the same number of swine (fifteen) that he had in 1860, although he produced only half the corn and none of the oats he harvested in 1860.

While James was helping Moses Carver in the fields, George was assigned to help Aunt Susan, who taught him to do household chores, including cooking, cleaning, sewing, and all of the tasks associated with laundry, including ironing. Those skills would serve him well throughout the remainder of his life.

Perhaps it was George's assisting Aunt Susan with gardening that nurtured his seemingly innate fascination with plants. In an 1897 reminiscence, he reported that flowers especially intrigued him: "Day after day I spent in the woods alone in order to collect my floral beauties [sic]." Often, he transplanted these flowers into a small, hidden garden that he maintained out of sight of the Carvers, because "it was considered foolishness in that neighborhood to waste time on flowers." Occasionally, George's effort at transplantation failed, leaving him emotionally distraught: "[M]any are the tears I have shed because I would break the roots or flower of some of my pets while removing them from the ground."[11]

Plants thrived under the child Carver's care. At least in his own telling of the story, he became known as the community "plant doctor," and
neighbors brought sickly plants to him. Carver remembered that "all
sorts of vegetation succeed[ed] to thrive under my touch," an experience
that must have nurtured his notion that he was a special person with extraordinary powers and abilities. That notion remained with and guided
him throughout his life.[12]

Carver did not attend school as a very young child. There was no state
compulsory education law in Missouri when he was of elementary school
age. Indeed, Missouri law required blacks and whites to be educated separately, and townships were not required to provide schools for blacks
unless there were at least twenty black school-age children in the political
subdivision. Fewer than ten black children of school age, including Carver, lived in Newton County's Marion Township in 1870. There is some
evidence that George and Jim tried to attend a local white school near
the Carver farm but were prohibited from doing so.[13] The 1870 federal
census indicates that neither George nor Jim could read or write. However, that same census also reveals that there was a fourteen-year-old white
boy named Nicholas or "Nickles" Holt living in the Carver household in
1870, who was also attending school. Is it possible that this child, and/or
his books, served as a source of learning for Jim and George Carver?

All of the evidence suggests that Carver learned to read and write at
an early age, helped, perhaps, by the young school-attending boy in the
house, or perhaps by Aunt Susan, with whom he seemed to have a strong
bond. Although some sources have suggested that Moses Carver was
illiterate, the 1870 and 1880 federal censuses would suggest otherwise.
George's only book, he reported in 1922, "was an old Webster's Elementary Spelling Book" which he "almost knew . . . by heart." More often than
not, however, the book was unable to answer the many questions that
filled the young Carver's mind. Years later, Carver summed up his early
intellectual curiosity by commenting simply that "From a child I had an
inordinate desire for knowledge."[14]

Carver's thirst for knowledge led him to leave his early childhood
home as an adolescent. Thus began more than a decade of wandering by a
young man who seemed to be in search not only of formal education but
also of a destiny. He remembered years later that the Carvers supported
his decision, explaining, "Mr. and Mrs. Carver were perfectly willing for
us to go where we could be educated the same as white children."[15]

The Carvers heard that there was a school for blacks in the county seat
of Neosho, a town of about three thousand persons, some eight miles

away. George set out on foot to become a student in that school. He was probably at least twelve years of age when he did so.

At that point in his life, the boy Carver had rarely been off the Carver farm and certainly had never been out of the county of his birth, save for the kidnapping episode that had occurred during his infancy. It is difficult to imagine the complex of emotions he must have felt as he set out on the three-hour walk to Neosho. He allegedly knew no one in the town, had rarely visited there, and surely must have felt anxiety about being on his own with no money, no resources upon which he could draw, and not even a place to stay when he arrived at his destination. Still, he must also have been excited at the thought of the adventure that he was embarking upon and the prospect of at last getting a chance to go to school. It is worth noting that Carver embarked upon his formal education at about the same age that most black male youths in his community and state were ending theirs. The vast majority of African American male youths in rural and small town post-Civil-War Missouri ended their formal education when they reached their teens.

Arriving in Neosho near or after dark, Carver spotted a barn and decided to sleep in it for the night. The next morning he realized that his choice of locations had been a good one; the barn was owned by Andrew and Mariah Watkins, a childless black couple who agreed to provide George with room and board in exchange for his help with chores.[16]

The Neosho in which Carver found himself living during the mid-to-late 1870s was a thriving, fast-growing community of roughly 3,300 persons, approximately 400 of whom were identified in the 1880 federal census as either "black" or "mulatto." Thus, African Americans constituted roughly 12 percent of Neosho's population, a considerable increase over the previous decade. In 1870 Neosho's total population had been 2,023, 129 (6 percent) of whom were African American. This was only a slight increase over the 106 slaves in Neosho in 1860.[17]

Why the African American population of Neosho more than tripled during the decade of the 1870s remains a mystery, but it must have been quite a sight for the young Carver, to see hundreds of people like himself walking the streets of the town. The migration of African Americans into Neosho during the 1870s almost certainly had something to do with the arrival of the railroad in the town in 1870, and it may well have been connected to the existence of the black school there. One is reminded of W. E. B. DuBois's comment about the freedmen's yearning for educational opportunities. DuBois wrote in his 1935 book, *Black Reconstruction,* "they [the freedmen] wanted to know; they wanted to be able to interpret the cabalistic letters and figures which were the key to more. They were consumed with curiosity at the meaning of the world. . . . [As a consequence] they were consumed with desire for schools."[18]

It was not unprecedented in Carver's Missouri for African American parents to flock to a town that offered formal educational opportunities for their children. Nor was it unheard of for black parents to abandon a community when the number of African American children of school age dropped below the threshold that required public support for a school.

Carver's exposure to African American life in Neosho would have been his introduction to the notion that blacks could be something other than farmers or farm laborers, although the 1880 federal census reflects that a number of African Americans in Neosho were still making their living in some way connected to agriculture. But there were even more blacks working simply as "laborers" or "day laborers," or "servants," the vast majority in the latter class "living in" the households of whites and serving whites much as they and their slave ancestors had done during the antebellum period. The black "professional" class in Carver's Neosho consisted of the two ministers in town and the one black teacher. Thus, as an adolescent or young teenager, Carver, the black child raised by whites, experienced a world in which blacks were heavily dependent upon whites, the same kind of dependency he would try to free Alabama blacks from a generation later when he lived and worked at Tuskegee.

Mariah Watkins seems to have influenced Carver in a number of ways, even though he lived in the Watkins home only a short period of time. "Aunt" Mariah took in laundry for hire and required George to help her, thereby forcing him to hone a skill that he would employ for his own survival many times over the next decade or more. She also served the community as a midwife and home remedyist. Her knowledge of plants and their purported curative powers appealed to George and, no doubt, laid the groundwork for his lifelong conviction that illnesses could be cured through the proper use of plants and the products that could be extracted from them.[19] One thinks, for example, of Carver's work on infantile paralysis patients during the 1930s.

Yet another way in which Aunt Mariah influenced George was through her regular reading of the Bible and her encouragement of George to do likewise. Many years later, Carver reported that he had had a religious conversion experience when he "was just a mere boy . . . hardly ten years old." Led to pray by a white playmate who told him about the Christian God, Carver attended a Sunday School class intermittently as a child. Moses and Susan Carver, by contrast, were not churchgoers.[20]

According to one of his contemporaries, George was heavily influenced by his Sunday School teacher, Mrs. Flora Abbott. Widely known for her fondness of children and her knowledge of the Bible, Mrs. Abbottt "constantly stressed the fact that the Lord heard and answered the prayers of a child just as surely as He did that of their parents."[21]

Mrs. Abbott encouraged members of her class to pray and to believe that their prayers were answered. George became one of Mrs. Abbott's star pupils and she rewarded his studiousness and attentiveness with gifts and praise. While still a child, he apparently developed what became a life-long practice of rising before dawn and walking in the woods to talk with God and to know Him better through His creations.[22]

Carver's conversion to Christianity gave him a sense of a deeply personal relationship with God who, he was convinced, frequently spoke to him through dreams and other forms of direct revelation. His earliest recollection of such an experience, one that he often spoke about throughout his life, came through a childhood dream. Longing for a pocketknife of his own, George dreamed of a knife sticking in a partially eaten watermelon in one of Moses Carver's fields. Upon waking the next morning, George walked to the spot on the farm revealed to him in his sleep. There, he saw the scene he had just dreamed of—the object of his longing, a knife, sticking in a partially eaten watermelon. The experience made a firm believer of him: dreams were to be believed and God was to be trusted.[23]

In Neosho, in addition to encouraging George's Bible study, Mariah Watkins also took him to regular church services at the local African Methodist Episcopal Church. Religion remained the dominant, shaping force in Carver's life for the rest of his years.

Once settled in with the Watkins family in Neosho, Carver enrolled almost at once in the town's "colored school," a one-room schoolhouse that either then, or soon thereafter, would be named for the slain sixteenth president of the United States. Established in 1872, the school was taught by Stephen Frost, a young black man who arrived in Neosho in 1875, probably in his mid-twenties, who likely had little or no formal training as a teacher. Sometimes an ability to recite the ABCs was the only qualification that a black teacher in postwar Missouri had to possess. Some critics of the black educational system at the time argued that even that expectation often went unenforced.[24]

The illiteracy rate among African Americans in Missouri remained high during the generation following the Civil War, one legacy of the prewar prohibition against teaching blacks—slave or free—to read or write.

Before the war, whites opposed educating blacks, fearing that literacy would lead to unrest, dissatisfaction, and rebellion. After the war, many whites opposed public funding for black schools, angry at the notion that they were required to pay taxes for the education of black freedmen, whom they regarded as their intellectual and social inferiors. In some counties, schoolhouses for African Americans were burned, teachers of black students were verbally and physically abused, and county officials tried to find ways to avoid their legal responsibility of establishing schools for blacks, including underreporting or refusing to report the number of black school-age children in the county.

The fewness in numbers of educated blacks in postwar Missouri, the reluctance of black parents to have their children taught by white teachers whom they tended not to trust, and the white hostility toward educating blacks at public expense, all meant that qualified African American teachers were hard to find and well-equipped schools for blacks were almost non-existent, especially in rural and small-town Missouri.

Carver did not stay long in Neosho, perhaps less than a year. Stephen Frost and the Lincoln School apparently had little to offer him. A wanderlust struck Carver, prompting him to want to leave Missouri for Kansas, a place regarded by many former slave-state African Americans as "the promised land" because of its historical association with the abolitionist John Brown.

By the late 1870s, thousands of Southern blacks began to move up the Mississippi River to various points in Missouri, from which they traveled overland to Kansas in search of a better life. They were fleeing the South in the wake of the so-called Compromise of 1877, a political deal between congressional leaders that allowed Republican Rutherford B. Hayes to become president of the United States in exchange for the removal of the federal troops remaining in the South, sent there after the war to protect the civil and political rights of African Americans. This so-called Exodus, named to commemorate and identify with the flight of Jews from their captivity in Egypt to freedom in Israel, marked the end of Reconstruction in the South and the reemergence there of state governments that were hostile to African Americans' efforts to enjoy social and political equality.[25]

Carver seems to have hitched a ride sometime in 1878 or 1879 with a black Exoduster family passing through Missouri en route to Kansas. He may or may not have still been in Neosho to read an item in the *Neosho Times* on April 10, 1879, when the local editor reproduced an article from the *Times-Journal* of St. Louis, warning Southern (and presumably local) African Americans not to abandon the familiar South for the unfamiliar state of Kansas: "If they go to Kansas and settle, they will stay there, for they will never be able to return unless they are sent back. The South will suffer by it and so will the negroes," adding that "they [the Negroes] are badly fooled and trapped." Whether he read this dire warning or not, George Carver joined what became the first major migration out of the South by African Americans; he could have been no more than fourteen or fifteen years old at the time, and still with few resources available to him to start a new life. And yet, like all of the other migrants, a new and better life was just what George Carver sought.

He took with him, of course, the sum of his experiences in Missouri. Although an African American orphan raised in a community and a state that regarded blacks as less than equal to whites, he had been aided and cared for by whites who were genuinely fond of him and perhaps even loved him. He had developed a sense that he possessed unique gifts and that he had a specialness that transcended race, a feeling no doubt nurtured by his Christian conversion experience and the treatment he received from his Sunday School teacher. Given all of his experiences and the confident hope that must have sprung from them, the teenage Carver must have been excited indeed. Given all that he had been through, all that he had seen, all that he had experienced, it must have occurred to him that he had become a person "of more than ordinary ability."

Chapter 6

Nathaniel C. Bruce, Black Education, and the "Tuskegee of the Midwest"

This mid-1980s photo of the Bartlett School Building gives a visual indication of the famous black school once known as the "Tuskegee of the Midwest." (courtesy of the State Historical Society of Missouri)

Black American leaders of the early twentieth century, almost without exception, identified education as a key to black progress.[1] They disagreed, however, on the kind of education black students needed.[2]

The philosophy of Booker T. Washington, the black leader who founded Tuskegee Institute in Alabama in 1881, dominated most discussions about blacks' educational needs. Born a slave in the South at a time when most blacks were illiterate and unskilled, Washington advocated vocational and agricultural training for blacks so they could achieve financial independence as a necessary prelude to obtaining social and political rights. "Our greatest danger," Washington proclaimed at the 1895 Atlanta Exposition, "is that in the great leap from slavery to freedom we may overlook the fact that the masses of us are to live by the production of our hands, and fail to keep in mind that we shall prosper in proportion as we learn to dignify and glorify common labour and put brains and skill into the common occupations of life."[3]

Alternatively, other black leaders, most notably the freeborn, northern intellectual W. E. B. DuBois, decried Washington's concentration on vocational training and urged, instead, liberal and professional education for blacks. Washington "depreciates institutions of higher learning," DuBois argued, "but neither the Negro common schools, nor Tuskegee itself, could remain open a day were it not for teachers trained in Negro colleges." DuBois maintained that a "Talented Tenth"—a college-educated, black elite—would be the key to racial elevation.[4]

Nathaniel C. Bruce became the most vocal and visible advocate of the Washington philosophy in Missouri during the first half of the twentieth century. A student of Washington's, Bruce was convinced that his mentor had the right answer to the question of how black progress could best be achieved, and subsequently he dedicated his life to black education. His first teaching assignment came in St. Joseph, Missouri, soon after he left Tuskegee. He later established a school in Chariton County modeled after his Alabama alma mater. Indeed, Bruce often referred to his school as "the Tuskegee of the Midwest." Originally called the Bartlett Agricultural and Industrial School and, later, the Dalton Vocational School, Bruce's institution served thousands of black Missourians from the time it opened in 1907 until it closed its doors at the end of the 1955–1956 school year.[5]

Born in 1868, on a farm near Danville, Virginia, Bruce attended Halifax County Public Schools while helping his father, an ex-slave, on the family farm. He left home at the age of fourteen to attend the Shaw Normal and Industrial High School in Raleigh, North Carolina. After completing high school, he went on to Shaw University, where he received a bachelor of arts degree, graduating with honors.[6]

Bruce's thirst for knowledge carried him farther. He continued his education, first at Bates College, then at Harvard, Hampton Institute, and finally Washington's Tuskegee Institute in Alabama. Bruce came to Missouri as a principal of a black high school in St. Joseph. After serving for a brief time in that position he, like many of his fellow students from

Tuskegee, set out to establish a school of his own based on the Tuskegee model.[7]

In 1907 Bruce established his Chariton County school "in a log barn on 8 acres of land owned by John Ewing, an ex-slave, who then owned 120 acres adjoining the little town of Dalton." Initially, Bruce had five students, three boys and two girls, each of whom spent half of the day in a classroom and the other half in the field. His goal, as expressed in a school brochure, was "to train the negro youth 'back to the land' and for efficient service in the home and on the farm."[8]

The school's early years were anything but auspicious. Bruce rented land in the Missouri River bottom in 1908 and 1909, but floods in both those years destroyed his entire crop. He and his students lived on corn bread and water in the absence of a more substantive food supply or money.[9]

After the 1909 flood, Bruce moved his school to higher ground. Simultaneously, his plight came to the attention of several prominent citizens of St. Joseph, Columbia, and St. Louis: Mr. and Mrs. Herschel Bartlett, Judge and Mrs. W. K. James, Professor Joseph D. Elliff, Dr. Calvin N. Woodward, Mr. and Mrs. Adolphus Busch I, William B. Ittner, and Charles Nagel, each of whom made contributions that allowed Bruce to purchase twelve acres of land from George D. Dalton. Later in 1909, Bruce and his students erected the first permanent building, the Busch Building, on the school's campus. This frame structure housed four classrooms and a boys' dormitory. Bruce named the school the Bartlett Agricultural and Industrial School, after its chief benefactor.[10]

In 1911 the Bartlett Agricultural and Industrial School was reorganized under a board of trustees. The Bartlett School operated with the day-to-day supervision of Bruce and the guidance of a fifteen-person board dominated by Judge James and Mr. Bartlett. The teachers' salaries and operating expenses during this period came almost exclusively from private donations supplemented by money earned from crops and livestock raised at the school. The board purchased an additional sixty acres of land in 1912 and that year constructed the Bartlett Building, containing two additional classrooms, an auditorium, and a girls' dormitory.[11]

By 1913 the hard work of Bruce, his staff, and their students began to pay off. Professor T. R. Douglas, secretary of the Missouri Corn Growers' Association, observed the fine corn crop grown by Bruce and urged him to enter a statewide contest sponsored by the association. Bruce not only entered the contest but won the *Missouri Ruralist* trophy with a yield of 114 bushels per acre despite a drought. In the February 20, 1914, issue of the *Missouri Ruralist*, he explained how he had done it. Hard work had been the key:

> The winning acre . . . had been in clover for three years. We turned it under, plowing very deep, in March, and disk harrowed and let it lay.
>
> . . . Late in April, we disk plowed it with a new Deering small two-horse disk riding plow and disk harrowed it a week or 10 days later, about the seventh of May. On the eighth we smooth harrowed it twice and put on the check row planter, planting the corn on top. . . . When the corn was just peeping up we saw that we had a fine, uniform stand. The prize acre was harrowed with the rest, and in a few days smooth harrowed again. Three days later we put in the five-tooth single-horse harrow plows, and two days after that gave our corn a deep cultivation with four teams and our best trained plow and cultivator plowing boys. . . . Ten days or two weeks later we went at it with thorough, but level cultivation.[12]

Such diligent efforts by Bruce and his students gained widespread attention for the school. The Bartlett School won first prize for the highest Missouri corn yield again in 1915. Bruce and his students also competed

N.C. Bruce and a student of Bartlett Agricultural School are shown judging corn. (courtesy of the State Historical Society of Missouri, Missouri Ruralist Photographs, 020832)

in the Panama-Pacific International Exposition, held in San Francisco, where they finished second nationally in corn production. Their effort was rewarded with a three-thousand-dollar prize contributed by Huston Wyeth of St. Joseph and Clarence H. Howard of St. Louis. Bruce used the money to build a new barn and silo and to purchase ten head of Holstein and Jersey cattle. "Place Missouri black boys on Missouri black land, behind the world-famed Missouri mule," Bruce rightfully boasted, "and nothing can beat the combination for raising corn or other crops."[13]

Bruce used the favorable publicity generated by his prizewinning corn to plead for state support of his still-struggling school. Calling his school "the first and only 'back to the soil' institution for black people not only in Missouri but in the West," Bruce argued that state support of the Bartlett School would be an investment in an improved black citizenry:

> We have shown and are going to keep showing that black people can make for themselves their best place and opportunity back upon black land. Our school needs, has earned and deserves to be equipped for just such service. It can be useful not only to the black people of Missouri but to all the West for the Negroes of this section are eager to learn better farming methods. Tuskegee has done and can do no better than Bartlett School when it gets one-hundredth part of the equipment that Tuskegee has had.[14]

A 1914 editorial in the *Boonville Weekly Advertiser* praised the Bartlett School for "doing good work among the negroes by training them [in] habits of industry, policies of honesty and teaching them self-reliance." This same editorial revealed, however, the white racism and stereotyping of the era when it noted that while blacks in Missouri "have been well treated" by the state in making provisions for their education:

> yet the per cent of illiteracy among them is appalling in many instances. Then again so few of them who go to school ever amount to anything . . . they cannot expect to improve their condition so long as they gather in towns and cities and are content with eking out an existence on a day's work now and then. There are opportunities on the farms awaiting the negroes who are willing to work. . . . Why do they not take advantage of these opportunities and become self-supporting citizens?[15]

Each year, beginning in 1907, the Bartlett School also sponsored the annual Missouri-Mid-Western States Negro Farmers' and Farm Women's Conference, which sometimes attracted as many as fifteen hundred "country life" blacks to its farm produce exhibits. As president of the organization, Bruce "carried the gospel of better farming" to thousands of rural Missouri blacks. Not surprisingly, the conference's objectives paralleled the Bartlett School's: "We urge [blacks] to stay on their jobs at home and make good in producing the largest possible yield of every edible and useful crop. Avoid all strikes, all quarrels possible, and live peaceably with all our neighbors, while others are profiteering, fighting and fussing and whining to keep out of work and to get greater pay for less work."[16]

By 1920, over five hundred students had been enrolled at Bartlett since the school's beginning. More than two hundred had graduated, and Bruce proudly noted "not one has sought employment in the city." His students' impressive achievements included the following:

> 36 graduates now own and operate their own farms. Sixteen of the school's graduates are managing farms for white farmers. Nine are in charge of farms owned by negroes. Of the girl graduates, 29 have married negro farmers and the remaining graduates hold positions of trust in good homes. The school has its record of loyalty, too, 28 boys having served in [World War I], two of them giving their lives for their country.[17]

Bruce's accomplishments brought begrudging admiration from white segregationists such as John F. Case, editor of the *Missouri Ruralist*. In July 1920, after visiting the Bartlett School, Case wrote an article praising the school but urging caution:

> I was impressed as every other visitor has been, with the intelligence, courtesy and hospitality of the men and women in charge of the school work. . . . These black folks have won the respect of the people in their section and the admiration of every visitor who has witnessed the remarkable work that has been done in crop production. There is no disposition on the part of these folks to ask or expect race equality but they do ask equal opportunity for the deserving negro boy and girl. . . . I have doubted sometimes whether an education brought happiness to the black man or woman, for undoubtedly in many instances it brings longing for social equality with white folks that could not and should not be gratified. . . . I do not believe in mixed schools. . . . Mixed schools breed trouble and unhappiness for the black child and if ever a negro graduated from one of them has brought honors to his race as [Booker T.] Washington and Bruce have I never heard of it.[18]

Bartlett School's board of trustees warmly endorsed Bruce's call for state support for the school. Board president Judge W. K. James led the lobbying effort. He and other proponents of state support pointed with pride to the school's success, while documenting the miserliness of Missouri's support of black education historically.[19]

Meanwhile, Bruce received support from another source. Missouri governor Frederick D. Gardner organized the Negro Industrial Commission on Lincoln's birthday, February 12, 1918. In the early days of America's involvement in World War I, Gardner had inquired of numerous black leaders how blacks could best be organized to support the war effort. The collective response of those leaders had been that blacks had to be allowed to help themselves, without white interference. Subsequently, Gardner appointed a commission of blacks whose purpose was "to discover, ferret out, survey and recommend remedies, educational, moral and industrial, for the betterment of negroes of Missouri."[20]

Commission members, all of whom espoused Washington's self-help philosophy, traveled the state encouraging blacks to plant gardens, offering them animal husbandry tips, explaining how to better cultivate crops and how to avoid food waste, and generally "urging and stimulating [the black] race's old time loyalty, fidelity and hearty, persistent labor."[21]

Not surprisingly, the first chairman of the Missouri Negro Industrial Commission was Nathaniel C. Bruce. And from the very beginning of its existence, the commission offered as one of its major legislative recommendations the establishment "of a sub-experiment station under control of the state and U.S. through our white College of Agriculture, the same as Arkansas, Mississippi, Georgia, Virginia, North Carolina, South Carolina and other states have for years given their negro farmers, to the great benefit of the state and to their country life negroes."[22]

Bruce, of course, hoped that the Bartlett School would become that station. For the next several years, he and his fellow commissioners argued in their biennial reports for the establishment of a state-supported experiment farm for blacks "because an experiment station among Negroes [would] increase the productive efficiency many fold and [would] give to the state in increased crop yields and better livestock many times the cost of the maintenance of such an institution. . . . It [would] give the Negro farmer an opportunity to become as efficient and progressive as his white neighbor; an act of simple justice."[23]

Finally, the effort paid off. In 1923 the Bartlett School's board of trustees donated fifty acres of choice land to the state of Missouri for developing an agricultural extension model farm for the training of black youth.

With this inducement, the Fifty-second General Assembly (1923) appropriated fifteen thousand dollars "for the purchase of land, the organization and administration of a demonstration farm and agricultural school at Dalton, Missouri, for the negro race, provided that the purchase of the land, construction of buildings and equipment and the administration of the demonstration farm and school shall be under the supervision and control of the college of agriculture of the university of Missouri."[24] With the takeover, the institution's name changed to the Dalton Vocational School. In 1924 the school was placed under the general control of the University of Missouri's College of Agriculture and the money used to buy more land and erect new buildings, including a model farmhouse, a trade shop, and hog and poultry houses.[25]

On September 2, 1924, a dedication ceremony held at the Dalton Vocational School commemorated the state takeover. The September 1, 1924, *Missouri Ruralist* noted that "it would be a great thing for Missouri if every Negro boy and girl now living on a farm could go to Dalton." A subsequent *Ruralist* issue observed that the state takeover "marked an epoch in human progress in Missouri so far as the Negro race is concerned."[26]

Dignitaries from all over the state attended the ceremony on a day filled with speechmaking and thanksgiving. The list of speakers included Frederick B. Mumford, dean of the Missouri School of Agriculture; Judge W. K. James, president of the school's board of trustees; Congressman W. L. Nelson, a board member; John F. Case, editor of the *Missouri Ruralist* and president of the State Board of Agriculture; Nathan B. Young, president of Lincoln University; and Andrew Clay, president of the Colored Farm Bureau. Young and Clay "brought messages of hope and courage to the younger people, urging the older people to send their boys and girls to the experiment farm, where they might learn to be self-supporting, while making better farmers, cooks, stock raisers and better home makers which means, always better citizens."[27] However, perhaps the most telling remarks were offered by a white farmer named Felby Littrell whose land lay in the vicinity of the Dalton School. Littrell commented: "These colored folks have won the respect of their white neighbors. At one time there was bitter feeling here but it is changing. Many of the colored boys and men have worked for me and they make good hands. I hope this school will be developed into one of real service to the colored people of this state."[28]

Bruce's effort to move the Bartlett School under the University of Missouri was not his first attempt at gaining state support for his fledgling institution. As principal of the Bartlett School and as chairman of the Missouri Negro Industrial Commission, Bruce became a highly visible spokesman for black education. In 1918 he sought to capitalize on his visibility and tried to become president of Lincoln Institute, the state-supported, black normal school in Jefferson City. Bruce hoped to reorganize Lincoln as a vocational and industrial college in order to funnel resources to his Bartlett School. Instead, Clement Richardson of Tuskegee moved into the position and quickly acted to expand industrial training at Lincoln Institute.[29]

Richardson's presidency lasted only four years. In 1923 Nathan Young replaced him. Young soon incurred Bruce's wrath by directing Lincoln's resources away from vocational training and toward liberal arts education. Bruce, unhappy with what he thought was Young's improper approach to black education, spearheaded a campaign among some of the state's black educators against the new president. It was not Young's first such conflict. Earlier he had studied and taught at Tuskegee, where he collided with Booker T. Washington over educational philosophy. The dispute eventually resulted in Young's resignation from Tuskegee.[30]

In 1924 a personal window of opportunity opened for Bruce when State Superintendent of Schools Charles A. Lee appointed him State Inspector of Negro Schools. Later that same year, Bruce left the Dalton School to devote more time to his position as state inspector. H. L. Drew, who had been trained at the school by Bruce, became acting principal.[31]

As State Inspector of Negro Schools, Bruce traveled the state championing his program of vocational education. By the mid-1920s his advocacy of such training for blacks, to the exclusion of academic training, began to rankle his fellow blacks more and more. In 1926, before the Moberly School Board, Bruce advocated that black youth be trained "in the work they must do if they get any work to do at all." Blacks must be trained to "take pride in any work they had to do whether cooking, washing, ironing, scrubbing or driving nails," rather than in "high book learning." "The Negro," Bruce urged, "must be taught his place and how to work like his old parents." Furthermore, he added that blacks "make the best servants and the best house workers of any race when they are taught pride in their work."[32]

On June 11, 1926, Roy Wilkins, *Kansas City Call* columnist and future executive director of the NAACP, attacked Bruce's narrow-mindedness. Bruce's pronouncement, Wilkins wrote, "leaves most of us dazed and unbelieving and some of us angry and crying for blood." Bruce's comments, he continued:

[are] more than disasterous. The harm is not in Mr. Bruce's belief that this kind of "practical" education . . . is good for Negroes, but in his unqualified recommendation of it as a general program for all Negroes to be placed in local school systems of the state INSTEAD OF HIGH BOOK LEARNING AND TRAINING [original emphasis]. . . . We can't get along without the higher book learning and the man who says so is either playing to a "cracker" "hill billy" gallery for a mess of pottage or else he is woefully ignorant.[33]

Whether as a result of the controversy created by his comments or not, Bruce resigned the inspector's position the next year, only to be replaced by his nemesis, Nathan B. Young.[34]

The Dalton School survived Bruce's departure and remained under the control of the University of Missouri until 1929. In that year, the Fifty-fifth General Assembly transferred control of "the demonstration farm and agricultural school for the negro race . . . at Dalton, Missouri," from the University of Missouri to the all-black Lincoln University.[35] The 1929 law also provided that black children living in a school district that made no provision for their education could attend the Dalton School without paying tuition. That same year, John W. Butler, a Bruce student and a former farm and demonstration agent, became acting principal.[36]

Upon Butler's death in 1934, E. M. Parrish, the vocational agriculture instructor, received the interim principal appointment. The following year, Beverly R. Foster was elected principal. Foster had a bachelor of science degree from Lincoln University and had done further study at Fisk and Denver Universities.[37]

The school continued to grow throughout the 1930s. Enrollment reached 42 in 1931, and more than doubled over the next decade. The 1942 term's enrollment totaled 109 students (49 boys and 60 girls), taught by ten instructors, seven of whom were Lincoln graduates. Even though appropriations never proved adequate, state money continued to provide the main source of the school's financing.[38]

A fire destroyed the Bartlett Building in 1932. At the time, it housed fourteen girls and three female instructors. The building was a total loss, unrecoverable by insurance, since the policy had been allowed to lapse because of insufficient funds.[39]

Although the fire dealt the school a temporary setback, the Missouri legislature appropriated money for a new building in 1937. F. C. Heariold, superintendent of buildings and grounds at Lincoln University, designed the building, and students and faculty, in true Tuskegee fashion, pitched in to help build it. Dedication of the new building occurred on May 18, 1938. Principal Foster presided over the cornerstone-laying ceremony. William J. Thompkins, a Lincoln alumnus and recorder of deeds in Washington, DC, delivered the keynote address, and others on hand included W. B. Jason, acting president of Lincoln University; Roland Wiggins, State Inspector of Negro Schools; W. G. Mosely, field agent at Lincoln University; and Nathaniel C. Bruce. Named for Herschel Bartlett, one of the school's early benefactors, the building cost $38,335.56 to construct. The Bartlett Building, a two-story brick structure designed for classrooms and containing an auditorium and a library, remains standing today.[40]

During the ten years that passed between the mid-1930s and the mid-1940s, the school received approximately $173,000 of state funds, or an average of $17,300 per year. In 1938 the Dalton School purchased a bus for the transportation of students from outlying areas. The school also continued to use its previous means of transportation—two privately owned automobiles—to transport sixty-eight nonresident students from Salisbury, Keytesville, Triplett, and the other small communities in the area.[41]

By the early 1950s, the school received approximately $100,000 each biennial legislative session. Despite modest increases in funding over

Dalton Vocational Classroom, 1980s (courtesy of the State Historical Society of Missouri)

the years, the Dalton School still received less than it needed to operate adequately. A memorandum to the general assembly written in 1951 summed up the situation: "This school is without a physical education gymnasium and auditorium, adequate shops for both vocational agricultural and vocational industrial arts, a good barn for livestock and grain storage, and a library room with equipment and books."[42]

That year, the Dalton Vocational School served nineteen school districts in Carroll, Chariton, Howard, Linn, and Saline Counties. Students from the outer districts were "transported by buses at distances up to 55 miles one way" to the school. By statutory provision, these districts remained exempt from tuition and did not have to pay transportation costs, causing a further drain on the school's limited finances.[43]

The 1951 memorandum also pointed out that "teachers in [the Dalton School] are among the lowest paid in the state." For example, when Eliot F. Battle, a Tuskegee graduate, was installed as principal in September 1953, he began at a starting salary of $3,200 for a twelve-month period. The average white male high school principal in the state earned slightly over $4,000 per year. The average white high school teacher for that year earned almost $3,400. Victoria Jones, with twenty years of teaching experience, earned $2,160, and the average Dalton teacher made only $2,110.[44]

Despite poor teacher salaries, the Dalton School boasted several fine instructors who distinguished themselves by their many years of loyal service. E. M. Parrish, who held a bachelor of science degree from Kansas State University, was hired for the 1929–1930 school year and taught vocational agriculture at the school until 1944. Throughout most of the school's history, the majority of its teachers came from Lincoln University. During the 1932–1933 school term, Victoria N. Jones, a Lincoln University graduate, began work at Dalton. Over the next twenty-four years she taught math, history, and social studies and served as the school's librarian. She continued to teach there until the school closed in 1956. Another Lincoln University graduate, Reginald S. Robinson, taught English and speech at the school for twenty-two years.[45]

Despite financial inequities, the Dalton Vocational School continued to provide educational opportunities for black students who had limited alternatives. Ironically, the force that ultimately destroyed the Dalton School was an occurrence that men such as Nathaniel C. Bruce and others could only have dreamed of: the 1954 *Brown v. Board of Education* decision, in which the US Supreme Court ruled segregated education unconstitutional.[46]

Following the Supreme Court decision, the Sixty-eighth General Assembly appropriated $42,500 (a reduction of $7,500 below the operational costs for the 1954–1955 school year) for the operation of the Dalton Vocational School for one last year, 1955–1956. Dalton students from Marceline, Salisbury, and the dozens of other small communities in and around Chariton County began attending school in their own towns. The Dalton School closed for good at the end of the 1955–1956 school year. The superintendent of an area school district expressed interest in leasing the property, but when the arrangements fell through, Lincoln University's board of curators recommended to the general assembly that the state sell the school property.[47]

In 1957, the Sixty-ninth General Assembly passed House Bill 562, which authorized the board of curators to transfer the land and property of the school "to any state agency." The bill further stipulated that, if not conveyed to a state agency within two years, the property could be sold by the board of curators "on the most advantageous terms obtainable."[48]

Apparently, no state agency wanted the property, and it stood idle for several years, making it fair prey for squatters, vandals, and the ravages of harsh Missouri winters. In 1960, when no state agency had expressed an interest in acquiring the land during the stipulated two-year period, Lincoln University advertised the buildings and approximately 123 acres of land for public sale "by Special Warranty Deed." Bids ranged from $4,558 to a bid of $15,498, made by Donald Grotjan of Brunswick. On July 8, 1961, Grotjan declared himself unable to purchase the property because a bank had refused to finance purchase by "Special Warranty Deed."[49]

Following Grotjan's failure to obtain a loan, none of the other bidders expressed an interest in buying the land. Subsequently, the board of curators approved the request of Denzil Kahler for grazing rights to the land, with the understanding that he would maintain the property's upkeep. Finally, in 1971, a black Chariton County farmer and Dalton Vocational School alumnus, Roland L. Hughes, and his wife, Rosia, purchased the property for twenty thousand dollars. By the time the Hugheses had acquired the property, most of the campus buildings had deteriorated beyond repair. The Bartlett Building, however, remains standing, a silent testimonial to Bruce's vision and the school's accomplishments.[50]

Chapter 7

"The Black People Did the Work"

African American Life in Arrow Rock, Missouri, 1850-1960

In his fine history of Arrow Rock, Missouri, published in 2004, historian Michael Dickey made this observation: "It is clear slavery fueled the economic wealth of Arrow Rock and created much of the leisure time enjoyed by upper class whites."[1] After slavery ended in 1865—and indeed throughout much of the first half of the twentieth century—Arrow Rock's freedpeople and their descendants continued to play a central role in the village's economy as laborers while simultaneously building for themselves a community and a culture largely apart from white society. Thus, while a majority of African Americans in Missouri became urbanites late in the nineteenth century, rural and small-town black life persisted in Arrow Rock late into the next century on the strength of black institutions built during the 1880s and 1890s.[2]

Located in the string of Missouri River counties known as Little Dixie, Arrow Rock achieved considerable prosperity during the decade of the 1850s. This prosperity was tied to hemp production and the town's location along the Missouri River, which facilitated the shipment of agricultural products, especially hemp.[3] Historian R. Douglas Hurt described the town's circumstances during this period as follows: "By the late 1850s, Arrow Rock was . . . a booming town with warehouses along the levy and mercantile stores, furniture shop, a branch of the Bank of Missouri, the private Western Exchange Bank, and a steam-powered planning [*sic*] mill lining main street. Wagons laden with hemp creaked over the ungraded main street as the drivers headed for the waiting steamboats."[4] In 1910

Rena Brown, seated, worked as a seamstress and laundress in private homes and as a cook at the Tavern in Arrow Rock. (courtesy of Friends of Arrow Rock, Inc.)

longtime Arrow Rock resident William Barclay Napton reminisced about this time period: "From 1850 to 1860 the county steadily advanced and prospered. . . . The large land owners and slave holders were particularly prosperous from the growing of hemp, which had become the most important crop of the county. Miami and Arrow Rock were the principal shipping points for hemp and other products and were then the most flourishing towns in the county, all the surplus products of the county being shipped by steamboat down the Missouri river."[5] In 1850 an Arrow Rock hemp producer put the matter more succinctly: "Hemp is not now a great staple from the Missouri river, but it is *the* great staple."[6]

The relative shortage of free agricultural labor in Saline County, and the labor intensity associated with the production of hemp, led to a dramatic increase in the number of slaves in the county and in the area around Arrow Rock during the decade of the 1850s. By 1860, as Dickey has pointed out, "Enslaved persons only made up 9.7% of Missouri's population and about 3% of the total in the United States. In contrast, the total population of Saline County was 14,699, and one third, or 4,876, were slaves."[7]

The increase in the number of slaves in Saline County during the 1850s, the dependence of whites on their labor, the growth in the number of slaves running away from their masters during that period, and the uncertainty of the future of slavery in the wake of the fight over its expansion into Kansas after mid-decade combined to create tension between blacks and whites. Unfortunately, that tension manifested itself in the lynching of four African Americans in Saline County in 1859. One of the lynchings, the murder of a slave of William L. Price, occurred in Arrow Rock in July 1859.[8]

Given the dependency of whites on slave labor throughout the Boonslick, it should come as no surprise that many of them reacted negatively when Missouri formally abolished slavery on January 11, 1865. Two months later, in March 1865, Union Gen. Clinton B. Fisk, commander of the District of North Missouri, wrote the following assessment of the response to abolition in central Missouri: "Slavery dies hard. I hear its expiring agonies and witness its contortions in death in every quarter of my district. In Boone, Howard, Randolph, and Callaway [and he could have added other Boonslick counties, especially Cooper and Saline] the emancipation ordinance has caused disruption of society equal to anything I saw in Arkansas or Mississippi in the year 1863." Fisk continued: "I blush for my race when I discover the wicked barbarity of the late masters and mistresses of the recently freed persons. . . . Some few have driven their black people away from them with nothing to eat or scarcely to wear. . . . The consequence is, between [guerrilla] Jim Jackson and his colaborers [sic] among the first families, the poor blacks are rapidly concentrating in the towns and especially at garrisoned places. My hands and heart are full. . . . There is much sickness and suffering among them; many need help."[9] Violence against black men was especially rampant during the immediate post-emancipation period, as some whites tried to intimidate blacks into remaining as slaves and punished those who sought a new life of freedom.

Many Boonslick blacks responded to this violence, as Fisk suggested, by fleeing the countryside and seeking protection in towns or villages where federal soldiers were garrisoned, or in the bordering free states of Kansas, Illinois, or Iowa. Boone, Howard, Cooper, and Saline Counties all lost African American population during the decade of the 1860s. Saline County's black population fell from 4,899 persons in 1860 to 3,754 in

1870, a decline of more than 24 percent. The number of blacks living in Arrow Rock Township, which included the village of Arrow Rock, declined by more than one-third during the decade, from 1,109 in 1860 to 711 by 1870.[10]

At least two prominent white Arrow Rock residents took note of the negative impact that emancipation and the decline in the black population had on Saline County's postwar agricultural economy. Writing in 1914, T. C. Rainey, who had arrived in Arrow Rock in the fall of 1865 by way of Tennessee and Springfield, Missouri, remembered the circumstances as follows: "The negroes were freed, and the former owner[s] not well trained to hard labor. Farms and fences were neglected, the roads in miserable condition, and the people without capital and discouraged."[11] More ominously, Judge William Barclay Napton set pen to paper in his journal soon after the war and slavery ended, bemoaning the loss of "the type of civilization" made possible by slavery and rather dramatically noting, "Thus ends one of the finest types of civilization known to this century."[12]

The majority of African Americans who remained behind in Arrow Rock after slavery's demise went about the business of trying to make a living much as they had always done—working for whites as servants and laborers. Indeed, Rainey provided a description of one such postwar circumstance that prompts a modern-day reader to think that little if anything had changed in the lives and circumstances of black servants living in the region at the time. This incident occurred "sometime during the [18]70's," when an elderly neighbor sent "a negro boy" to fetch Rainey for a visit. As Rainey approached his host's house, he noted the presence of "negro cabins" and commented that "several of his black people had never left him." The "darkies" cared for Rainey just as they would have done during the days of slavery, and Rainey was treated to a meal prepared by a black woman: "Everything prepared just as well as it can be by an old Virginia housekeeper and her cook."[13]

By 1880, a decade and a half after slavery was officially abolished in the state, the number of African Americans living in Arrow Rock Township had further declined, from 711 in 1870 to 562 in 1880, leaving the black population in the township little more than half of what it had been two decades earlier. Seventy-seven blacks continued to live in the village of Arrow Rock. This number represented 25 percent of the village's total population of 305 persons. In a measure of how little the lives of many African Americans had changed since emancipation, fourteen (58 percent) of the twenty-four households in which blacks lived were headed by whites. Thus, a majority of blacks worked as live-in help in white households. For example, James Tippen, his wife, Mollie, and their three children lived in the household of Rachel McGilton, a white hotelkeeper. In the census, James's occupation was listed as "anything," and Mollie was identified as a "cook." Likewise, Frank Switzler, a "servant," and his wife, Adaline, a "domestic servant," lived and worked in the household of Lavinia Bradford. Two of the Switzlers' five children, both adolescents, are identified in the census as "servants" while also being listed as attending school.[14]

Clearly, the situation of living in white households and working as resident servants dramatically limited African American autonomy. Elizabeth Clark-Lewis, in a richly textured book titled *Living In, Living Out: African American Domestics and the Great Migration,* documents the humiliation and deprivation under which live-in servants functioned. Live-in servants had no clear starting or stopping time for work. They were literally trapped in the white household, with no time of their own to control. They could be made to do whatever the white head of the household wanted done, whenever he or she demanded. It was difficult for husbands or wives who lived in to fulfill family responsibilities to each other or to their children, since their first responsibility was to the white head of the household.[15]

Despite these restrictions, Arrow Rock's African Americans tried to create their own institutions and their own spaces away from white control. Having been denied access to education during slavery, blacks sought to establish their own school in a way that was reminiscent of black scholar W. E. B. DuBois's comment about black freedmen generally in the immediate postwar period: "[Former slaves] wanted to know. . . . They were consumed with curiosity at the meaning of the world. . . . They were consumed with desire for schools." DuBois added: "The uprising of the black man, and the pouring of himself into organized effort for education, in those years between 1861 and 1871, was one of the marvelous occurrences of the modern world; almost without parallel in the history of civilization."[16] An 1866 Missouri law stipulated that "separate schools for colored children" should be established in townships where the number of school-aged black children exceeded twenty.[17]

The first publicly supported school for African Americans in Arrow Rock was established in 1869 as a consequence of a trip to the area by James Milton Turner, a prominent black leader who was engaged by the Freedmen's Bureau and the Radical Republican–controlled Missouri Department of Education to establish schools for freedpeople throughout the state. Turner was drawn to Arrow Rock by the local school board's failure to build a school for blacks. He arrived by buggy from Boonville on November 9, 1869, and immediately confronted the local school board spokesman, Henry S. Wilhelm, a tailor who had a thirteen-year-old black female servant named Elizabeth Pearson living in his household. Turner asked Wilhelm what had happened to the portion of local tax money that was supposed to be used to finance a school. Wilhelm pleaded ignorance, saying the board had not gotten the money due it. According to Turner, Wilhelm offered, instead, "to use money belonging to white children & open a school in [a] colored church building now in course of erection and run the same [for] four months."[18]

Turner was uncertain that he could trust the board spokesman. "I think," Turner wrote his supervisor, "old man Wilhelm talks most too kind to be relied upon." To ensure that Wilhelm delivered on his promise, Turner threatened the local man with the wrath of Radical Republicans in the state capital of Jefferson City and then "called a meeting of colored people & made them promise to complete the House in 15 days." At the meeting, Turner also "told the colored people to tease old man Wilhelm," then in his mid-fifties, "until he gives them a school that he may be rid of them."[19]

The church building was completed and a school soon in operation. The school that was established in the fall of 1869 served the entire Arrow Rock Township. According to the 1870 federal census, there were sixty-six African Americans attending school, including Wilhelm's live-in servant, Elizabeth Pearson. Many of the students were adults who had been denied access to education prior to emancipation. Of the sixty-six students enrolled in 1870, eleven (almost 17 percent) were twenty years old or older. Another fourteen (21 percent) were between fifteen and nineteen.[20]

The earliest record of an African American teacher in Arrow Rock appeared in 1873. On April 10 of that year, Albert Spears was issued a certificate to teach. He taught off and on for several years, into the 1890s. Curiously, the Missouri-born Spears is listed in the 1870 federal census as a twenty-year-old Arrow Rock resident who was unable to read or write. In addition to employment as a teacher, he was also a preacher, serving as a minister at the Fairview Colored Baptist Church north of Marshall between 1876 and 1881.[21] Other important African American teachers during the generation after the war and beyond were Harrison Green, a Michigan-born black man who received a certificate to teach in August 1874 and taught periodically throughout the 1880s, and John Thomas Trigg, a Saline County native whose teaching in Arrow Rock extended from 1889 into and through most of the decade of the 1920s. Trigg died in Marshall on December 11, 1932.[22]

The late 1860s structure that housed a combination school/church represented, of course, another way in which African Americans sought to exercise control over their lives apart from the larger white community. For former slaves, freedom meant not only building their own schools but establishing their own churches, calling their own preachers, and praying their own prayers, all forms of self-determination that African Americans had been denied during the days of slavery. The land upon which this first church stood was deeded by prominent white resident William B. Sappington and his wife, Mary, to the "Ruling Deacons in the Colored Baptist Church of Arrow Rock" on June 24, 1871. The deed transferring the plot of land "upon which the said Baptists have a new church erected and completed" reveals that the Sappingtons had allowed the deacons to erect a church on the property before transferring ownership to them.[23] One suspects that the erection of the church might have been a condition of the land transfer.

John Brown was apparently the first minister called to lead the African American Baptists in Arrow Rock. The Missouri-born Brown is listed in the 1870 census as a "preacher," aged twenty-five years. The 1880 census lists four African American men in Arrow Rock Township, in close proximity to the town of Arrow Rock, as ministers, although there appear to have been only two black churches.[24] In addition to the Baptist church, there was an African Methodist Episcopal (AME) congregation by 1870, with Henry Brown as its minister. A church to house the AME congregation was finally built in 1877. It was constructed on land sold by local whites Thomas and Mariah Martin to black church trustees Nelson Robinson, James Tyre, Newton Hill, Robert Falls, Stephen Steward, Lee Gorman, and Thomas Brown.[25]

Yet another way in which Arrow Rock African Americans asserted their independence and group solidarity during the generation after the Civil War was in the establishment of fraternal and sororal lodges. Such organizations served as vehicles for social interaction and also provided a sense of community and support, especially for orphaned, widowed, or destitute members. Historian Robin D. G. Kelley points out the importance of groups such as these in his book *Race Rebels: Culture, Politics, and the Black Working Class*. Kelley writes:

> Grass-roots institutions such as mutual benefit associations, fraternal organizations, and religious groups not only helped families

with basic survival needs, but created and sustained bonds of fellowship, mutual support networks, and a collectivist ethos. . . . Fraternal
and mutual benefit societies, in particular, provided funds and other
resources to members in need and to the poor generally, including
death benefits (mainly to cover burial costs) and assistance for families whose members became seriously ill or lost their job.[26]

The first black lodge to be established in Arrow Rock was Brown Lodge
No. 22 of the Ancient Free and Accepted Prince Hall Masons, probably
established as early as 1877, although the earliest extant membership list
is for 1880.[27] The Prince Hall Masons of the United States trace their
origins to an eighteenth-century free black man named Prince Hall, who
established the first all-black Masonic lodge in America in Boston, Massachusetts, in the mid-1780s. The first black Masonic lodge in Missouri
was established in St. Louis in 1851.[28]

According to historian William Muraskin, the black Masonic sense of
history is crucial to an understanding of the organization. By tracing its
foundation to Hall and (so they argued) Masonry's origins among black
Egyptians, the fraternity "erased from the mind of the black Mason his
actual descent from slaves." In the process, it also gave him a new heritage. As a Mason, Muraskin contended, "the black man . . . ceased to be a
poor, insignificant member of an oppressed group" and instead became
"a member of the most important and idealistic institution the world has
ever seen!"[29]

Thus, Prince Hall Masonry gave African Americans victimized by
white racism a creative way in which to respond. Black Masonry served
significant psychological and social functions for its members. Members
paid dues that created a relief fund for fellow Masons and their depen-
dents who were down on their luck. A portion of the annual dues was
used to pay for the burial of members and their families. Obituaries of
Arrow Rock African Americans from the late nineteenth and early twentieth centuries often commented on the fact that a Masonic burial was
provided. In 1915, for example, when John Tyrus died, the *Arrow Rock
Statesman* noted that, after his funeral, "his remains were interred in the
Sappington burying grounds by the members of the Masonic and Brown
Lodges of which he was a member."[30]

Another role played by the Masons was that of enforcer of community
morals. The Masons were conscious of white allegations of black immo-
rality; they sought to establish a code of behavior that would place their
members above reproach or criticism. Un-Masonic conduct, "UMC" as it

was referred to, was not to be tolerated. According to the group's constitution, "Profanity, gambling, drunkenness, the keeping or frequenting of wine shops and disreputable houses, are offenses against good morals.... [A]ny member ... adjudged guilty of the above, upon the evidence of two members, shall be suspended for the first offence [sic]. For a persistence in the same he shall be expelled." At the June 1888 annual statewide Masonic gathering in St. Joseph, Missouri, for example, Lewis Edwards of Arrow Rock was expelled, and Frank Brown and Charley Wright, also of Arrow Rock, were suspended for un-Masonic conduct. Brown and Wright were suspended again in 1889, along with Steven Steward and Thomas Martin.[31]

In Arrow Rock, the building housing Brown Lodge No. 22 was the place where black men congregated to participate in Masonic rituals, to make decisions relating to the relief and burial funds, to discuss and decide allegations of un-Masonic conduct, and generally, and not insignificantly, to socialize away from the scrutiny of whites. The land upon which the building was erected was purchased by the Masons from William B. Sappington on March 2, 1881. The septuagenarian Sappington had three live-in black servants as late as 1880.[32]

Membership rolls from the early 1880s indicate that there were approximately twenty-seven members of Brown Lodge. The leader, or "Worshipful Master," of the Arrow Rock Masons in 1880 was Harrison Green, clearly one of the leading local African American figures during the generation after the Civil War. A native of Michigan, the thirty-three-year-old Green appears in the census as a "Mulatto," boarding in the Arrow Rock Township household of a mixed-race carpenter, Isaac Finnel.[33]

Formed in 1890, the Grand United Order of Odd Fellows of America Lodge No. 3201 was another black fraternal organization in postwar Arrow Rock. The Odd Fellows, as they were known, traced their origins in America to a black man named Peter Ogden, a ship steward, who started the first black Odd Fellows lodge in New York City in 1843. They, too, provided burial insurance, relief for the needy, and a forum for social interaction. An article in the *Arrow Rock Enterprise* in 1893 commented on the celebration of the third anniversary of the Odd Fellows in the town. A band from Slater provided marching music and led "the procession, which marched to Bingham's Grove, where festivities of various kinds were indulged in." Later that night "orations were delivered by various ones, after which a dance was had."[34] In 1891 the Odd Fellows purchased a house at the corner of Morgan and Seventh Streets that served as their meeting place through the remainder of the decade.[35]

The Odd Fellows had a women's auxiliary known as the Household of Ruth. Additionally, for many years there was an active juvenile division of the Odd Fellows and the Household of Ruth. On May 23, 1927, Edward S. Lewis, District Grand Secretary of the Grand Lodge of Missouri, wrote to Elizabeth Taylor of Arrow Rock, bemoaning the fact that the "Juvenile Society" in Arrow Rock had declined to "two or three members." This was especially disturbing, Lewis wrote, since "for many years [Arrow Rock] was one of the largest Juveniles in the state." Lewis chided "Sister Taylor," reminding her that there were "42 members in the H[ouse] H[old]" and that "the Juvenile should still be in a flourishing condition if the proper interest was manifested by the parents." Lewis went on to say, "The Juveniles are the foundation of our Order, and the Juveniles of to-day [*sic*] should be the members of the H.H. and the Lodges of tomorrow."[36]

The strength of black institutions such as the churches, school, and lodges notwithstanding, Arrow Rock remained a decidedly racist town during the late nineteenth century. Racism manifested itself in a variety of ways, including the use of the local newspapers to assert racial control and superiority. Sociologist Herbert Blumer, in an important 1958 essay titled "Race Prejudice as a Sense of Group Position," made the point that dominant racial groups use public forums such as newspapers to ascribe qualities to other racial groups as a means of legitimizing their domination.[37] In Arrow Rock and Saline County, whites controlled the newspapers, and they used those newspapers to portray blacks in ways that they thought supported their notions of superiority. Thus, blacks were most often mentioned in the newspapers in the context of some crime that they had committed or were alleged to have committed. Terms such as "coon" and "nigger" appeared all too frequently, as did allegations of black laziness and "cussedness." On one occasion, a newspaper threatened that "some of them [blacks] should be put to work forcibly if necessary."[38]

By contrast, the African Americans who were praised, and whose lives were celebrated, were often former slaves who were thought to have served their masters well. Thus, when "Aunt Liza Hutchinson, colored," died in 1892, she was remembered fondly as a former slave, "a good old woman," who had been brought by her master from South Carolina more than four decades earlier.[39] Even when blacks acted in a manner approved by whites, a local newspaper found a way to offer a backhanded "compliment," as was the case when the editor of the *Arrow Rock Enterprise* condescendingly noted that African Americans had been well behaved at a recent social event: "The colored people are to be congratulated on the good behavior prevalent throughout the day, as not a single breach of the peace took place."[40]

By 1900 the population of Arrow Rock had grown to 358 people, 113 (31.5 percent) of whom were African Americans. By the turn of the century, black residents of Arrow Rock had bolstered their efforts to define freedom on their own terms with new economic relationships and forms of social and cultural independence. Although a majority of Arrow Rock blacks had lived and worked in white households in 1880, all twenty-seven households in which blacks lived in 1900 were headed by African Americans. Living-in had stopped, and blacks had established their own households in their own homes. Indeed, thirteen of the twenty-seven households were located in houses owned by the black residents themselves. A more concentrated black community had emerged on and near a single street (Morgan Street) on the northern border of the village. The genesis of this new community stretched back to the 1880s, when African Americans began buying property along Morgan Street from whites who sold them land for modest sums—perhaps, one is tempted to speculate, because they feared losing their traditional labor force.[41] The community was further nurtured in 1892 when, as the *Arrow Rock Enterprise* reported, the old school for whites was torn down, "and the brick and lumber conveyed to the lot in the northern part of town where the work of erecting a negro school is progressing rapidly."[42]

These African Americans were often still working for whites, of course. Indeed, blacks continued to provide the primary labor force for Arrow Rock into the mid-twentieth century. As one elderly white woman summarized in a 1997 interview, "Everything everybody did, the black people did the work."[43] But by the turn of the twentieth century, African Americans had escaped residency in white households and, with this escape, had arrived at a new level of independence. This independence was abetted by the survival strategies they adopted. For example, by 1900 a number of the households (seven, 29 percent) had either extended family members or boarders living under the same roof, which was a way of sharing living expenses and child-care responsibilities. Both husbands and wives often continued to engage in the wage economy. Eleven (31 percent) of the thirty-five black women fourteen years or older in Arrow Rock in 1900 were listed in the census as laundresses or servants. An even greater percentage of black women worked for wages by 1910. By that year, the total population of Arrow Rock had actually declined to 336, but the black population had gone up to 148, or a surprising 44 percent of the village's total population. Seventeen (40 percent) of the forty-two

Brown Chapel, the Freewill Baptist church, was erected in late 1869. It also housed the first African American school in Arrow Rock. (courtesy of Friends of Arrow Rock, Inc.)

women aged fourteen years or older were working as "servants," "general house laborers," or "laundresses."[44]

The emergence of a relatively large African American community on Arrow Rock's northern edge nurtured the growth of the village's black institutions. At some point in the late nineteenth century, perhaps as early as the 1870s but certainly no later than the 1890s, the Arrow Rock Freewill Baptist Church joined an association composed of numerous west-central and western Missouri Freewill Baptist churches. In August 1893 the association's annual meeting was held in Arrow Rock. In an article titled "Colored People from Far and Near," a local newspaper noted, "The climax was reached when at least two hundred visitors came into town from all points within twenty miles of Arrow Rock. Both of the colored churches were filled to overflowing both morning and afternoon."[45]

These association meetings became gatherings to remember during the first half of the twentieth century. Bishop M. H. (Marvin Henry) Williams, who was born in nearby Union Hill in 1916, recalled attending association meetings in Arrow Rock as a child during the 1920s. By

1920 the town's black population had dropped to 116, a figure that still represented nearly 41 percent of Arrow Rock's total population of 286. According to Williams, association meetings began on the first Sunday in August and ran for an entire week, through the following Sunday. Williams remembered these meetings attracting as many as three hundred people. Men "would always relinquish their seats so the ladies could sit down. And they would [go outside] and stick their heads in the windows."[46] One of the most popular preachers at these gatherings was the Reverend Will Todd. In 1920 the fifty-seven-year-old Todd, a Missouri native, lived in Arrow Rock with his wife, Annie, a son, and a stepson. Saline County native Fielding Draffen remembered that the Reverend Todd "was a legend in Saline County. He was a fire and brimstone preacher." Draffen further recalled, "I can remember hearing my grandparents say 'we can't miss Sunday in Arrow Rock, because Reverend Will Todd is preaching.'"[47]

The fact that hundreds of people attended the week-long association meetings created a challenge for the black community of Arrow Rock as housing and food had to be provided for out-of-town guests. Bishop Williams remembered that a housing committee would be set up within the Brown Chapel congregation. Members of the committee would contact all of the church members in the community, asking them to host visitors. Draffen remembered, "At the end of every meeting, the host minister would stand up . . . just before the benediction, and he would say, 'Has everyone been placed or does everyone have a place to stay?'" If local church members could not provide enough space, nonmembers of the Arrow Rock black community would be asked. "We had lots of friends," Bishop Williams recalled. In addition to a housing committee, there was also a food committee, which had to arrange for the feeding of this large group of people.[48]

Although Arrow Rock's black population declined during the decade between 1910 and 1920, it had rebounded to 137, or 45 percent of the town's population, by 1930. An important reason for this growth appears to have been an increase in employment opportunities for black men in particular. The US Army Corps of Engineers opened a rock quarry along the Missouri River bluff below Arrow Rock, probably in 1929, and stone quarried at that site was used to channelize the river. The 1930 federal census listed twenty-two African American men working as "rock breakers" at the "Government Quarry."[49]

Apart from the quarry, the largest single employer of African Americans in Arrow Rock in 1930 was the Huston Tavern, then operated as both a hotel and a restaurant. Five individuals worked there, including Rena Brown, a sixty-three-year-old "cook" who lived with her husband, Hooker, who worked as a farm laborer, and her two adult daughters, Marian and Adaline, both of whom worked as laundresses for private families.[50]

Life was especially difficult for African Americans in Arrow Rock during the Great Depression. After the quarry closed during the early 1930s, black men continued to seek jobs as agricultural laborers, but such work was increasingly difficult to find. Not only was the farm economy in serious decline but mechanization was displacing farmworkers. As Marvin H. Williams remembered it, "many farmers began to get various machinery," especially tractors and combines. Black men who were fortunate enough to find work on farms could expect to earn up to $2.50 per day.[51]

Women continued to seek employment as domestic servants, but as Pearl Adams remembered, "We had a hard time! A hard time." She recalled, "When I first went to work, I made 50 cents a day. [I] clean[ed] house, cook[ed], [did] whatever had to be done." Like many other Depression-era children, Adams remembered her mother supplementing the household food supply by raising hogs, chickens, fruit, and vegetables. The staple diet consisted primarily of navy beans and corn bread, with wild greens doused with bacon grease supplementing the diet in spring and summer. Sugar, salt, flour, and coffee were among the few store-bought items purchased. Adams recalled, "Most of them [black village residents] left after that [the Depression] because of work. Wasn't any work around."[52] Marvin Williams concurred. Black Arrow Rock residents left for cities such as St. Louis, Kansas City, and Chicago in search of work. The result was that the village's black population declined during the Depression decade, from 137 in 1930 to 95 in 1940, a nearly 31 percent reduction.[53]

The 1940 federal census reveals that there were 95 African Americans living in thirty separate households in Arrow Rock that year. In contrast to the image of twenty-first-century African American urban family life, twenty-four of the thirty households (67 percent) were headed by males. Twelve of the thirty residences were owned by their occupants. The stability of the African American community is further evidenced by the fact that all of the black residents of Arrow Rock in 1940, save one, had lived in the "same place" or the "same house" five years earlier.[54]

In 1939 the most common occupation for black men in Arrow Rock was working on "road construction." While road construction was somewhat seasonal, men who were able to find this type of work in 1939 were employed for as few as sixteen weeks to as many as forty-two weeks. Wages for this type of work brought the laborer approximately $12.00 per week. Other black men worked at a rock quarry that had recently reopened. Quarry work was both less stable and less remunerative than roadwork. William Huston Van Buren, for example, worked at the quarry for twenty-six weeks in 1939. That work earned $78.00 for him, a total of $3.00 per week, or one-fourth of what road construction workers earned. Carl Edwards, a thirty-one-year-old black man, worked thirty-five weeks at the quarry and earned $200.00, or just under $6.00 per week. Seven black men listed their occupation as working at the quarry, while a majority of the remaining black men living in Arrow Rock worked as farm laborers. Jess Napier was one of the few black men who found steady farmwork. He earned $300.00 working fifty-two weeks on a farm in 1939, an average wage of $5.77 per week.

The steadiest work of all in 1939 came for those employed at the Old Tavern. Earl Parker worked fifty-two weeks there in 1939, as a porter and table waiter. His work earned him $156.00, or $3.00 per week. In 1939 Minnie J. Parker, wife of road-construction worker Lester Parker, earned $182.00 for fifty-two weeks of work as an Old Tavern cook. That meant an average weekly salary of $3.50 per week.[55]

Despite a decline in Arrow Rock's African American population during the decade of the 1930s, a sufficient number of blacks remained in the village during and after World War II to support at least two postwar black businesses. One was a combination bar and restaurant, run in the lower level of the black Masonic hall by William Huston "Creaker" Van Buren. Thelma Van Buren Conway, Creaker's wife, remembered working as a waitress in the establishment, which served "hamburgers, hot dogs, rabbit, fish and chicken," along with an occasional barbecued raccoon. Thelma's sister, Rosella, also owned a restaurant, sometimes referred to as "Whittie's," or "Over East."[56] Whittie's doubled as a popular dance hall where people such as Betty Banks Finley learned to jitterbug.[57] No doubt one of the most popular musicians to play for these dances during the era of World War II and beyond was John T. Banks, a fiddler and mandolin player, remembered by longtime Saline County resident Bill Kearns as someone who "could play all the popular music of the day (the 1920s and 1930s) from foxtrots and rags, and other dances in vogue, and he also could play the old-time square dance tunes he had absorbed from growing up in the community."[58]

By the 1940s and 1950s, a white-owned restaurant, the Huston Tavern, employed approximately twenty African Americans at any one time, according to longtime manager Mary Lou Pearson. According to her, blacks were "hired at the tavern as waiters and waitresses, houseboys, people to do all the work." "They made my living for me," Pearson recalled, adding, "[I] couldn't have done it without them." Notwithstanding this reality, it was the mid-1950s before Mrs. Pearson would serve black customers because she feared violating the segregationist social customs of Little Dixie, thereby upsetting her white clientele. Change in this policy came in association with two rather dramatic episodes at the tavern.[59]

The first occurrence happened during "the first year [1956] that the black kids started going to school with the white kids." At Christmas time, Pearson invited all of the students to the tavern for lunch, forgetting that black children would be among those attending, including the daughters of her head cook, Ruth Banks. When the black students arrived, Pearson tried to discourage them from eating inside, offering to make them a plate that they could take outside. But then she felt ashamed of herself: "I just started crying because I was so upset with myself."[60]

At roughly the same time, Pearson turned away a racially integrated group associated with nearby Missouri Valley College. As Pearson related the story, someone in the group complained to Missouri's governor who, in turn, called Pearson and told her, "Mary Lou, we have to let them [African Americans] in any time they come." Pearson complied with the governor's directive.[61]

Segregation continued into the era of World War II and beyond in Arrow Rock and the rest of Little Dixie, but African American institutions also remained strong. Sometime during the war era, the Freewill Baptist Church began hosting annual dinners on Sundays in early June. Variously referred to as "Rally Basket Dinners" and "Homecoming Basket Dinners," these gatherings brought together hundreds of African Americans, although usually only for the day. People ate on the yard in front of the Freewill Baptist Church and in the streets. Hortense Nichols remembered these occasions as "just an old fashioned basket dinner. . . . Everybody cooked . . . everybody brought a washing tub full of food . . . a number two washing tub."[62]

Nichols remembered church as "our biggest entertainment."[63] But it was much more than that. The African American sociologist Andrew Billingsley, writing in an important book titled *Climbing Jacob's Ladder,* explained: "It is a mistake . . . to think of the black church in America as simply, or even primarily, a religious institution in the same way the white church might be conceived."[64] C. Eric Lincoln, another well-known student of the African American church, has written, "Beyond its purely religious function, as critical as that function has been, the black church in its historical role as lyceum, conservatory, forum, social service center, political academy and financial institution, has been and is for black America the mother of our culture, the champion of our freedom, the hallmark of our civilization."[65]

When a black family in Arrow Rock needed help of any kind, Pearl Adams remembered, the first place they turned was the church: "People would pitch in and help. . . . They'd just take what they had and carry it to the family to help them out. . . . Somebody got sick and they'd go cut wood and bring it in. The women would cook and wash and wouldn't think nothing about it."[66]

In a measure of how one-sided race relations were during the Jim Crow era, however, whites felt comfortable participating in black church–related activities, if only as spectators who drew entertainment from what they regarded as quaint African American practices. During the early post-emancipation period, for example, T. H. Rainey reported a large group of whites gathered on the bank of the Missouri River to watch "the colored people" baptize "new converts to the Baptist faith." Rainey commented, "Very rarely in my life have I witnessed a scene so picturesque, or listened to music so natural and delightful."[67] Similarly, during the 1930s and 1940s, longtime Arrow Rock resident Mary Burge and others remembered attending black funerals and revivals. Whites seemed to relish what they regarded as the theatrical elements of these occasions—the singing, shouting, and sometimes fainting. By contrast, the town's African Americans rarely if ever attended white church services. It was whites who made the rules of social interaction. "We were," Mary Burge summarized, "just a city divided."[68]

Arrow Rock's African American school continued to thrive into the mid-twentieth century, in tandem with the black church and the social and fraternal lodges, despite the fact that there was a decided lack of appreciation of the value of formal education among at least some black parents of the era. In a 1996 interview, for example, Ruth Wilson Banks Perry, born in 1906, recalled that in her early life and in her home, education was not considered very important for children. "All we knowed was work," Perry recalled. "They didn't send us to school." Ruth further remembered her mother telling her she "didn't need no education." Instead, Ruth was taught by her mother's white employer. Years later, Ruth recalled the white woman's advice: "She said when you get up big you gonna have to know how to count money and write your name . . . she said if you know how to count money can't no body beat you out of nothing."[69]

The school for African American students in Arrow Rock was destroyed by fire in about 1930. A frame structure built to replace that school was also destroyed by fire in 1948 and was replaced with a brick building that still stands in Arrow Rock today. At least one year of high school for black students was offered during the 1930s and 1940s. Black students who sought education beyond that level had to go to racially segregated schools in Sedalia, Jefferson City, or Boonville or to the Dalton Vocational School in Chariton County.

By the 1960s Arrow Rock's black population had dwindled to an all-time low. Racial integration resulting from the 1954 *Brown v. Board of Education* decision and the civil rights acts of the 1960s, combined with increased economic opportunity in urban areas such as Kansas City, attracted away most of the African Americans who had called Arrow Rock home. Teresa Habernal, whose family was among the last black families to live in Arrow Rock, recalled that she was one of only two black students attending the town's racially integrated school during the late 1950s. By the 1990s only one African American resident remained in Arrow Rock, then a village of fewer than eighty residents. When that one resident, Sue Hall, died in 2009, Arrow Rock's African American population remained only a memory.

For more than a century, however, African Americans were a key factor in Arrow Rock, Missouri, life. They were brought there against their will in the antebellum period as part of what historian Ira Berlin calls "The Passage to the Interior," the forced migration of black slaves from the eastern seaboard into the interior of the United States. After multiple generations in the rural Missouri River valley, their descendants became part of another, even greater, migration, one that carried African Americans into urban, industrial centers of the Midwest and North. In that regard, the lives of black Arrow Rock residents from 1850 to 1960 characterized and dramatized the lives of countless other black Americans who both shaped and were shaped by the complex effort of Americans to deal with the issue of race over the course of a century.[70]

Chapter 8

"Just like the Garden of Eden"

African American Community Life in Kansas City's Leeds

For more than two decades a growing number of American scholars have devoted their research to uncovering the ways in which African Americans forged rich and rewarding lives during the late nineteenth and early twentieth centuries within a society often committed to the devaluation of people of color.[1] Despite this intellectual effort, our understanding of African American community life during the age of segregation is incomplete, especially in regions of the country outside the Deep South.

The border state of Missouri witnessed creative and energetic efforts by African Americans to achieve dignity and autonomy in the face of racial oppression during the so-called Jim Crow era.[2] Indeed, an in-depth look at black life in the Kansas City, Missouri, community of Leeds from approximately 1915 to 1960 adds detail and texture to the story of the African American response to segregation.

Kansas City's African American population grew dramatically during the last decade of the nineteenth century and the first two decades of the twentieth century. In 1890 there were 13,700 African Americans who called Kansas City home. Thirty years later, that number had more than doubled, to 30,719.[3]

The growth of Kansas City's black population was part of a larger story of African American migration from southern to midwestern and northern states, and from rural to urban areas in Missouri. In 1890 47 percent of Missouri's black population lived in cities; by 1900 the figure had jumped to 55 percent. By 1910, nearly 67 percent of Missouri's African Americans lived in cities, almost three times the national average.[4]

White Kansas Citians, much as their urban cousins across the state in St. Louis, responded to this influx of African Americans by restricting them from living in white residential neighborhoods. Thus, during the first two decades of the twentieth century, Kansas City blacks increasingly concentrated in what historian Sherry Lamb Schirmer calls the "Vine Street Corridor," a strip several blocks wide, extending from about Tenth Street on the north to Nineteenth Street on the south.[5]

Although this neighborhood quickly became crowded and, as Schirmer writes, "developed many of the earmarks of a ghetto," it had much to offer its African American residents. The high concentration of blacks in the area resulted in the building of a number of important social, cultural, and commercial institutions. Crispus Attucks School, named for the African American killed by British soldiers at the Boston Massacre in 1770, was erected at Eighteenth and Brooklyn in 1893. Fourteen years later, black population growth in the Vine Street area prompted the building of a new Attucks School at Nineteenth and Woodland, only two blocks east of Vine. Additional elementary schools for African American students were built in or near the Vine Street Corridor over the next several years. The city erected a black high school—Lincoln High—just to the west of Vine Street, at Nineteenth and Tracy, in 1906. Black churches also anchored themselves in this neighborhood, which by 1912 had perhaps as many as three thousand residents.[6]

Despite the advantages of living in a predominately African American neighborhood with strong black cultural and social institutions in the Vine Street area, not all black Kansas Citians wanted to live there. During the era of World War I (1914–1918), an alternative, if smaller, African American community began to develop west of the Blue River, south of Raytown Road. Incorporated into the city in 1909, this area was not platted and laid out into lots until 1915. On October 29 of that year, J. W.Couch and his wife, Laura, filed a plat for what became known as "Couch's 1st Addition." The neighborhood extended from Thirty-third Street on the north to Thirty-sixth Street on the south, and from Raytown Road to Hardesty Avenue. Although white, the Couches began building houses in their new subdivision and selling them exclusively to African Americans.[7]

Roughly a decade later, during the mid- to late 1920s, the demand for housing in this area led to two more subdivisions being opened for African Americans, just east and southeast of Couch's 1st Addition. Known collectively by local residents as "Allen's Addition," this neighborhood extended to the Blue River on the east.[8] By the late 1920s, residents of

Couch's and Allen's Additions had begun to refer to the joint neighborhoods as Leeds, a name that also referred to a white industrial community east of the Blue River.[9]

What attracted African Americans to this area that lay roughly two miles east of the Vine Street Corridor, and even farther from the heart of downtown Kansas City? Interviews with longtime residents of Leeds provide insight into the motivations of early settlers. First of all, property proved far more affordable in the Blue River area than in the Vine Street Corridor. In addition, the white owners of the property would sell the land to blacks on installment plans. This allowed African Americans to become landowners rather than renters, as was the case with a majority of the residents in the Vine Street area. Taking advantage of this option, some early Leeds residents moved to the Blue River area from the Vine Street Corridor. Dolly Mosby Malone, for example, born in 1911 in the 2500 block of Woodland, two blocks east of Vine Street, moved with her parents to Couch's Addition in 1917. She recalled in an interview that "the rent in Kansas City caused them [her parents] to move."[10]

Thus, the Leeds community, and the opportunity to buy land there, provided Kansas City blacks with the chance to own their own homes, a possibility that had been extremely important to African Americans since the early post-emancipation period.[11] The 1920 federal census reveals that 96 of the 108 households in the community at the time were occupied by residents who lived in homes they owned, an astonishing 89 percent. Only twelve of the households were listed as renters.[12]

The houses in Leeds were not, by any stretch of the imagination, elaborate or extravagant. A majority of the early houses erected in Couch's Addition were two-room, frame, shotgun structures built by the white developers who owned the land. Malone remembered, "Regardless of how large your family was, you got a two-room house." Most of the houses included porches, which served as bedrooms in the summer. To ward off mosquitoes, a large tub filled with smoldering rags would be kept nearby.[13]

The houses lacked bathrooms, central heat, even foundations—they were built on wooden piers sunk into the ground. At least some of the houses had dirt floors. Gertrude Gillum, who moved to Leeds in 1921 at the age of six, mentioned that "some [women] would sweep designs in the floor and they did not want you to mess up their floors." Buyers "paid some money down and then you paid so much a month." The developers "came through on Sunday" to collect the money due them.[14] The Reverend Kenneth E. Ray, born four years after his parents moved to

Couch's Addition in 1928, said his father told him that he paid a hundred dollars down on the family's first house.[15] The houses in Allen's Addition, built during the late 1920s and 1930s, tended to be more substantial than the early houses in Couch's. Most were built as single-story, front-gable, frame bungalows, featuring full basements and full-length screened-in front porches.[16] Mary Garth, whose family was among the first to move to Allen's Addition, recalled that at the entrance to the neighborhood from Raytown Road, "there was a big sign . . . and it had a house on it and under it was printed 'exclusively for colored.'"[17]

In addition to providing African Americans with an opportunity to own their own homes, the community of Leeds offered migrants a better way of life than they could attain in the city. Parents, especially, found Leeds' wide-open spaces, where children could run and play, inviting. The Reverend Kenneth Ray summarized the attitudes of many when he reported that his father moved from Arkansas to Leeds because he was "looking for a place where he could raise his family and have a garden and not have to worry about the inner city."[18] Comments such as this underscore the fact that the people who chose to make Leeds their home were very family-oriented. The 1920 federal census indicates that 105 of the 108 households in the community had both a father and a mother living in the home.[19]

The fact that so many of the Leeds residents came either from the South or from rural Missouri was another important reason that they congregated in the area. Although within the city limits of Kansas City, the area remained very rural. Southern and rural blacks quickly discovered that they could replicate their southern semi-subsistent lifestyle. Stories about gardens and livestock in Leeds are woven tightly throughout the community's collective memory. Longtime residents recalled that most neighborhood families established large vegetable gardens in which they raised a variety of items, including mustard greens and collards, sweet potatoes, green beans, asparagus, and corn. Residents also raised fruit such as peaches, pears, blackberries, and raspberries. Harvest time was a time of sharing with neighbors. The Reverend Kenneth Ray's father "had one of the biggest gardens in Leeds and at that time people would not only plant for their families but they would also have enough left to help people in need." Food grown in gardens and not consumed in season would be preserved for the winter months through canning, with the canned goods usually stored in cellars dug beneath family homes.[20]

In addition to the ubiquitous vegetable garden, many residents raised chickens, not only to ensure a supply of eggs but also to provide meat for the family table. Other residents raised ducks and guineas for the same purposes. Thinking back, Rosa Mae Gillespie said, "There was a man named Gillman and he had cows . . . and we used to get milk from those cows."[21] Easter Hubley, born in Leeds in 1923, remembered the community as a place where "the Lord took care of everybody. I can say I never did have a hungry day. Everybody shared things. Where we lived we had hogs and chickens and every October we had a big hog kill and everybody was there. Everybody would bring their hogs to our house and kill them. The people would go around to the homes and collect garbage and that is what they would feed to their hogs. After they killed the hogs they would separate the meat and salt some and smoke others."[22]

To augment their diet of homegrown food and meat, community residents hunted and fished. They also gathered fruits, nuts, and greens growing in the countryside beyond the houses. "Leeds was just like the Garden of Eden," reminisced Mary Garth, who moved there when she was about six years old, during the early 1920s. "You could go over that hill at Leeds and find all kinds of fruit and some of the sweetest strawberries over there."[23] Charles Jones, whose family moved to the area in the 1930s, recalled that a number of community men, including his father, made wine from wild berries and grapes.[24]

Jones also stated that most Leeds residents relied on fish and wild game for food. Men and boys in the community hunted rabbits and squirrels in the nearby woods. "Back then you could walk out of your back door and hunt," Jones said. Wild game not only supplemented his family's diet but also provided him with spending money. He sold the rabbits he killed with a .22-caliber rifle for twenty-five cents apiece.[25]

As with other foodstuffs, neighbors shared fish and wild game with each other. The Reverend Thomas McCormick noted, "There were a lot of [neighborhood residents] who lived for hunting in the winter and fishing in the summer and our family would always share in the results. Nobody went hungry unless you did not like fish or rabbit or squirrel." Those children who claimed not to like rabbit often found themselves eating it anyway, disguised as hamburger. Hunting in the area continued into the era of World War II and beyond.[26]

For those few residents who did not grow, gather, or hunt their own food or for those who wanted to supplement their fare with store-bought goods, there were several neighborhood grocery stores. The dominant grocery store in Couch's Addition during the pre–World War II era and beyond was O. M. Scott's Grocery Store, located at 3400 Hardesty Avenue. Scott, an African American, lived with his family in the upstairs of the large two-story building that housed the store. Turner's Grocery Store on East Thirty-sixth Street Terrace was the most popular store in Allen's subdivision. Like Scott's, Turner's was also a black-owned and -operated business. All of the neighborhood grocery stores allowed patrons to buy on credit.[27]

At the far eastern edge of the black Leeds community, near the intersection of White Avenue and Raytown Road, Denzil Maple, a white man, operated a grocery store. Located just west of the Blue River, Maples Grocery served a large black clientele from Leeds. Across the Blue, several blocks east of White Avenue, a Jewish-owned grocery store known as Friedmans also attracted some black Leeds shoppers. Although African Americans were welcome at Friedmans and Maples, Vivienne Starks Smith recalled, "A lot of people didn't go [to either one]. . . . You had a lot of black people just as prejudiced as white people.[28]

The residents of Leeds lived a semi-subsistent lifestyle. Jobs with a steady income proved hard to find in the community, especially during the early 1920s. The most common occupation recorded for heads of household in the 1920 federal census of the area is "laborer," with the place of employment listed as "working out."[29]

Gertrude Gillum recalled, "Until they built the Chevrolet plant out in Leeds [in late 1928], most of the men worked in construction."[30] Men often traveled into downtown Kansas City to work on construction sites

Lawrence Jackson and his "jitney" that was used as a taxi in Leeds (courtesy of JoAnn Jackson)

as day laborers. In the 1920s, Lella Jo Birks's father, a construction day laborer, "would go to the corner and a truck would come by and pick him up" and take him to a job site.[31]

During the early 1920s, it appears that most men had to leave the neighborhood to find work. A few found employment at one of Kansas City's packinghouses, and some worked as elevator operators, cooks, or janitors in downtown hotels or office buildings, but they, like the construction workers, had to leave Leeds. The most common way to go downtown was to walk to Thirty-first Street and Raytown Road, at the northwest edge of the neighborhood, and catch a streetcar. In later years, during the early 1930s, at least one enterprising Leeds resident operated a cab or "jitney" service that carried those who could afford it to and from the streetcar stop. Cab fare ranged from five to fifteen cents, depending upon the distance traveled.[32]

The streetcar served as a stark reminder to Leeds residents of the reality of racism that surrounded their island community. Although the streetcars were not segregated, African Americans usually found themselves outnumbered by whites on the cars. They were often subjected to racial epithets and derogatory comments. Sometimes white riders would not move over in a seat, thereby refusing to allow black riders to sit beside them. Added to the irony of being forced to face racial hostility on a supposedly integrated public transportation vehicle, the streetcar took Leeds riders from their friendly, collegial community to an area of the city stratified on the basis of race and class.[33]

A minority of Leeds women joined the men for the trek downtown each day, largely to work as maids in private homes. The majority of neighborhood women, at least during the 1920s, remained behind with their children and busied themselves with the day-to-day chores of housekeeping and child rearing. These chores were made difficult by the absence of "modern" conveniences in the community. For example, no running water existed in the houses. The bulk of the water used in the homes came from community hydrants located in each block. According to Hazel Nicholson, "You had to go out into the garden where there was a water faucet and we would have to bring the water into the house and heat it on the stove to wash the dishes." The absence of running water also made it difficult to do laundry. Ruby Robinson remembered her mother boiling the laundry in a large iron pot in the yard.[34]

Not only was there no running water in Leeds homes during the 1920s and early 1930s, there was also no electricity or natural gas. Kerosene lamps provided lighting, and wood or coal heating stoves furnished warmth during the winter.[35] Refrigeration came in the form of iceboxes, cooled by large blocks of ice delivered by men who hauled their product in horse-drawn wagons through the unpaved streets of the neighborhood. Coal and milk were delivered in the same manner. According to Ruby Robinson, "The coal man would bring the coal and the ice man would bring the ice and the milk man would bring the milk. We had a man for everything."[36]

Church attendance was important in Leeds. The Reverend Kenneth Ray reported, "Church was always an important part of our lives. Our parents and grandparents were there and they saw that we had a good religious education." One of the earliest neighborhood churches was Gilbert Memorial (African Methodist Episcopal), organized in 1918 at 3608 Bellaire Avenue by the Reverend A. A. Gilbert. The congregation moved from house to house until they built a church at 3704 Topping Avenue in 1920.[37]

Other early churches included the Green Grove Baptist Church, at 3300 Oakley Avenue, and Pilgrim's Rest, a Baptist church organized in September 1918 at 3400 Hardesty Avenue.[38] *The Call*, an African American newspaper established in Kansas City in 1919, regularly published accounts of activities at these churches during the early 1920s. In January 1922, for example, *The Call* reported on "watch meeting services" at Pilgrim's Rest that lasted "throughout the old year, into the New Year." *The Call* noted that "the Services were well attended Sunday all day and night," and the "offering for the entire day [was] $27.90." Likewise, "a glorious watch meeting was observed" at Green Grove Church, where "a large number partook of the Lord's Supper."[39]

According to Hazel Nicholson, churches provided the major social outlet for Leeds residents in her youth. She and her family attended Sunday school and worship services every Sunday morning and then returned in the evening for Baptist Youth Training Union (BYTU). Church attendance was important to Hazel's parents. If she did not attend Sunday morning services, her parents would not allow her to go downtown to the Lincoln Theatre for a Sunday matinee, a favorite activity.[40]

Churches held social activities throughout the year that were often attended by community members who may or may not have belonged to the church. Gilbert Memorial AME Church, for example, always held a children's fashion show on the Monday after Easter so that, as Nicholson remembered, "every kid could strut his or her stuff." Gilbert Memorial also held popular "Tom Thumb Weddings," presided over by child ministers.[41]

The significance of the churches was reflected in the fact that ministers were among the most highly respected members of the community.

Often they would be invited into the homes of congregants for Sunday dinner. In a late-life reminiscence, Ruby Robinson still marveled "at how fast [the preacher] could eat and talk."[42]

Because all of the neighborhood's schoolchildren attended the local public school, it was probably a more important community institution. The school opened in September 1917 in the Green Grove Church with an initial enrollment of about twenty-five. By the end of the first school year, enrollment had climbed to thirty-nine students. Whitfield Ross, the first teacher and principal, lived in Leeds until his accidental death on December 31, 1929. In September 1919, Ross hired a second teacher, Annie C. Goins. By the end of the 1919–1920 school year, enrollment at the Green Grove School had grown to ninety-six students. In June 1920, the Kansas City Board of Education voted to erect a new eight-room school building on the crest of a hill on East Thirty-sixth Street, between Oakley and Hardesty Avenues.[43] Vocational education students from Lincoln High School, under the supervision of their instructor, W. T. White, did much of the building of the new school. The Reverend Thomas McCormick recalled, "My father related to me he was on the crew that came out from Lincoln High School that built Dunbar School."[44] The new school was named Dunbar in honor of the prominent African American poet Paul Lawrence Dunbar, born in Dayton, Ohio, in 1872. Dunbar was at the height of his popularity in the United States during the second decade of the twentieth century.[45]

On November 16, 1920, the day that Dunbar opened, the entire student body marched in a parade from Green Grove Church to the new school. "I was happy," Dolly Mosby Malone said, "because it was a big improvement. We did not have to have school in the church with those hard benches. Also, the new school had better bathroom facilities." The "bathroom facilities" were still outhouses with a wooden partition dividing boys' and girls' toilets.[46]

As more families with children moved into the Leeds community, the school grew dramatically. By the close of school in 1921, enrollment had jumped to 151 students. At the end of the next year, 231 students attended Dunbar. Seven faculty members were employed by 1922, including Bessie Taylor, who oversaw the department of sewing and a school garden that was maintained as part of a vocational training program.[47]

Each school day began with a prayer, usually the Lord's Prayer recited in unison, followed by a recitation of the pledge of allegiance to the flag. Often the pledge was followed by a song—"Good Morning to You." The students sat in desks discarded by white schools and arranged in rows.

They often used hand-me-down materials, including textbooks from the white schools. There was no school lunch program. Students either returned to their homes for lunch and then went back to school for afternoon classes or carried their lunches to school in paper bags. Former students who attended Dunbar stated that they had been taught by "excellent teachers" who took a keen interest in them, both as students and as people. One former student commented, "[The teachers] just did not let you fail. They made you learn."[48]

Although many Dunbar teachers lived outside the community, in or near the Vine Street Corridor, they tended to remain at the school for long periods of time, and they got to know their students' families well. Parents trusted teachers and thought of them as partners in the shaping of the neighborhood's children. This partnership extended to discipline. Corporal punishment was common at Dunbar, and according to the Reverend Ray, "If the teacher would paddle you at school . . . that meant you would also get one at home." On one occasion, Ray's father came to school and whipped his son in front of the whole class for talking back to a teacher. Community monitoring of truancy minimized the incidence of skipping school.[49]

One of the high points of the school year for Dunbar children was the day of the Christmas program, when each class put on a performance. Parents helped to make costumes, and children practiced their programs to perfection. The most eagerly anticipated day of each school year, however, was May Day, which featured an outdoor picnic on the playground behind the school. Students participated in square dancing, foot races, and an assortment of games. Each class put on a program or performed a dance, often wearing costumes made of paper that fit over outer clothing. A flagpole in the middle of the schoolyard was transformed into a May pole, with long streamers extending from its top. One former student remembered, "Each child got hold of [a] streamer and [would] go round and round the May pole and we would sing."[50]

A large vacant lot across the street from the school served as a neighborhood playground. Widely known by the neighborhood children as "Big Dusty," this site hosted baseball games throughout the summers. Girls and boys alike played baseball, the neighborhood's dominant sport. Ground rules specifying how many bases could be taken on errant balls traveling into adjacent yards governed the playing of games.[51]

Liberty Park, bordered on the north by Raytown Road and on the west by Thirty-fourth Street Terrace, provided another place for public gatherings and entertainment. The seventeen-acre park opened with great fanfare in mid-June 1922. Described by advertisements in *The Call* as "The Negroes Playground" and "The Only Place of its Kind in the United States that is Run for the Exclusive use of Negroes," the park became a popular gathering place for both adults and children, especially on weekends.[52] Gertrude Gillum said, "[Liberty Park] was a regular amusement park and they had merry-go-rounds, Ferris wheels, concession stands [and] a dance hall." Delores Ray remembered, "You always had to pay to get in but the kids had a place they could slip in by the fence and they did not pay nothing." Lawrence Jackson summed up many residents' view of the park: "That park was jumping." [53]

The Call proclaimed that the park had "the finest dancing pavilion in Kansas City," adding that "the music for dancing is furnished by George Lee's Orchestra." In addition, *The Call* reported, a radio was being installed so that "free Radio Concerts" could be held at the park. This was especially popular with area residents who did not own radios. African Americans from throughout the city found Liberty Park an attractive place to gather. It provided a welcome alternative to Kansas City's Swope Park, where blacks were confined to a segregated area commonly referred to as "Watermelon Hill."[54]

Liberty Park also featured a lake that served as a swimming pool in the summer and an ice-skating rink in the winter. Occasionally, a baptism was held in the lake. The park had a baseball field, as well, where teams comprising young men from Leeds challenged teams from other parts of the city. One of the most popular community teams was the Leeds Clowns. Among the most beloved annual activities at Liberty Park was a Fourth of July celebration that included the shooting of fireworks.[55]

Gypsies found Liberty Park a favorite camping place in the summer, sometimes staying for weeks at a time. Each evening, the Gypsies performed a musical for all who wished to attend. Although the gatherings attracted sizeable crowds, some area residents remained in their houses, fearing that other Gypsies might steal from neighborhood homes during the nightly performances. Dora Craven was warned, "Don't go down there [to the park]. [The Gypsies] will steal you and make slaves out of you."[56] Across Raytown Road from Liberty Park, near Thirty-fourth Street, stood a neighborhood bar known as the Liberty Tavern. It was a favorite gathering place for men of the community, and women sometimes frequented the tavern as well. Rosa Mae Gillespie recalled, "We all went down to that tavern and that is where we learned to drink." The Reverend Kenneth Ray, however, remembered the tavern as "the only place we could not go in Leeds when we were kids." [57]

In May 1929 Sarah Rector, a wealthy African American woman, opened a dance hall called Del Ray Gardens on Thirty-fourth Street, near the southern border of Leeds. An article in the *Kansas City American* announced the opening and explained that "special permission from city authorities will allow the Garden to remain open all night."[58] Rector's dance hall attracted well-known bands and a large clientele from the Vine Street Corridor; Leeds residents who could afford the admission also went there for entertainment. At one point during this period, the rowdy reputation of Del Ray Gardens seems to have attracted a vigilante group of whites, remembered by a number of people as members of the Ku Klux Klan. The group marched through Leeds toward Del Ray Gardens in an apparent effort to intimidate community members into "cleaning up" the dance hall.[59]

Children and adults also sought entertainment in their own homes and yards and in the streets of Leeds. Young people depended upon each other when it came to having fun. Hazel Nicholson recalled that children often gathered at her house because her mother "was always home and

Dunbar School (courtesy of the Kansas City Public Library Special Collection)

would look out for all of us." They played jacks, marbles, cards, school or church, or made mud pies. Yvonne Starks Wilson loved to play school: "I used to teach school on the front porch. . . . I had the kids on our front porch and I would try to teach them math. . . . We spent a lot of time on the front porch." According to Delores Ray, "In the winter time we used to sleigh ride down those hills and some of the boys would . . . build a fire to keep us warm. Everybody had sleds. We even had a pulley rigged up so you could pull yourself back up the hill."[60]

Often in the evenings, after dinner, family members gathered to sing and play music. Dolly Mosby Malone remembered, "My father played the mandolin, my brother played the drums and my sister played the piano. And my mother played the mandolin and piano . . . and I had another brother that played the horn."[61] Sometimes in the evenings, families gathered to study the Bible or listen to the radio. Few people, for example, missed listening to a live broadcast of a Joe Louis fight during the 1930s or early 1940s.[62] Indeed, one could walk through the streets of Leeds during the broadcast of a Louis fight and hear the play-by-play coming from radios perched on porches and in living rooms throughout the neighborhood. The recounting of community interest in Louis's fights calls to mind the one described by Maya Angelou in her autobiography, *I Know Why the Caged Bird Sings*. Angelou described how neighborhood blacks gathered in a store to hear a Louis fight:

> The last inch of space was filled, yet people continued to wedge themselves along the walls of the Store. Uncle Willie had turned the radio up to its last notch so that youngsters on the porch wouldn't miss a word. Women sat on kitchen chairs, dining room chairs, stools and upturned wooden boxes. Small children and babies perched on every lap available and men leaned on the shelves or on each other. The apprehensive mood was shot through with shafts of gaiety, as a black sky is streaked with lightning.[63]

Joe Louis was a source of racial pride for African Americans all over the country, and his popularity in Leeds prompted neighborhood women to form a social club known by a variation of the heavyweight's nickname, the "Brown Bombers."[64]

Dolly Mosby Malone and her teenage friends "had a club called 'The Gays' and we would get together for socials and dances, all the young people. . . . We went from house to house." Parents were not fearful of crime or criminals. Consequently, they allowed their children to roam all over the neighborhood. Mary Woods recalled, "In the summertime we would go crawdad fishing in the Blue River." Gertrude Gillum allowed her son Ronald to roam at will without concern about his well-being: "I remember we had a next door neighbor that had four boys all about the same size and Ronald would get up, eat a bowl of cereal, and leave the empty bowl on the table and go with these neighbor's boys and be gone all day and when they came home about 5–6 o'clock they always smelled like dogs." A favorite place for the boys to play was a wooded area between their neighborhood and a city-run correctional center, the Kansas City Municipal Farm, widely known as the Leeds Farm.[65]

While most parents seemed to have had little fear for their children so long as they stayed in the Leeds neighborhood, some parents were reluctant to allow their children to go into the city for fear that they might get into trouble. Dolly Mosby Malone's parents did not permit her to attend movies downtown when she was a child. She "did not get to see a movie until I was eighteen years old. The superintendent of the Sunday School . . . took me downtown to the Gem Theater to see 'Moon over Israel' and I never forgot that. It was a silent movie." Likewise, the Reverend Thomas McCormick remembered, "My father was not too keen on us going to town."[66]

Graduation from Dunbar School, for those who went on to high school, meant a daily trip out of the neighborhood to attend Kansas City's racially segregated Lincoln High. Some students experienced discrimination and ridicule because they lived in Leeds. A number of city students regarded Leeds—with its absence of running water, electricity, and paved streets—as a backward, even primitive, place to live. They sometimes made fun of and picked on students from Leeds.

Leeds students devised a variety of strategies to deal with the situation. They tended to travel together and to remain in groups at school whenever they could, hoping thereby to ward off taunts and verbal and physical threats. Students who owned two pairs of shoes wore one pair for the walk from their home to meet the streetcar at Thirty-first Street. There, they changed shoes before boarding the streetcar, leaving behind the dust- or mud-covered shoes that signaled they lived in Leeds. The soiled shoes would be retrieved in the afternoon after school and worn home.[67]

Some Leeds students at Lincoln High claimed that the negative treatment extended also to teachers and administrators. Ronald Gillum recalled, "The high school counselors did not encourage the Leeds kids to go to college. [If you were from Leeds,] you were encouraged to go to a trade school." Gillum also remembered occasional announcements: "All kids from Leeds [should] report to the auditorium." Once in the auditorium, students would be told "how bad we were and they said we were lower than 'pine scum' and he said 'you are all living out there in squalor.'"[68]

Dating exacerbated the tension between Kansas City youths and their "country cousins." Leeds boys, in particular, resented city boys who tried to date girls from the neighborhood. As the Reverend McCormick said, "We did not appreciate the boys from town coming out to Leeds to see the girls."[69]

The self-subsistent, cooperative lifestyle of the Leeds residents, no doubt, helped to sustain them through the Great Depression. One manifestation of the willingness of community members to help each other was what Dora Horn Craven remembered as "tax parties." When someone could not afford to pay their property taxes and was threatened with the loss of their property, friends raised money by throwing a party, charging admission, and giving the proceeds to the person(s) who needed money for taxes.[70]

The community's connection to Kansas City's Democratic political boss, Tom Pendergast, also proved beneficial. During the 1930s, African Americans throughout the country were moving from their traditional alliance with the party of Abraham Lincoln, "the Great Emancipator," toward the party of Franklin D. Roosevelt.[71] Tom Pendergast openly courted African American support in Kansas City, including Leeds. Isola Richardson recalled that "you could always tell when it was election time. They would come down and grade and oil Hardesty Street." Pendergast's principal lieutenants in Leeds appear to have been Mary Evans and Darie Richardson. A precinct captain, Richardson and his wife, Myrtle, lived at 3316 Oakley Avenue and operated the Liberty Tavern on Raytown Road. Evans and the Richardsons, said Dolly Malone, were "with Pendergast." Isola Richardson stated that Darie Richardson "was over the garbage trucks for Pendergast." Lawrence Jackson called Richardson "a pretty big shot guy."[72]

Malone and others also remembered that Evans traded clothing for votes: "After the election [she] would bring clothes out to Leeds to give away." Mary Garth said that Pendergast would have bread and milk delivered to community members in exchange for political support. Alvin Brooks remarked, "During the Pendergast days if you were a precinct captain you got coal and food but if you were not on the list of some captain, you might not get anything." Others remember Tom Pendergast coming to Leeds, especially just before elections. Often accompanied by a milk or bread truck, he dispensed milk and bread to all who approached him. His favorite stops seemed to have been on Raytown Road, near Darie Richardson's tavern, and on the playground behind the Dunbar School.[73]

No doubt the community's connection to Pendergast made Leeds a focal point of Works Progress Administration (WPA) projects, which brought improvements to the community while providing much needed jobs for the men of the neighborhood. As historians Lawrence Larsen and Nancy Hulston have pointed out in their biography of Pendergast, the Kansas City boss influenced the allocation of WPA funds throughout Missouri by virtue of the fact that one of his associates, Matthew Murray, was in charge of WPA projects for the state.[74] Thus, Pendergast was in a position to make sure that some WPA money was funneled into the African American community of Leeds.

Longtime residents recalled multiple WPA projects in the area during the mid- to late 1930s, including the paving of several streets, the widening of the Blue River, and the building of a new bridge across the river. Easter Hubley recalled with great clarity the widening of the Blue River. Her father worked on the project until he drowned in an accident on the job in June 1938.[75]

World War II brought many changes to the Leeds community. Robert White, born in 1930 and reared in Leeds, recalled the war years as a prosperous time: "Everybody had a job and cars were beginning to show up." In addition, running water and indoor toilets were installed in many neighborhood houses during the early war years. Many men of the community, at least those not called into the armed services, went to work either at the Lake City Arsenal or at Pratt and Whitney, war industry plants outside of Leeds.[76] Women also worked in the defense plants, expanding upon a trend that had become increasingly apparent during the Great Depression, the tendency of Leeds women to work outside the home. During the depression, neighborhood women found jobs as domestics, seamstresses, and child-care providers in the homes of Kansas City whites. Extended family members or neighbors cared for these women's children. Yvonne Brooks Bullock recalled, "Mrs. Nelson took care of me because my mother worked. Back then in Leeds people never had to hire babysitters. There was always somebody to look after the children for you. Mrs. Nelson was a neighbor. She lived right across the street from us."[77]

A relative prosperity continued in Leeds after World War II. By that time, most of the men worked either at the Chevrolet factory east of the Blue River or in the railroad tie plant near the Chevrolet plant. Continued employment combined with the opening of housing in formerly all-white areas of Kansas City during the late 1950s led many Leeds residents to leave the community for better homes. One Leeds resident recalled, with perhaps only slight exaggeration, "The best house in Leeds wasn't as nice as some of the worst houses in white neighborhoods."[78]

Nevertheless, life in Leeds left a huge imprint upon the people who grew up there in the period between and during the world wars. According to Clara Horne Walker, one of the greatest legacies of Leeds was that it was a place where young people learned self-sufficiency. In Leeds, "boys learned to be men." They learned to do chores and to accept the responsibility of helping out their families, which, in turn, helped them to become good providers as adults. Consequently, Robert White asserted, "The word [was] out that if you marry a Leeds man, you have a good man." In addition, Walker recalled, girls learned to fill the roles of wife and mother by learning to cook and keep house.[79]

Just as important, life in Leeds taught residents to think of their neighbors as members of a large, close family. Yvonne Brooks Bullock recalled, "That was the best time in my life [living in Leeds]. My friends say to me 'you just love Leeds,' and I say, yes, everybody out in Leeds was just like a family." The Reverend Kenneth Ray commented, "Almost everybody from Leeds is my sister and brother and whenever someone dies in Leeds it is just like someone in our family." Ray summarized what was perhaps the greatest legacy of Leeds when he said, "Love in Leeds ran like water. . . . Everybody loved everybody."[80]

Chapter 9

The Whitley Sisters Remember

Living with Segregation in Kansas City, Missouri

The period between the two World Wars in the United States witnessed an unprecedented migration of African Americans from the South to the North and from farms to cities.[1] Federal government policies and attitudes mitigated against agricultural prosperity, especially for small farmers. Likewise, mechanization of many agricultural tasks displaced black field hands. Hence, many African Americans abandoned the pre-

This group photo taken in Hartville includes Frank and Opal Whitley. (courtesy of the Irene Whitley Marcus Collection, the State Historical Society of Missouri)

industrial lifestyle they had known in rural America for the competitive, industrial, fast-paced life of the city. Among the communities that experienced this so-called Great Migration was Kansas City, which saw its African American population increase by 26 percent during the decade of the 1920s alone, driven as much by rural Missouri blacks moving to the city as by southern blacks moving north.[2]

What was life like for these new urban migrants? To whom did they turn for help in their effort to adjust to urban life and what institutions served them as acculturating forces? This essay seeks to answer these questions, largely by looking at the lives of three of the migrants: Gertrude, Geneva, and Irene Whitley, who moved to Kansas City, Missouri, with their parents, Frank and Opal Whitley, in 1920.[3]

Mr. and Mrs. Whitley had grown up in Hartville, Missouri, in Wright County, deep in the Missouri Ozarks. Their grandparents had been among the Exodusters who left Tennessee during the late 1870s and early l880s.[4] By 1920, the Whitleys were having trouble surviving as farmers in the Missouri Ozarks. Additionally, Mr. Whitley had some sort of run-in with local law enforcement officers. The young couple decided to leave the region with their three daughters. They chose Kansas City because Mrs. Whitley's parents, John and Sallie Denton, lived there. The Dentons, too, had lived in Hartville earlier but had left Wright County in 1900 for Iola, Kansas, where Mr. Denton worked for a time at a cement plant. In 1914 the family moved to Kansas City, where Mr. Denton found work in the Wilson Packing House.[5] In an action that was quite common among "Great Migration" families, the Whitleys moved in with the Dentons in a small house that had no indoor plumbing at 2446 Flora Avenue, near the southern edge of a black neighborhood identified in 1913 by sociologist Asa Martin as "the Bowery."[6]

The 1920 census, taken in January before the Whitleys arrived, indicates that fifty-two-year-old John Denton and his forty-seven-year-old wife, Sallie, lived with their three children: Lawrence (sixteen), Georgia (fourteen), and Hobart (twelve). When the Whitleys arrived later in the year, the number of occupants doubled and then soon increased again as more migrant family members moved in.[7] Throughout their childhood, and through several moves within the neighborhood, the Whitley sisters shared their grandparents' home with other extended family members. The house that they remember best was at 2223 Lydia Avenue. They were forced to move from Flora because of the landlord's objection to children. The Whitleys remember that there were usually at least seven children living in the household at any one time. Such an arrangement made for

The Whitley sisters as young girls
(courtesy of the Irene Whitley Marcus
Collection, the State Historical Society
of Missouri)

Opal Whitley (courtesy of the Irene
Whitley Marcus Collection, the State
Historical Society of Missouri)

little privacy and cramped quarters. During warm weather, the Whitley
sisters joined scores of other neighborhood children and some adults
who slept on blankets in nearby parks. There was a positive side to the
congregate living experienced by the sisters: it gave them playmates and
made their house an exciting place to be. Indeed, the sisters remember
that every house they lived in was referred to by neighborhood children
as "the big house" because it was always the gathering place for many of
their friends. Boredom was never a problem for the Whitley sisters. Indeed, as Irene expressed it, "we didn't know that word [bored]."[8]

Tragedy struck the Whitleys soon after the family arrived in Kansas
City: Mrs. Opal Whitley contracted double pneumonia and died in November of 1920, leaving Mr. Whitley without a wife and Gertrude, Geneva, and Irene without a mother. Gertrude, only four years old at the time,
still remembers the night her mother died. "I will never forget. . . . I woke
up and saw them carrying her out. . . . I asked my grandmother, I said, 'is
my mother coming back?' She said, 'no, she won't be back.'" Mr. Whitley,

who had been unable to find work, left soon after his wife's death for California, where he hoped to find employment. He left his daughters to be cared for by their late-middle-aged grandparents, John and Sallie Denton.[9]

Growing up without a mother and without the presence of their father was not as difficult for the Whitley sisters as one might assume. Geneva and Irene, who did not remember their mother and barely knew their father, called Mr. and Mrs. Denton "Papa" and "Mama." Today, all three sisters continue to honor the memory of the couple who raised them and still marvel at the sacrifices and support shown by their grandparents and their Aunt Georgia, their mother's sister, who also shared the household. Still, the sisters believe that the near-orphan experiences of their early childhood nurtured and solidified their extraordinarily strong bond of sisterhood. Even now, the sisters tend to do things together. As Geneva said in a 1998 interview, "When we go out now and if we are not all three together, someone will ask 'where is the other one?'"[10]

Among the earliest memories of the Whitley sisters is that of attending the Bethel African Methodist Episcopal Church at 2329 Flora Avenue, in the block next to the one that contained the Denton home. Gertrude, the eldest of the daughters, remembers that soon after her mother's death, when she was only four years old, Ms. Eula Pryor from the Bethel Church came to her grandparents home to take her and her sisters to Sunday School. Thus began a lifelong relationship with the church that continues to the present day. In a 1998 interview with the authors, Gertrude Whitley Bardwell remembered the Bethel AME Church as "the connecting link" that held the people she knew and loved together. Bethel Church, by the way, was still a relatively new church in 1920. In fact, in 1920 the congregation still met in the church basement, which had been built in 1912. Bethel was the first AME church in Kansas City to be built south of Eighteenth Street. Its very presence reflected the migration of African Americans into south Kansas City.[11]

The Whitley sisters remember that, as children, they attended church three times on Sunday (Sunday School, morning worship, and night service) and several times during the week. During the summer, when the heat became unbearable and the Kansas City Monarchs and Blues were out of town, the Whitley sisters would join other church members for an interdenominational Sunday night church service at the baseball stadium at Twenty-second and Brooklyn. The church was much more than a religious institution: it was a place of social interaction and relaxation, a place where African Americans could enjoy themselves without being scrutinized by whites. Gertrude, Geneva, and Irene remember the church as a place where they participated in games, plays, and musical performances. As they grew older, they joined the choir and sang favorite hymns, such as "Precious Lord," "My Faith Looks Up To Me," and "Amazing Grace." Choir participation was so much fun that often friends of the Whitley sisters would join the choir without joining the church. As adults, the Whitley sisters became members of "The Daughters of Bethel," an adult group of women church members who held recitals, dramatizations, dinners, and other fund-raising events to further the church's mission. Although the Bethel AME church has experienced a dramatic decline in membership over the years, especially during the last two decades as African Americans have moved out of the neighborhood, the Whitley sisters continue their regular attendance at the church whose services they were introduced to more than seventy-eight years ago.[12]

Another important institution that shaped the early lives of the Whitley sisters was the all-black Wendell Phillips School, located down the street from their house at Twenty-fourth Street Terrace and Vine, in a facility that had been known as the Bryant School until 1912.[13] Like a great many other African Americans who had been denied access to formal education Grandfather and Grandmother Denton, both of whom were illiterate, wanted their grandchildren to go to school. Geneva remembers, in particular, that "Grandpa was so proud of us because we could read, so, you see, that was a void we filled because we could read and we kept them up to date on everything." In some ways, the school was an extension of the church, inasmuch as both institutions sought to instill in students a strong moral core. Although Wendell Phillips School was a public institution each day began with a prayer. Teachers were extraordinarily dedicated to molding students into responsible and contributing adults. Each of the Whitley sisters relishes the opportunity to tell stories about the dedication of their teachers, including the principal, Henry L. Cox, who served Wendell Phillips School from 1916 to 1947. Teachers placed great emphasis on mastering the English language and learning the skills that would help one to get a good job. Among the skills that every girl at Wendell Phillips learned were sewing and cooking. All girls took sewing in the fourth grade; according to Irene, "first you made a sewing bag to carry supplies. Then you made a dress."[14]

After completing elementary school, the Whitley girls and all other high school-aged blacks in Kansas City attended Lincoln High School, located at Nineteenth and Tracy, from 1908 until 1936. In 1936 the old Lincoln High building became the R. T. Coles Junior and Vocational High

School and a new Lincoln High was built at Twenty-first and Wood-land.[15] One of the things that the Whitley sisters recall most about their high school days was how school officials often brought well-known African Americans to their school for lectures and presentations, so that Lincoln students would have positive role models of their own race. Among such people that the sisters remember best is George Washington Carver, whose fame as a scientist and educator had peaked by the time the young women were in high school. Gertrude remembers Carver as a man of small stature with a "screechy voice," who was very patient with the students when showing them his many experiments with the peanut and sweet potato. She remembers that "Everyone sat enthralled at his presentation."[16]

The sisters also remember the unbridled commitment shown by their teachers and the way in which the teachers took an interest in their total development. Irene, in particular, remembers Lincoln as a "well-behaved school: you did not even raise your voice in the halls. They even told you how to walk. They would say 'stand up straight and throw those shoulders back, and stop grinning like a Cheshire cat.'"[17]

A third institution that played a key role in the maturation process of the Whitley sisters was the YWCA, which began during the era of World War I.[18] During the 1920s and 1930s, the YWCA was located at Nineteenth and Paseo, within walking distance of the Whitley sisters' home. The YWCA official best remembered by these women is Elsie Mountain who became executive director in 1928 and continued in that position until 1943. Ms. Mountain came to Kansas City from Ohio and, according to Gertrude, took the YWCA to "unknown heights."[19]

Ms. Mountain is described by Gertrude as "a stately and cultured woman whom all the girls admired. She was a power." One of her greatest accomplishments, certainly the one that had the greatest effect upon young women such as the Whitley sisters, was the establishment of the "Girl Reserves" in 1930. Described as a guidance group for elementary and high school girls, the Girl Reserves taught young girls "the path that they should follow." Ms. Mountain took her girls on tours throughout the city, including to white churches, where the young black women put on musical and dramatic programs for their audiences. She used the Girl Reserves to teach manners and proper etiquette. Every spring she had the YWCA host a "Vocational Training Symposium" where professional women, mostly teachers and social workers, would come to promote their professions and to encourage the girls to continue their education and seek a professional life. Gertrude, in particular, still recalls a saying that was continually drilled into the young members of the Girl Reserves: "To everyone is given a high way and a low way, and everyone must choose the way that she would go."[20]

An example of what happened to girls who took the "low way" existed just outside the neighborhood: it was the Florence Home for Negro Girls, established in 1925 at 2446 Michigan and later (in 1930) moved to 2228 Campbell. The Florence Home stood outside the neighborhood, just as unmarried teenage girls who found themselves pregnant were perceived to stand outside the realm of acceptable behavior. The leading force behind the establishment of the Florence Home was Mrs. Elizabeth Bruce Crogman, an Urban League volunteer who spent a considerable amount of time at the Jackson County courthouse and was troubled by the lack of social services available to black youths who appeared before the court. Although Mrs. Crogman worked at the Florence Home for approximately twenty-five years, the Whitley sisters remember best Dorothy Johnson, a social worker at the home. She and Mrs. Crogman made the Florence Home a comfortable place for pregnant, unmarried young women to stay with their babies when they had no place else to go. Unwed mothers, according to the Whitley sisters, were often shunned by community members. In spite of this general negative attitude toward pregnancy among unmarried girls, birth control was not a topic for discussion at the YWCA, or the church, or even at home. Sex and birth control were taboo subjects. According to the sisters, it was understood that carrying oneself as a lady meant not engaging in premarital sex. Young girls were taught to carry themselves in such a way that respect for their bodies was demanded from young men. Sex was reserved for marriage.[21]

The Urban League, which Ms. Crogman served during the 1920s and 1930s, was another important institution that shaped life in the neighborhood where the Whitley sisters lived, although they remember it as having less direct impact upon their lives than did the church, the school, or the YWCA. The Urban League of Kansas City had its origins in an effort "to provide rest and recreation for black soldiers who passed through Kansas City after demobilization in 1919." According to a 1980 "Salute to the Urban League," written by then-executive director Dr. Thomas A. Webster, the Urban League quickly moved to assist "Great Migration" era blacks who were moving to Missouri's westernmost city: "Most of the Urban League staff members met waves of black families as they arrived at the railroad stations. They acquainted them with the facts of urban living. They took them to jobs and to housing. They also informed them about school attendance and other requirements of the city. They stressed

The Whitley sisters in the mid-1930s were an attractive and popular trio of young ladies who obviously represented the careful upbringing of their grandparents and the influence of their beloved Aunt Georgia. (courtesy of the Irene Whitley Marcus Collection, the State Historical Society of Missouri)

proper dress, good work habits, and punctuality on the job." The first Urban League headquarters in Kansas City was in the Shannon Building, which was located at the corner of Eighteenth and Vine Streets, at the northern end of the neighborhood occupied by the Whitley sisters.[22]

As the Whitley sisters entered their adolescent and teenage years, they sought entertainment and social interaction supplementing their church, school and YWCA activities. Among their most pleasant memories are events associated with attending movies at the old Lincoln Theatre, also located near Eighteenth and Vine. The Lincoln was managed by and operated for African Americans. A friend of the Whitleys, Barbara Pullam Thompson, also remembers the Lincoln Theatre fondly, although she recalls that her parents allowed her to go to a movie on a Sunday afternoon only if she had attended Sunday School at the Bethel AME Church first—no Sunday School, no movie. Another favorite attraction in the neighborhood was the series of Sunday afternoon band concerts that were held during the summer at Parade Park, located just north of Seventeenth Street, along The Paseo. The sisters' uncle, Lawrence Denton, played with the band and a great many of the residents of the neighborhood attended these gatherings, although Ms. Thompson remembers that her mother would not allow her to attend because she feared that there might be drinking among people attending and the crowd might be too rowdy.

This fear on the part of Ms. Thompson's mother also kept young Barbara away from summer baseball games at the Muehlebach Stadium, located at Twenty-second Street and Brooklyn Avenue, within walking distance for both the Whitley sisters and Ms. Thompson. The irony of Ms. Thompson's mother not allowing her to attend Kansas City Monarch games was that her father, Arthur "Chic" Pullam, Sr., had played for the Monarchs prior to his marriage to Barbara's mother.[23] Geneva and Irene Whitley, by contrast, often attended the Monarchs' opening game. Opening Day of the new baseball season was an especially important event. Opening Day activities featured a parade to the ballpark and a crowd of participants that sometimes swelled to nineteen thousand people. Irene and Geneva remember Opening Day as a time when men and women dressed in their finest clothes and came to the ballpark as much to be seen as to see. As Irene remembers it: "No matter what the temperature was, we put on [our best clothes] so we could be dressed up for that day. All the women wore hats, and even though it was in the springtime, some of the women wore their furs. A lot of people that went did not know much about baseball, but they *had* to be there for the opening game."[24]

The Whitley sisters entered their teenage years during the Great Depression. The first time that they were separated for any length of time came in September 1933 when the eldest, seventeen-year-old Gertrude, graduated from Lincoln High School and decided to enroll as a freshman at Lincoln University in Jefferson City.[25]

Up to that time, no one in the family had ever gone to college. But Gertrude was an exceptional student; she was hardworking, disciplined, and ambitious, the valedictorian of her class. She wanted to go to college, if it was at all possible. She and her grandmother visited the principal at Lincoln High and asked if there were any scholarships available, because there was no way that her family could afford to send her without considerable financial assistance. Grandfather Denton had lost his job at the packinghouse in 1930 and had been able to find work only at a much less-well-paying job.[26]

The high school principal told Gertude and her grandmother that traditionally two scholarships were granted to graduating seniors: one to Fisk University and the other to Lincoln University. The class salutatorian wanted to go to Fisk. That left the Lincoln University Curator's

Scholarship of fifty dollars available to Gertrude. Although she knew little about Lincoln University, Gertrude jumped at the chance for a college education.[27]

Fifty dollars was a lot of money in the heart of the Depression, but even then it would only go so far. The fifty dollars had to be spread over two semesters, and tuition alone was $18.75 per semester. After paying tuition for the first semester, Gertrude had $6.25 left, with which she paid one month's room rent (approximately $4.00 per month). The $2.25 left over would not pay the $14.00 semester meal charge. Hence, Gertrude had to rely upon the help of family and friends to raise the balance of funds needed for school. Her father in California, who was making $68 a month, committed to sending her $10.00 per month. Her grandparents and her Aunt Georgia, who worked as a maid in a white beauty shop at Thirty-first and Troost, helped out as they could. Sisters Geneva and Irene, both still in high school and occasionally working odd jobs, pooled their money and sent a few dollars occasionally. Friends and neighbors also helped in whatever way they could, all of them drawing pride from their effort to help someone in their neighborhood who was furthering her education. In fact, Gertrude's arrival on campus in September 1933 came as a consequence of a generous neighbor, Mr. Jeffry Jett, who owned a car and agreed to take her, her grandparents, and Aunt Georgia to Jefferson City.[28]

Gertrude enjoyed the same success in college that she had enjoyed in high school. She was elected president of the freshman class and did well in all of her classes. Unfortunately, the university's finances did not allow for the renewal of the scholarship for a second year. Gertrude had to drop out of college. Moving back home, she took a job as a domestic in the home of a white family. She remembers working twelve-hour days, five days per week, for a total of $5.00. Since she had to pay $1.25 for "car fare" to get back and forth to work, she only cleared $3.75 at best. She gave her grandmother $1.75 of this, to help out with bills. In the fall of 1936, Gertrude's dream of returning to college was fulfilled when she became a recipient of a National Youth Administration (NYA) grant that provided her with an opportunity to return to Lincoln University and to work there. The NYA was one of many New Deal programs initiated by President Franklin D. Roosevelt in response to the Depression. Gertrude worked in Dean W. B. Jason's office and earned $15.00 a month. She graduated from Lincoln University in 1939. Soon thereafter, she was hired as a teacher in another New Deal–funded program: a daycare center operated by her church, Bethel AME. Interestingly, the person who recommended her was Eulah Pryor, the same woman who had taken her and her sisters to Sunday School nearly two decades earlier.[29]

Geneva, the middle sister, graduated from high school in 1935 and also worked as a domestic for a while. In 1936 her sewing ability earned her a job with the NYA in a factory at Fifth and Troost. She had been sewing for people in her neighborhood since she was a child. Soon, her sewing talent earned her a promotion to a supervisory position, and she remained on the NYA job through 1939. Irene graduated from Lincoln High in 1936 and took a job caring for the daughter of a woman who worked with her aunt. Her pay was $3.00 per week. Throughout the 1930s, the Whitley sisters continued to live with their grandparents, aunt, an occasional uncle, and cousins. Even after they married in the early 1940s, for a number of years they and their husbands shared the house with and cared for Grandfather Denton, Mrs. Denton having passed away in 1937.[30]

The Whitley sisters had no desire to leave the neighborhood of their youth. It was a neighborhood where residents looked out for and took care of each other. It was a multidimensional, self-contained neighborhood: people lived their private and their public lives there and virtually all of the needs of residents could be met without leaving the neighborhood. Food, fuel, even clothing could be purchased in the neighborhood. Health care was available, with doctors and dentists in black-owned businesses from Twenty-fourth Street to Eighteenth and Vine and the public City Hospital No. 2 and private Wheatley-Provident Hospital nearby. Geneva remembers Dr. P. C. Turner, superintendent of City Hospital No. 2, as the physician whom she and other family members went to most. Gertrude recalled that "He [Dr. Turner] was very refined, very professional, but not distant. You felt like you could talk to him and you felt like he really had your interests at heart. People trusted him and they liked him."[31]

Entertainment and opportunities for social interaction abounded.[32] As young women, the Whitley sisters joined social clubs whose members created their own social and cultural entertainment, at a time when African American social and cultural life in Kansas City was curtailed by law and custom. The group most often mentioned by the sisters is "The Twin Citian Club," formed at the height of World War II, when many young black men from Kansas City had been taken from the community for the war effort.[33]

Gertrude, the eldest of the Whitley sisters, was among the charter members of the Twin Citians, and the group's first president. The club's first meeting was held on January 9, 1943, at 2432 Park, the home of the

Whitley sisters. Initially, the Twin Citians gathered to play bridge and to put on programs that consisted of artistic presentations, musical selections, and readings. Later, anniversary parties and balls were held, and benefit functions were hosted to raise money for worthy causes.

In 1958, the Twin Citians spearheaded an assault on segregation in Kansas City. Unhappy with "discriminatory practices in the restaurants and coffee shops operated by downtown department stores," they organized a group known as "The Community Committee for Social Action of Greater Kansas City," which, in turn, organized a successful Christmas season boycott of stores such as Jones, Macy's, Kline's, Peck's, and Emery, Bird, and Thayer.[34]

Unfortunately, much of the neighborhood in which the Whitley sisters grew up and lived their early adult years is being destroyed today. The Bruce Watkins Memorial Highway is cutting a wide path of destruction through the very blocks where the sisters lived. The physical destruction of the neighborhood follows a decline in the area that began nearly half a century ago. Ironically, the sisters blame the very racial integration that they once pursued for the decline of their neighborhood. Not that they want to return to the days of racial segregation, when they could not go into many white-owned businesses in Kansas City, or when they could not try on clothing at many retail establishments downtown. Still, they recognize that racial segregation forced African Americans of all classes to live and work together in shaping a common destiny. During the 1920s and 1930s, the Whitley sisters were likely to run into the Reverend D. A. Holmes, one of the most prominent African Americans in Kansas City whose Paseo Baptist Church was only a few blocks from their house. But they might just as easily encounter the notorious gambler Felix Payne, who lived only two blocks from them and who could be easily spotted in his trademark "pink shirt and Kelly green pants."[35]

The civil rights movement of the 1950s and 1960s created new vocational and professional opportunities for blacks, especially those who were better educated. These were the people who were the quickest to leave the neighborhood. Paradoxically, they were also the people that the neighborhood needed most.

Chapter 10

The Missouri Industrial Home
for Negro Girls

The 1930s

Late nineteenth-century industrialization brought social changes that shocked and frightened many Americans.[1] Populism, a farmers' protest movement that reached the height of its force in the 1890s, tried unsuccessfully to forestall the nation's movement away from an agrarian lifestyle. When that effort failed another group of reformers, the Progressives, emerged on the scene. They accepted the inevitability of industrialization but sought to control its excesses and alleviate, or remove altogether, the suffering it brought in its wake. The one group of people that these turn-of-the-century Americans hoped to save above all others was the children. Progressives saw urban children as being at once the most victimized by industrialization but also the most salvageable.[2]

The Progressives possessed a self-confidence that bordered on arrogance: *they* knew what these vulnerable children of the cities needed better than anyone else, better even than the youngsters' parents. Moreover, as historian David Rothman has pointed out, the "Progressives were not afraid to introduce the coercive force of law" in dealing with children. Indeed, Progressives had unlimited faith in the state to become a surrogate parent whose power to deal with errant but educable children should be unrestrained.[3] A favorite Progressive tactic for dealing with juvenile delinquency, therefore, was the establishment of state-operated correctional facilities where children were to be taught to develop resources that would ensure their survival even in vice- and poverty-ridden industrial America. These facilities, intended as substitute homes, had administrators who served as surrogate parents for wayward but not-yet-lost juveniles. As a result, this put the governors of such facilities in the position of having, as Rothman has written, "to administer, all ironies and confusion intended, non-institutional institutions. Their routines had to be not only normal—that is, approximating life in the outside community—but intimate—recreating the close ties of the family."[4]

Unfortunately, the unbounded faith in the state-as-parent created an early twentieth-century juvenile justice system that gave judges and institutional superintendents almost total power over "delinquents" without giving them the economic, philosophical, or political wherewithal to accomplish their avowed goals. Not surprisingly, by the mid-1930s, at least one major study of the nation's juvenile justice system soundly condemned the system and argued that nearly 90 percent of the nation's juvenile delinquents were becoming recidivists.[5]

A detailed look at one midwestern facility for juvenile delinquents graphically illustrates how ill-prepared and unequipped were the facility's operators to handle their charges. The Missouri Industrial Home for Negro Girls at Tipton housed more than one thousand black juveniles between the time it opened in 1916 and its closing in 1956.[6] Throughout that forty-year period, the institution generally failed to help its inmates prepare to enter the mainstream of American life. Political patronage determined who would govern the institution, leaving well-meaning but ineffective leaders with poorly trained staffs to deal with an often too-large number of girls whose background and behavior would have challenged even the most sophisticated juvenile delinquency experts.

This essay focuses primarily on life in the Missouri Industrial Home during the 1930s, not because that decade is more important than any other but because, through historical accident, the case files of seventy-seven inmates incarcerated during that period have been deposited in the Missouri State Archives and are available to researchers. The rarity of such records' becoming available to historians makes their use all the more imperative.

The seventy-seven girls whose files have been spared the ravages of time represent slightly more than 25 percent of the number of inmates incarcerated during the decade of the 1930s. While it would be impossible to say categorically that the seventy-seven were "typical" of all Tipton residents during those years, they were typical in at least two important ways. First of all, their average age was 14.39 years upon entering the institution. Second, 83 percent of them came from the urban areas of Kansas City and St. Louis (see Tables 1 and 2).

ETHEL BOWLES
Superintendent

(courtesy of the Missouri State Archives)

Ethel Bowles, a black woman, served as superintendent of the Missouri Industrial Home for Negro Girls for most of the 1930s. Bowles's appointment to head the training school was clearly the result of political patronage.[7] Democratic governor Guy E. Park's election as governor in 1932 ended twelve consecutive years of Republican rule, and the blacks who helped to carry out that coup expected to be rewarded.[8] A Republican superintendent of the home, Elizabeth Shelby, still held office at the time. But as one staunch Democrat indicated to Park, the Tipton job represented "the highest office for Negro Democrats in Missouri," and party loyalists expected the Republican to be removed.[9]

Park complied with requests to remove Shelby and sought the advice of a St. Louis group known as "The Negro Democratic Organization" in his search for her replacement. That group offered the name of Ethel Bowles as "the one woman in St. Louis who is particularly well-equipped for this position and whose appointment would be well received by all of the leaders of the Negro Democratic Party and mutually satisfactory to the Negro Race of Missouri."[10]

Bowles got the job, taking over in June 1933, at the age of thirty-nine. A graduate of the Knoxville Normal College and the Chicago School of Dramatic Arts, she taught history, civics, and Latin at Lincoln Institute (later Lincoln University in Jefferson City, Missouri) and served as secretary to the president of that school from 1916 to 1920. An active member of a number of St. Louis social service agencies, Bowles administered the distribution of welfare benefits to St. Louis County blacks for several years prior to her Tipton appointment. That work experience, rather than any formal training, made her the first professional social worker to govern the Industrial Home.[11]

The facility that Bowles took over in mid-1933 still reflected not only the goals of its founders but also their biases. The legislators who voted to create Tipton were frankly troubled over the question of what to do with black female juvenile delinquents. Late nineteenth-century white girls who ran afoul of the law in Missouri were sent to a home in Chillicothe. Although Missouri law did not prohibit sending black girls there, custom did. The Chillicothe home's superintendent wrote in 1903 that accepting "colored girls" into the institution "would create a disturbance among the inmates and virtually put an end to the reformatory features of the institution." Subsequently, a separate building for blacks was erected at the Chillicothe facility, but overcrowding caused the building to be used for whites instead.[12]

In 1908 the problem of no home for black girls came to a head when a twelve-year-old girl was sent to the Missouri State Penitentiary. Shocked by the spectacle of a child serving time with hardened criminals, the Missouri legislature appropriated money to establish the State Industrial Home for Negro Girls the next year. Difficulty in finding a community that would allow a correctional facility for black girls to be built in its midst postponed the opening of the Tipton home until 1916.[13]

The law that appropriated the money for the Missouri Industrial Home empowered the state to incarcerate any black girl between the ages of seven and twenty-one who committed a crime not punishable by death or life imprisonment, "whose associations are immoral or criminal, or bad and vicious, or who is incorrigible to such extent that she cannot be controlled by her parents or guardians in whose custody she may be."[14] Once these "delinquent colored girls" had been "rescued" from a nascent life of crime and placed in the Tipton institution, officials there resolved to structure their lives around "meaningful" labor in an atmosphere that was as much like a home as possible. If, as the commissioners who planned and oversaw the facility believed, strength of character was

a natural result of a good family life, then Missouri's black female delinquents would have a good family. Indeed, the commissioners reported in
their first biennial report that the manager of the institution was to be
"known as Mother" and that she would teach the girls "the many little
things taught children by a mother."[15]

The goal of these original formulators of reform school policy was
summarized in this first biennial report:

> The idea of the present board is to equip each girl with a thorough
> knowledge of household work and the duties of a housekeeper, so
> that they may readily find good homes because of their efficiency. It
> is the intention to teach them to cook, scrub, wash, iron, sew, mend,
> care of chickens, bees, garden, small fruits, in short, to be thorough-
> ly qualified domestics or housekeepers, and it will be our aim to
> cultivate in them a love of country life, and to find homes for them
> in the country. Believing that a knowledge of the care of poultry
> may be a means of livelihood to many of our girls, they are being
> trained in the profitable care of chickens. The improvement in the
> department of unruly girls assigned to the care of poultry is quite
> noticeable. Having something that is alive and helpless committed
> to their care arouses good thoughts and impulses, and reclamation
> is thereby made easier. The same theory holds in the beneficient re-
> sults from gardening.[16]

This education in the domestic arts was to take place in a school that
went through the eighth grade, and which was heavily laced with religious guidance. Indeed, God, "Mother," and domesticity became the Missouri Industrial Home for Negro Girls' own trinity.[17]

This emphasis on vocational training for black girls reflected contemporary attitudes toward the role that blacks and women should play
generally in American society. Booker T. Washington's philosophy of
developing marketable skills rather than intellectual acumen still influenced most *black and white* thinking about how blacks should be prepared for adult life.[18] Moreover, early twentieth-century girls who had
no parents to care adequately for them were supposed to learn skills that
would allow them to survive until they could achieve the *real* purpose of
their existence: marriage to a good man who would take care of them.
Learning the "domestic arts," then, had a double advantage: it made girls
not only marketable but marriageable as well.[19]

Ethel Bowles did nothing to change the purpose or practices of the
Missouri Industrial Home for Negro Girls. She, like all her predecessors,

insisted upon being called "Mother," and she declared it her aim "to help these young girls make their adjustments by changing mental attitudes, removing ignorance, rebuilding health, and instilling a moral code which reveals their responsibility to themselves, to their family, to their community, and to their God."[20] Bowles proposed to do this through a strict regimen of work, worship, and play. While she did not consider "academic" education unimportant, she saw the main purpose of learning to be "to fit [the girls] for service" to their communities.[21] Aware that "the larger proportion of our girls find an outlet for making a livelihood by cooking and serving," she acknowledged that learning domestic skills was particularly stressed.[22]

It was one thing to express the intention of remolding the character and habits of delinquent girls; quite another to accomplish it. The facility was overcrowded, for one thing, making it very difficult to give the girls the close attention they needed so desperately. When Bowles took over in mid-1933, the home housed eighty girls, five more than its capacity as defined by a State Survey Commissioner.[23] Moreover, money for a well-trained staff was always in short supply. Throughout the institution's

The Missouri Industrial Home for Negro Girls (courtesy of the Missouri State Archives)

existence, for example, its employees were paid considerably less than similarly employed whites at the Chillicothe Home for White Girls.[24]

The best that Bowles could do in her effort to change her errant charges was to adopt the system of discipline used by her predecessors, which had come to be known as the Merit System.[25] Two merits were given each day for perfect performance in the following categories:

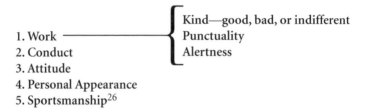

1. Work
2. Conduct
3. Attitude
4. Personal Appearance
5. Sportsmanship[26]

Kind—good, bad, or indifferent
Punctuality
Alertness

In addition, Bowles added a new twist to the Merit System. In an effort to ensure uniformity of behavior and a strict sense of order, she divided the inmates into four groups, each with opportunities to earn various privileges. Consistent perfect performance under the Merit System placed one in the most prestigious group, the "COCs" (Cream of the Crop). The girls in this group had "the highest honors, privileges, etc. [wore] nice dresses and [were] eligible to leadership." At the other end of the scale, a "Fourth Group" of girls enjoyed a "minimum of privileges."[27] A private investigative body, the Osborne Association, in a 1938 report described how dress was used to reward and punish: "Group One [COC] has no uniform, each girl being permitted to choose her own dresses; Group Two wears pin-striped shirtwaists and skirts; Group Three wears striped overalls, and Group Four is dressed in blue denim work dresses."[28]

Monthly evaluations that tallied the merits earned by each girl contain brief comments regarding her strengths and weaknesses. Positive comments frequently found on monthly reports of girls with high merit-point accumulations and Cream of the Crop status reflected a girl's apparent pliability and the relative ease with which she could be managed. This attitude is reflected in such statements as: "Anxious to please—does her very best and tries to do her whole duty and learn";[29] "willing, over-anxious to win favors, easily handled";[30] "wholesome, clean, obedient, reliable";[31] and the curiously "positive" statement of appreciation that a particular girl "seems reconciled to her fate."[32] Alternatively, criticism often clearly revealed what kinds of behavior were considered unacceptable: "Must yet learn neatness and remember all girls are extremely forgetful. Keeping them busy may greatly alleviate the defect";[33] "fussy, hard

Inmates in front of the Missouri Industrial Home for Negro Girls
(courtesy of the Missouri State Archives)

to get along with," "not interested, very, very poor worker," "Doesn't apply herself seriously to anything," "worst trait: deceitfulness, quarrelsome";[34] "sore because she's here";[35] and "Worst trait: refusing to tell on others."[36] Exactly what the matron meant who wrote on one girl's evaluation that "hope" was her worst trait remains unclear, but presumably it meant an unwillingness to adjust to the reality of life at Tipton. Indeed, nothing unsettled the superintendent and her staff more than an uncooperative inmate with a "bad attitude." The Osborne Association's 1938 report notes that Bowles, "In answer to a direct question as to what are considered the most serious offenses . . . stated that a 'bad attitude' is considered much more serious than any overt acts."[37]

Supplementing the merit system as a means of internal control was another incentive: the prospect of early release from the institution for good behavior. Girls who compiled a higher number of merit points could look forward to getting out "on 7/12 time, (serv[ing] 7 months out of each year)." Efforts were made to parole girls to "The most desirable homes" and always with the reminder that "they are subject to return any time for misconduct or violation of instruction measured out to them."[38]

The merit system and the possibility of parole were the most publicized tools of control used by "Mother" Bowles. Less talked about was the resort to corporal punishment when all else failed. Bowles's biennial reports to the legislature make no mention of physical punishment and give the impression that punishment was entirely negative: the withholding or withdrawal of privileges and rewards. But corporal punishment was used and, although Bowles indicated to the Osborne Association that

"We . . . are earnestly striving to eliminate this type of punishment," she offered the following justification for whippings:

> Some of our girls come to us wholly untrained, unbelievably near the animal stage without the least rudimental knowledge of clean and decent living and with no respect for law and order. We have found that the nearest approach to them is through fear. Then we are able to develop "Pride" and "Self Respect" and make them realize that they *must* respect some authority or observe some rules of law and order. If not, they will be hurt physically their bodies are the only things they are conscious of, apparently.[39]

One of the most graphic examples of Bowles's use of corporal punishment appears in the case file of a nineteen-year-old St. Louis girl named Clara, labeled by Bowles as "a sex problem." Clara was a member of the COC group until she "became involved" sexually with another girl. According to Bowles's testimony, she demoted Clara to the Fourth Group and placed her in "isolation" after discovering her homosexual behavior. Subsequently, another girl named Alice managed to sneak into Clara's room for a night of sexual activity with her. Both girls were then locked in their respective rooms "and not allowed to mingle with the rest of the girls for 2 ½ months."

The two girls were finally released from their rooms after promising to stay away from each other. They did not, and this time the threat of further punishment evoked a violent response in Clara. According to Bowles's account, she was punishing yet another girl (by cutting her hair) when Clara entered the room and, after a brief exchange of words, tried to wrestle the scissors from Bowles, shouting that she would never submit to having her hair cut *again*. Ultimately, it took Bowles, her husband, a matron, and the night watchman to subdue Clara. Bowles described Clara as the worst case she had had since becoming superintendent (at the time, five years) and bluntly told Col. J. E. Matthews, director of the Department of Penal Institutions: "I have punished this girl many times during the four years she has been here, even whipped her in December, but she had always admitted I was right and that she more than deserved whatever punishment she received." In view of Clara's intransigence, Bowles recommended she be "returned to the Court as an incorrigible whom we are unable to handle at the Industrial School for Negro Girls."[40]

The case of Clara illustrates that homosexuality was a problem at the home, although just how widespread it was would be impossible to say.

David Rothman contends that "sexual offenses were invariably among the leading three or four causes of disciplinary action" in early twentieth-century homes for juvenile delinquents.[41] No statistics are available on the incidence of homosexual behavior, and even if there were they would be very unreliable inasmuch as a great deal of such behavior must have gone undetected. Also, matrons often defined girls merely as "sex problems," by which they meant *both* masturbation and homosexuality.[42]

That homosexuality caused both *institutional* and *individual* tension is clearly evident in the case of a young girl named Lillian, who was thought to have "more intelligence than the average" at Tipton. Her case history reveals that her "conduct was almost perfect with the exception of the sex problem. She was usually in the C.O.C. but would occasionally become involved and drop to the 4th group. She was seldom in between. Eith[er] the top or the bottom."[43]

Not only did Lillian suffer the loss of privileges that came with a demotion to the Fourth Group; she also lost self-respect because she had disgraced herself and disappointed Mother Bowles. Her letters reveal her own inner conflict as she pleaded for both understanding and forgiveness, acknowledging at once that her behavior was deviant and immoral but that she was unable to change it:

> I'm writing this against my will, but not for my benefit, but for the benefit of others I have gotten in trouble with. You have beat me, and you have done everything that you could do to break me of the most disgraceful habit that one could have. . . . Please lock me up forever, I can't live like this and I don't want to. I've tried but I never go any length of time before I fall again for the same thing. So let me go, you have wasted too much precious time on me and it is in me and I know it, but you don't know. . . . I try to have some respect for myself.[44]

Lillian's release was contingent upon her ability to control her homosexual encounters. Arrangements had been made to parole the young woman to a family that had already arranged for her to finish high school. But when Lillian's future foster parents found out about her homosexual activities, they refused to take her. This change of heart nearly destroyed Lillian. Her feelings of complete abandonment and hopelessness are evident in a letter to Superintendent Bowles, written a few weeks after her date of release was canceled. Again, the letter abounds with expressions of appreciation and apologies and pleas for forgiveness:

I hope you will not misunderstand my letter or think me ungrateful for I don't mean to be. . . . I'm more than grateful for everything that you have done for me[,] knowing that my conduct all along [has] not been worthy. . . . Mr. and Mrs. Carter are the only people that I have [believed] in, that I would have like[d] to stay with except my father and if they wouldn't take me . . . [I] have decide[d] to go home [and] make the best of whatever I will have to face. . . . I do want to go home to my father, tho [*sic*] I feel as tho there is nothing for me to live for but I know there must be something. . . . But I will always be grateful toward you with all my heart.[45]

Lillian's pledge to be forever grateful to Mother Bowles did not reflect the attitude of all the Industrial Home's inmates. The desire of Bowles and her staff for order and stability in the home often clashed with the inmates' wish for freedom and flexibility. As a result, tension between the two groups remained high. The girls were often torn between a feeling of gratitude for efforts made on their behalf and a resentment of the restrictions placed upon them. One girl who had been in Tipton for ten years wrote two letters to Mrs. Bowles asking for more privileges. She began both letters with obsequious acknowledgments of Bowles's efforts to help her rehabilitate herself but went on to say that she needed much more than that:

Mother, couldn't I just be free. . . . Just let me be free, I could help around here and like that—anything so that I could be free and could have good time. . . . Tomorrow I'll be nineteen. . . . I wonder what it would be like to be free and could stay up as long as you like and see a movie or go in swimming or something like that. . . . I want to get loose to see people and mingle with them. . . . Please don't keep me any longer; Mother, if only you could understand . . . the constant grind of things, day after day and year after year is really getting me. Mother, please.[46]

Sometimes tension manifested itself in fights that broke out between the inmates. Violent responses to restrictions came from girls in all merit groups. Girls were still torn, however, between a need to assert their individuality and the guilt that resulted from having failed to abide by the rules. One inmate felt compelled to apologize not only to the girls on her hall but also to Superintendent Bowles after having been in a fight. She wrote that she realized "that I done wrong by fighting[;] after [everything] was over I was really & truly [sorry]. Just to think that I am a

Super C.O.C. and letting something like that [get] the best of me. But I have ask[ed] the hall for pardon, and they has [*sic*] forgiven me. Now I am asking you because I think it is my duty."[47]

Occasionally tension gave way to despair, as in the case of a St. Louis girl named Willa, whose parody of the 23rd Psalm was found in her Bible:

> Mother Bowles is My Shephard.
> I am in want. She maketh me to lie
> down on the floor. She leadeth me
> beside starvation. She torments
> my soul. She leadeth me in the
> path of death for her name sakes.
> Yea tho I walk thru the valleys of
> the shadow of death I fear evil
> for she is with me. Her rod and
> her staff they beat me.
> She breaks down my defence in
> the presence of mine enemies.
> She annointest my head with whelps.
> My cup is empty. surely hatred
> and revenge shall follow me all the days of my life and I shall
> dwell in hell for ever and ever.[48]

Willa's prediction that she would "dwell in hell for ever and ever" may have been prophetic for most of the Tipton girls. No records were kept of what actually happened to inmates once they left Tipton. Throughout the 1930s, there was no systematic plan for monitoring the behavior of released girls. As one historian of the home has written, "the only kind of supervision which they had was through correspondence from girls, some cooperation from state social agencies, and the cooperation of the Federated Women's Clubs of Missouri," whose members served as volunteer social workers.[49]

All that Superintendent Bowles and her staff could do was try to find a family that was willing to allow a girl to move in with them once a sentence had been completed. That did not always work out for the best, as letters to Mrs. Bowles make clear. At least thirty-one of the seventy-seven girls whose case files survive for the scrutiny of the historian continued to write letters "Home" to Tipton after being released. These letters contain expressions of gratitude to Tipton officials for their help and abundant apologies and pleas for help from those who were still struggling to adapt.

The girls who continued a correspondence with Bowles still viewed her as "Mother" and looked to her to provide the same sense of stability, order, and well-being she had tried to give them at Tipton. Mother Bowles's teachings—the memory of them, if not the practice—extended beyond the gates of the institution for many of the girls. Unfortunately, the memory of Tipton, its structured atmosphere, its "meaningful" tasks, only intensified the lack of such structure and meaning in the girls' life outside.

One St. Louis girl named Lucille corresponded with Bowles for almost four years after she was released. Life outside of Tipton was very hard for Lucille; she was ill and unable to work a great part of the first year she was free. She wrote asking for money and "a photo of mother to remember you by as [you] was so dear . . . and forgave all the mistakes [I] made." She continuously reported to Bowles that she "took [her] advice and took the right way" unlike so many other Tipton alumni she heard about.[50] When she was finally well enough to work and found a job, she was called a nigger by her employer, quit her job as a result, and when asked twice to return, refused. She worried that she had done the wrong thing and sought Bowles's counsel—and more money. Though there is no record of Bowles having sent the money, she did send encouragement, telling Lucille "keep your head up and remember my teachings."[51]

Another girl from St. Louis, named Hattie, suffered acutely from homesickness for Tipton, felt extremely lonely and desperate, and was unable to find work or resist the temptations that Mother Bowles repeatedly warned her against. In a letter to Hattie's probation officer, Bowles wrote: "Hattie is very smart, a good student, quiet and obedient and she has a sweet disposition. . . . Her main weakness as I see it is no 'back bone.' No 'will power' to resist temptation. Easily led. With a little help she can develop into a very useful woman. Without encouragement and help she will be just another little 'Lady of the Evening' as she is very nice looking."[52]

Bowles's fears were not unfounded. Hattie searched desperately for jobs during the depressed years of the 1930s with no luck. Desperate, she confessed to Bowles that she almost "slipped down" and "went back to what [she] came from" but was "saved" by a woman who gave her a job in a cafe.[53] More than a year and many jobs later, Hattie wrote:

> I certainly know what unpreparedness can do for a person who has been away and in for four years. . . . I really have learned what little a girl can do.

I tried several [jobs] and then found out about my condition. I hadn't been back hardly two months before it happened, however I am glad for one thing it is a boy and after all its men that gets [sic] the breaks. He's a very sweet little piece of humanity and is me all over again. . . . I love him dearly.

I have not been good and have not had any encouragement to be good. . . . I am not married nor receiving any help. When one errors, [one] must pay—so I am paying. You know I know I have been so wrong until it just hurts my heart. I have learned a lot about life.[54]

Superintendent Bowles responded immediately and congratulated Hattie on the birth of her son and sent him money. She told Hattie she hoped the baby would "have a lovely disposition . . . but more WILL power" than his mother. She closed the letter with the following question and "motherly" advice: "Tell me, Dear, why do you stay at the Grand Central [Hotel]? Remember your boy must grow up to be proud of you—not ashamed. Please do not think I am trying to preach—I am so concerned with your future. I do not want you to make any more mistakes. We all have to make some—but we do not have to wallow in them, do we?"[55]

Another girl who had difficulty adjusting to freedom was a Kansas City youth named Leona. In April of 1935, Leona, recently paroled to an aunt in Kansas City, wrote to "Mother Bowles" about what a "nice home" Aunt Bessie had provided for her and how good she had been. She assured the superintendent that she had "remembered every thing that you told me," adding "every thing that you told me was for my own good." She closed her letter by telling Mother that she was actively involved in a church group and that she was "trying to live the right kind of life." She signed the letter "from your Daughter."[56]

Apparently this girl's aunt felt that the former Tipton inmate was doing well also, for she too wrote to Mrs. Bowles explaining "how nice Leona . . . is getting along." Aunt Bessie heaped praise on Mrs. Bowles, telling her that "I feel proud as you are doing great work in training the girls," adding that "I will all ways pray for you that you will have all the best of luck."[57]

Despite Aunt Bessie's faith in the near-miraculous transformation of her young niece, the amiable relationship had fallen apart by midsummer. On July 24, 1935, Bessie wrote to Mrs. Bowles, informing her that she was uncertain about Leona's whereabouts. She complained that her efforts to help Leona live as a Christian had failed. Leona, she wrote, "wanted to go out and around bad places and have gangs of Boys laying around my home." Leona "talked bad" to her and "made lots of trouble at my home." Leona left Aunt Bessie's home after a particularly heated argument and stayed away for several days. When she returned apologetically asking to be taken in again, she and Aunt Bessie got into another fight, and this time Leona left for good.[58]

It is impossible to say how many of the girls who left Tipton ended up like Leona—well-intentioned and ostensibly resocialized but unable to move comfortably back into the mainstream of society. *They had never been* in the mainstream of society, and little that happened to them at Tipton altered the fact of their marginality. Not only did they have to overcome their own poor upbringing and poor family environment, they had to do it in a state whose Jim Crow system was firmly entrenched (even in the Tipton home) and a nation whose attitude toward women was that they should remain decidedly subservient to and dependent upon men. And, as if all that was not obstacle enough to overcome, the inmates of the 1930s had to return to a society sorely afflicted with the woes of the Great Depression. No wonder the odds favored recidivism.

Ethel Bowles and her coworkers could do little to help. They meant well—they cared about their charges and they wanted to be of assistance. But, first of all, they did not know how. They owed their jobs more to political loyalty than to professional training in how to deal with juvenile delinquents. Even if they had been well-trained, however, their caseloads were too heavy to give these girls, who so needed help, the kind of personal attention the girls required. As a result, Bowles and her matrons found themselves unable to be more than custodians of a building full of delinquents; their priority became the smooth running of the institution and not the reformation of its inhabitants. There simply was not the time, money, or knowhow to do that.

Nor were there the resources to support or even keep track of girls who left the strict confines of the home. In most instances, paroled girls did not go to the untroubled rural environments that the founders of the home had envisioned. Indeed, they usually went right back into the same environment that had contributed to their incarceration. The power of the state had removed these girls from that environment only temporarily. During that interim, however, neither the girls nor the environment changed appreciably. Whatever good intentions had motivated the people who built the system, the state-as-parent failed the black juvenile delinquents of the Missouri Industrial Home for Negro Girls.

TABLE 1: Ages at Which Girls Were Admitted to Tipton, 1930s

Year	11	12	13	14	15	16	17	18	19	Total	Ave. Age
1930			2	8	1	4				15	14.46
1931			7	9	11	15	4	2		50	14.98
1932			5	6	8	5	1			26	14.53
1933			5	3	11	10	3			32	15.09
1934		2	2	7	5	8	2			26	14.80
1935			2	2	5		3			12	15.00
1936			1	9	8	13	1			33	15.03
1937			5	6	12	5	3		1	32	14.96
1938			4	11	7	14	1		2	39	15.07
1939		2	4	13	6	6	1			32	14.40
										297	

TABLE 2: Place of Residence of Girls Admitted to Tipton, 1930s

Year	St. Louis City	Jackson County	Combined	Other	Total
1930	2 (13%)	8 (53%)	10 (66%)	5	15
1931	26 (52%)	14 (28%)	40 (80%)	10	50
1932	10 (38%)	11 (42%)	21 (80%)	5	26
1933	18 (56%)	9 (28%)	27 (84%)	5	32
1934	17 (65%)	4 (15%)	21 (80%)	5	26
1935	2 (17%)	4 (33%)	6 (50%)	6	12
1936	15 (45%)	14 (42%)	29 (87%)	4	33
1937	12 (38%)	14 (44%)	26 (82%)	6	32
1938	21 (54%)	9 (23%)	30 (77%)	9	39
1939	20 (61%)	5 (15%)	25 (26%)	8	33
				298	

Chapter 11

Black Culture Mecca of the Midwest

Lincoln University, 1921–1955

Nathan B. Young (courtesy of the Lincoln Collection,
Inman E. Page Library, Lincoln University)

In 1927 Nathan B. Young, president of Lincoln University in Jefferson City, Missouri, wrote to friends about his perception of the role he thought his university should play in the Midwest.[1] He indicated that it was "beginning to look as if [the university] were destined to become what it should be, the educational beacon light for the middle west." He described Lincoln as being "in the center of a circle of service to more than two million Negroes within a radius of three hundred miles."[2]

Founded in 1866 as a subscription school by black Civil War soldiers from Missouri, Lincoln became a normal school for African Americans in the 1870s, when it was taken over by the state of Missouri, and a college in 1887. Lincoln was Missouri's only public four-year institution of higher learning for blacks when its name was changed by legislation from "Institute" to "University" in 1921. The 1921 law gave the curators of Lincoln University the responsibility of reorganizing the school "so that it shall afford to the negro people of the state opportunity for training up to the standard furnished at the state university of Missouri whenever necessary and practicable." This law was an acknowledgment of Missouri's intransigent racism and white Missourians' unwillingness to open the state university at Columbia to African Americans. Ironically, this forced racial separation, combined with black creativity and the spirit of mission associated with the so-called new Negro movement on black college campuses in the early 1920s, brought a gifted and dedicated group of superior African American faculty members to Lincoln University. This cadre of brilliant teachers turned the school into a black culture mecca of the Midwest.[3]

The mission of transforming the school from Institute to University was left to Young, who came to Lincoln in 1923 after a strained sojourn as president of Florida A&M College. Young resigned the presidency of Florida A&M after a new Florida governor, Cary Hardee, began an effort to reorganize the historically black school around a theme of vocational education for blacks as opposed to academic education.[4]

Lincoln was a university in name only when Young arrived. The vast majority of its four hundred students were enrolled either in high school courses or in a two-year teacher-training program. Armed with a new legislative mandate and increased funding from the Missouri General Assembly, Young sought to attract better trained black scholars with graduate degrees and records of scholarship. He hoped to create, as he wrote to W. E. B. DuBois, a "First-class institution of Higher Learning in the Middle West." He raised salaries to a level unprecedented at black schools and established a system of sabbatical leaves for continuing education. As historian Raymond Wolters has pointed out, "[The] number of professors with graduate degrees tripled within four years. The faculty was soon graced with scholars who gave Lincoln a reputation for excellence among the Negro land-grant colleges—Harvard-trained Sterling Brown and Cecil Blue in literature and drama, William Dowdy of Cornell in biology, W. Sherman Savage of Ohio State in history, and Langston Fairchild Bate [the first black PhD at Lincoln] of Chicago in chemistry." These professors, and others who were attracted by the atmosphere they and Young created, made Lincoln, in the words of one of them, "the educational cynosure of the Middle West for our race group."[5]

One of the first people to take advantage of Young's new policy of supporting graduate study for the existing faculty was historian W. Sherman Savage. Born in Wattsville, Virginia, Savage graduated from Howard University with a bachelor of arts degree in 1917. He came to teach at Lincoln in 1921 and continued until his retirement in 1960. Savage took a master's of arts degree from the University of Oregon in 1925, becoming that school's first black graduate. He continued graduate study and in 1934 received a PhD in history from Ohio State University. A leading scholar on the history of African Americans in the West, Savage demanded superior scholarship of his Lincoln University students while simultaneously offering them a role model both as a teacher and a writer. His magnum opus, *Blacks in the West*, was published in 1976.[6]

One of the first scholars to arrive at Lincoln University after Young launched his new effort was Sterling Brown, the son of a Tennessee-born slave. Brown was a native of Washington, DC, where he attended Dunbar High School, an educational institution with a national reputation for excellence. Brown later attended Williams College in Massachusetts on an academic scholarship, graduating in 1922. Later that year he enrolled in graduate school at Harvard University, completing a degree in English in 1923.[7]

Upon leaving Harvard, Brown took a job teaching English at Virginia Seminary in Lynchburg, Virginia. He taught there for three years before moving to Lincoln University in 1926. Brown was only twenty-five years old when he arrived on the Lincoln campus, but he brought to his students a love of language, particularly poetry, and an already finely honed appreciation of African American folk culture. Brown loved the blues, black folk humor, and the ways of the common folk. He encouraged his students to observe blacks in their own neighborhoods and businesses and to put their observations into words. While at Lincoln University, Brown spent a considerable amount of time wandering around "The

Foot," a block-long black business district at the northeast edge of campus. Indeed, one of Brown's students recalled that "there were those who considered 'Prof' Brown a bit 'tetched' to be spending so much time with 'those weird characters' who frequented the 'Foot.'" One of Brown's favorite characters was a local waiter named "Slim," a storyteller who became the central figure in a number of "Slim Greer" poems written by Brown. One of Brown's often-quoted poems, "Checkers," was written about two men from different worlds who met regularly at "The Foot" barbershop:

> Mojo Pete is bad,
> Totes a gat,
> Shoots to kill
> At the drop of a hat.
>
> A man of God
> Is Deacon Cole,
> With the sins of the world
> Upon his soul.
>
> But Saturdays
> These strangers meet,
> The man of God
> And Mojo Pete.
>
> The barbershop loungers
> Lie no more
> Silently watching
> The weekly war.
>
> And although Pete
> Won't cuss at all
> The deacon's words
> Aren't biblical.
>
> "Pusson, what gits
> In de jam youse in,
> Better let somebody
> Play what kin."
>
> "Be not puffed up
> With anything,
> My son. Trust God,
> An' watch yo' King!"

Mojo disdains
His loud-voiced boss,
Forgets his Missis,
Rebbish, cross.

Deacon Cole forgets
A world drenched with sin,
Vexed by the trouble
His kingrow's in.

The phonebell jangles
Calling Pete;
Pete won't budge
Got de deacon beat.

And they play their game
Till the night grows old:
The Shepherd, and the lost lamb
From the fold.[8]

James Dallas Parks came to Lincoln University to teach art in 1927. A native of St. Louis, Missouri, and the nephew of John Draine, one of the original founders of the school, Parks began teaching with an undergraduate degree from Bradley Polytechnic Institute. Encouraged by Lincoln policies to continue formal study, he attended the University of Iowa, where he earned a master's of arts degree. A gifted artist, Parks encouraged his students to study and understand the role of the black artist in American society. He was a founder and longtime chairman of the National Conference on Artists. One of Parks's lifetime passions was the pursuit of details about the life of a little-known, but nonetheless important, antebellum African American artist named Robert S. Duncanson. The Cincinnati-based Duncanson, who lived from 1817 to 1872, is best remembered for his landscape paintings.[9]

In 1928 Sterling Brown urged a fellow Harvard alumnus, Cecil Archibald Blue, to come to Lincoln. A native of British Columbia, Blue had also attended Dunbar High School in Washington, DC. He graduated from Harvard in 1926 and took a job teaching at Johnson C. Smith College in Charlotte, North Carolina, before being attracted to Lincoln. Remembered by one colleague years later for his "impeccable use of the English language," Blue gained a modicum of fame in 1927 when he won the *Opportunity* short-story contest for his story "The Flyer." In 1941 Blue's story was reprinted in the now-classic collection of "Writings by Amer-

ican Negroes," *The Negro Caravan*. The collection was edited by Sterling
A. Brown, Arthur P. Davis, and Ulysses S. Lee, the latter of whom, also a
Dunbar High School graduate, taught at Lincoln in the 1950s. At Lincoln,
Blue quickly developed a reputation as a demanding teacher, a brilliant
thinker, and an indefatigable worker for what he called "this enterprise
known as Lincoln University."[10]

In the 1930s, Cecil Blue teamed with newcomer Lorenzo J. Greene to
enhance the cultural and intellectual life of the campus. Together Blue
and Greene, bachelors who called themselves "the color boys," shared a
residence, which they dubbed "The Monastery" and which became an
off-campus site for faculty-student interaction. All-night discussions
about Roosevelt's New Deal, international communism, and race relations were common. The Monastery's reputation spread beyond Jefferson City, and black intellectuals from elsewhere who came to Lincoln
during the 1930s often expressed the desire to go first to the Monastery.
Said Greene, in a 1981 interview, "No person of any note ever came to
Lincoln without coming to the Monastery."[11]

Greene, in my no-doubt-subjective judgment, was the most important
of the scholars attracted to Lincoln during its golden years. Born in An-
sonia, Connecticut, in 1899, the son of a teamster, Greene had attended
predominately white schools until his enrollment at Howard University
in 1919. Heavily influenced by Charles Wesley, Greene took an undergraduate degree in history from Howard in 1924 and then went on to do
graduate work at Columbia University in New York. In 1928, having completed his master's degree in history and having begun work on a doctorate, Greene went to work in Washington, DC, for Carter G. Woodson, the
founder of the Association for the Study of Negro Life and History and
the founder and editor of the *Journal of Negro History*. Woodson's journal
was the most significant scholarly publication on black life and culture
throughout most of the twentieth century.[12]

Greene's relationship with Woodson, although sometimes tempes-
tuous, was important because Woodson instilled in him an unbending
belief in the need for black pride based on past performance and present
possibilities. Greene brought that belief with him to Lincoln University
in 1933. Reflecting back on his early years at Lincoln in 1979, Greene had
this to say:

> Lincoln had an excellent faculty, drawn from such prestigious uni-
> versities as Harvard, Columbia, Chicago, Boston, New York, Pitts-
> burgh, Cornell, and others. A group of us planned to make Lincoln

an academic replica of Amherst. Student enrollment ranged between 300 and 350. We had the pick of black students from Missouri, Arkansas, Oklahoma, and other nearby states. Others came from
as far away as California and Massachusetts. . . . I had found my life's
work and loved it.[13]

One of the first activities Greene became involved in during the 1930s,
largely through Blue's influence, was the Lincoln University debating society. Greene served as the society's secretary and Blue as coach. The great
irony surrounding the society was that, although it debated representatives from all over the United States and, on one occasion, even hosted a
debate team from Oxford University, the Lincoln team was never allowed
to debate the University of Missouri's own team because of Missouri's
strictures against interracial educational activity.[14]

Those strictures were so powerful that they resulted in two changes
at Lincoln when two African Americans tried to enroll in professional
schools at the University of Missouri. Lloyd Gaines sought admission to
the state university's law school in 1936, and Lucile Bluford tried to enroll
in the much touted University of Missouri School of Journalism three
years later. In keeping with its commitment to maintaining "separate but
equal" educational facilities, even if separate would later be shown to be
inherently unequal, the Missouri legislature created first a Lincoln University Law School and then a Lincoln University School of Journalism.
The person charged with the responsibility of establishing and nurturing
the LU journalism school was Armistead S. Pride, a native of Washington,
DC, and yet another graduate of Dunbar High School. Pride came to
Lincoln in 1937 and taught for thirty-eight years. In 1950 he earned a
doctorate in English and journalism from Northwestern University.[15]

No single individual played a more important role in the promotion of
black culture during the 1940s and 1950s than did Thomas D. Pawley III,
a native of Mississippi who grew up in Virginia. Pawley, who was trained
in the theater, aspired to be an actor. In the summer of 1940 he contacted
Richard Wright, who was working on "Native Son." Pawley, who wanted
to act in the play, was told by Wright that production would not begin for
another month and he should come back then.[16]

Meanwhile, Cecil Blue, now English department chair, had written
Pawley and offered him a job teaching for the summer "in a place called
Jefferson City." Pawley came to Lincoln intending to stay only through
the summer. Instead, he ended up staying more than fifty years. Pawley
found Lincoln University to be "an exciting alternative to a professional

career in the theater." Years later, Pawley, by then a well-known playwright himself, reflected that "I found Lincoln University itself to be a very exciting place. . . . I found more black intellectuals [t]here than I found any place else." Thomas Pawley, more than any other person, was responsible for developing a theater program at Lincoln. Cecil Blue had written to Pawley that Lincoln provided "a lush field for the development of the theater."[17]

If the field was lush, it was so in large part because of the efforts of Hazel McDaniel Teabeau, who preceded Pawley at Lincoln by three years. Born in 1892 at Fort Smith, Arkansas, Mrs. Teabeau earned a bachelor of arts degree in English from Kansas University in 1915. While she was at Lincoln University, she did graduate work at the University of Chicago (master of arts, 1944, in English). In 1950 she became one of the first black students to enroll at the University of Missouri, and on August 7, 1959, at the age of sixty-six, she became the first African American to earn a doctorate from the University of Missouri. Although a teacher of English first, Mrs. Teabeau was a lover of drama; she promoted theater productions prior to Pawley's arrival and assisted Pawley for many years thereafter. Through the efforts of Teabeau and Pawley, the lush field produced a bountiful harvest of theater programs unequalled anywhere in the Midwest.[18]

Lincoln University students were introduced to the serious study of music by O. Anderson Fuller, who came to the school in 1942. Born in Roanoke, Virginia, Fuller moved with his family to Marshall, Texas, where his father was a dean at Bishop College. Fuller studied at Bishop before going to graduate school at the University of Iowa, where he studied under Dr. Phillip Greely Clapp. In 1942 Fuller became the first African American to earn a doctorate in music. Under Fuller's direction, Lincoln established a degree program in music, a program shepherded by Fuller as department head until his retirement in 1974. Among the more distinguished of Fuller's students was the opera singer Felicia Weathers.[19]

Fuller also had an impact on countless black high school students in the state. During the 1940s an annual state black high school music festival was held at Lincoln University, with band, orchestra, and choral competitions. And, as historian Nancy Grant has pointed out, "The University also sponsored music camps for black high school students from Missouri and neighboring states."[20]

The intellectual climate created by the presence of the unique gathering of African American scholars at Lincoln University during the 1920s–1950s served as an attraction for black and white artists and literary figures, who

Memorial Hall,
Lincoln University
(courtesy of the State
Historical Society of
Missouri)

came to the campus on a regular basis during those years. Carl Sandburg visited the campus in 1939, drawing an overflow crowd of "students, faculty members and townspeople" into old Page Auditorium on the third floor of Memorial Hall where, according to a front-page article in the *Chicago Defender*, he "charmed the audience by the ease of his manner."[21] In 1942 the Missouri-born Langston Hughes made one of many trips to Lincoln, where he "lectured, offered several of his poems, and sketched for his listeners some of his experiences of travel and contact."[22] In 1947 a performance by Paul Robeson, originally scheduled to take place on campus, was moved to the larger Jefferson City Junior College Auditorium because of the overwhelming response. Robeson's presence in the white school's auditorium on January 25 "shattered an established precedent denying Negroes use of the largest seating tax supported facility in the city." Said Mrs. Roena Savage, cochair of the program committee and wife of distinguished scholar W. Sherman Savage, "It took no less a figure than Robeson to help us break down the barriers which Negroes have encountered here for years when requesting use of the auditorium."[23]

Arguably the black literary figure of the era who caused the greatest stir on the Lincoln University campus was W. E. B. DuBois, who was the featured speaker on the occasion of the seventy-fifth anniversary of the founding of Lincoln University, in 1941. DuBois, who among other accomplishments was the editor of the recently established *Phylon* magazine, titled his address "The Future of the Negro State University." It was DuBois's hope that Lincoln University, and black colleges generally, would nurture black culture and black consciousness and, in so doing, provide a model to whites of how people should live.[24] In an interesting aside, and mindful of the recent Gaines and Bluford cases, DuBois asked the question in his speech, "Should Lincoln University try to become another University of Missouri?" He answered that it should not, commenting that "After all, among the great universities of America, the University of Missouri would hardly be placed among the first. It can be considered a sort of average of those plodding miscellaneous centers of crowds, dispensing education with varying degrees of efficiency."[25]

The apogee of intellectual activity was reached in the late 1940s with the establishment of the *Midwest Journal*, a self-styled "magazine of research and creative writing." First issued in 1948 and continuing for nine years, the journal was edited by Lorenzo J. Greene, with Sidney J. Reedy and Cecil A. Blue serving as associate editors.[26] Many scholars who would gain fame in the 1960s and 1970s as writers of black history had their early works published in the *Midwest Journal* during the 1940s and 1950s. August Meier, for example, who had become one of the most prolific writers of African American history by the 1970s, had two of his earliest essays published in the journal. Reflecting back on the *Midwest Journal* and its role from the perspective of the mid-1980s, Meier wrote: "Some very significant material appeared in the pages of that journal. It was well-edited, and with *Phylon* running only short pieces, *Midwest Journal* was the place to get something substantial published if the *Journal of Negro History* decided not to do it. . . . Qualitatively it was a journal every bit as good as the *Journal of Negro History*."[27]

From the beginning, the journal featured the work of prominent and promising writers. The first volume set the tone, carrying pieces by, among others, Herbert Aptheker, T. Thomas Fletcher, John Hope Franklin, Lorenzo J. Greene, Rayford W. Logan, Booker T. McGraw, Benjamin Quarles, and Melvin B. Tolson. Former Lincoln University student M. Carl Holman, a prize-winning poet and later the director of the National Urban Coalition, published a poem in the first volume entitled "Lines for a Soldier Killed after Peace."[28]

In the second number of the first volume, in the summer of 1949, Langston Hughes contributed two poems. "Low to High" was the first:

> How can you forget me? *But you do*!
> You said you was gonna take me
> Up with you—
> Now you've got your Cadillac,
> You done forgot that you are black
> How can you forget me
> when I'm you
> But you do.

And "High to Low" was the second:

> God knows
> we have our troubles, too—
> One trouble is you:
> you talk too loud,
> cuss too loud,
> look too black,
> don't get anywhere,
> and sometimes it seems
> you don't even care.
> The way you send your kids to school
> stockings down,
> (not Ethical Culture)
> the way you shout out loud in church,
> (not St. Phillips)
> and the way you lounge on doorsteps
> just as if you were down South,
> (not at 409)
> the way you clown—
> the way, in other words,
> you let me down—
> me, trying to uphold the race
> and you—
> well, you can see,
> we have our problems,
> too, with you.[29]

It was 1949, also, that Greene and the *Midwest Journal* first got into trouble with the Federal Bureau of Investigation. This was, one must re-call, a time of great political conservatism. The Soviets had, only a short time before, exploded their first atomic weapon in a test that revealed they were much further advanced in that area than Americans had thought possible. Additionally, the Chinese Communist revolution had occurred, solidifying the American fear of Communism as a monolithic force that threatened the United States with great immediacy. It was the atmosphere that gave rise to Joseph McCarthy and McCarthyism.

In 1949 Greene published two controversial essays. The first was a piece by Shu-yi Yang entitled "Role of Students in China's Struggle" in summer 1949. Yang praised the Chinese Communists in this article and talked about how they were "liberating" China. The second essay, in winter 1949, was entitled "The Freedom to Learn," by W. E. B. DuBois. In this essay, DuBois wrote that "What this nation needs most of all is the free and open curriculum of a school where people may study and read Marx, know what Communism is or proposes to be, and learn actual facts and accomplishments."[30]

Not long after the DuBois essay appeared, Greene was working in his Lincoln University office on a Saturday morning when a federal agent came to call, asking numerous questions about Greene, the journal, and the political ideology of both. Documents obtained from the US Justice Department in 1986 through the Freedom of Information Act reveal that the journal and Greene were under surveillance for some time.[31]

Ironically, 1949 was also the year that Lincoln University hired the most prolific and controversial scholar of its "golden years," the sociologist Oliver Cromwell Cox. An avowed critic of capitalism, Professor Cox published his classic book *Caste, Class, and Race* in 1948 and then, while at Lincoln, published his famous trilogy on capitalism: *The Foundations of Capitalism* (1959), *Capitalism and American Leadership* (1962), and *Capitalism as a System* (1964).[32]

Cox, too, ran afoul of the US Department of Justice, although the FBI first took notice of him before he came to Lincoln University. In 1944, while Cox was teaching at Wiley College in Marshall, Texas, an FBI informant reported that Cox had "questionable tendencies." Although the FBI apparently never considered Cox a serious threat to national security, the agency continued to gather information on him into the 1960s, throughout most of his tenure at Lincoln University.[33]

The dedication of a new library—the Inman E. Page Library—in 1950 brought to the campus one of the most distinguished gatherings of black writers ever to appear on the campus. The two-day program began with an address by the distinguished author and semanticist S. I. Hayakawa. Later in the day a program chaired by Thomas D. Pawley was entitled

"An Afternoon with the Poets." Participants included Langston Hughes, Melvin Tolson, Robert Hayden, and Sterling Brown. That evening a symposium entitled "The Negro Author Today" featured Arna Bontemps, Langston Hughes, Sterling Brown, and Lorenzo Greene. Cecil Blue presided on that occasion.[34]

The *Brown v. Board of Education* decision and the civil rights movement of the 1950s and 1960s changed Lincoln University dramatically. By the mid-1960s, with major universities being threatened with civil rights lawsuits if they did not create greater opportunities for African Americans, the composition of Lincoln University's faculty and student body changed significantly. Lincoln no longer had the "pick of black students" that Greene referred to. Now those students were being recruited elsewhere, enticed by scholarships and other promises. Indeed, black faculty were also being drawn away, so much so that Lincoln University president Walter C. Daniel expressed a widely felt concern when he talked about a "black brain drain" in early 1970. Ironically, Daniel himself left Lincoln two years later for the University of Missouri at Columbia.[35]

The changes in Lincoln University, not surprisingly, saddened many of the black scholars who had given their professional lives to the school. Perhaps Thomas D. Pawley best summed up the bittersweet effects of integration. When Pawley came to Lincoln in 1940, he found "a black Ivy League school . . . [which] attracted the best minds from the black middle class all over the middle west." Pawley encountered students such as M. Carl Holman who, he remembers, "challenged the hell out of me." Indeed, Pawley continued, in a sentence that captures the essence of his disillusionment, "There was a level of student and there was an interest in learning that I have not seen since, I regret to say."[36]

The golden years of Lincoln University lasted little more than a generation. But for that short time Lincoln University was a place where there congregated a score or more of dedicated, brilliant African Americans who served as role models to literally thousands of young black students and who introduced those students to the world of the mind and to the world of black culture in a way and to a degree not duplicated in the Midwest either before or since.

Chapter 12

Lake Placid

"A Recreational Center for Colored People" in the Missouri Ozarks

On October 8, 1934, during the heart of the Great Depression and in the second year of Franklin Delano Roosevelt's first term as president of the United States, two white men from Morgan County, Missouri, sold a 346-acre plot of land in the Missouri Ozarks to two black men from Kansas City.[1] The sellers were a prominent county physician, Dr. C. A. Wiest, and his son-in-law, a local farmer named Reed J. Blackman.[2]

The buyers were Dr. P. C. Turner and J. M. Sojourner. Dr. Turner served as superintendent of General Hospital No. 2 in Kansas City, the publicly supported but racially segregated hospital for African Americans in Missouri's second-largest city. A printer, Sojourner ran the Sojourner Press at 1604 East Nineteenth Street in Kansas City. The business served only a black clientele. Segregation defined the world occupied by Turner and Sojourner. State and local laws and customs dictated that African Americans live, work, shop, worship, and even play in separate facilities, away and apart from whites.[3]

Magnificent Swope Park, comprising more than thirteen hundred acres, served as the major public recreational area for Kansas Citians during the 1930s. The land had been donated to the city for recreational use in 1896 by real estate developer and philanthropist Thomas Hunton Swope. In accordance with plans drawn up by George Kessler, the landscape architect and designer who helped to make Kansas City a shining example of the Progressive Era's so-called City Beautiful Movement, the city developed the land as a park during the early 1900s.[4] No amount of landscaping, however, could hide the ugly fact that Swope Park was

Dr. P.C. Turner (courtesy of the Leonard Pryor Collection)

racially segregated, with blacks forced to go to a small section of the park widely referred to by members of both races as "Watermelon Hill."

Dr. P. C. Turner, the driving force behind the purchase of the Morgan County land, wanted a place to relax without having to suffer the indignities of racial segregation. This eliminated Swope Park and the segregated city park in his hometown of Independence, where Turner had grown up as the son of a postal worker and his wife at the turn of the century.[5] Turner, a hunter and a fisherman, loved the outdoors and dreamed of the opportunity to roam the hills of the Ozarks, unfettered by the rules and racism of reigning whites. He had been looking for just such a place since at least 1932. The Morgan County property seemed to fit his needs.[6]

Turner and Sojourner visualized the land as more than a place for their own personal use. According to the contract signed by the parties in 1934, ninety-six acres of the land were "to be used and set aside for a l[a]ke, Dam, Golf course, Park ETC [sic]." Individual lots measuring a hundred by thirty-three and one-third feet would be sold at prices ranging from fifty dollars to one hundred dollars, depending upon the location. Thus, from the very beginning, the purchasers conceived of the area as "a recreational center for colored people."[7]

Turner and Sojourner had little cash available, which was not surprising in the fifth full year of a national depression. Their lack of cash but eagerness to buy, combined with Blackman and Wiest's keenness to sell the land and the absence of other buyers, led to a creative way to finance the sale. Turner paid the sellers two dollars in cash (Sojourner apparently never provided any cash for the project) and agreed to pay Blackman and Wiest 40 percent of the amount earned from the sale of lots, "which sum is to be used to pay off a mortgage now existing against the said land." Once two thousand dollars had been paid, the buyers would then pay 20 percent of gross sales, "until the sum of $6,650.00 more has been paid." At that point, the sellers were to receive "thirty per cent of the gross sales until the sum of $13,350.00 more has been paid, making a total payment of $22,000.00 in all." Thus, Turner and Sojourner agreed to pay the considerable sum of more than $63.58 per acre for rocky, hilly, tree-covered, northern Ozarks land. This represented at least three times the per acre cost of similar land in the area. The advantage to Turner and Sojourner, of course, was that they could pay off their indebtedness to the sellers from the proceeds earned from selling lots. The contract placed no time limit on the arrangement, except that the buyers had to pay the sellers two thousand dollars by August 31, 1935.[8]

Almost immediately after purchasing the Morgan County property, Dr. Turner arranged to have a rustic cabin built by a local craftsman on the land as a "getaway." Here he and his wife could relax, and he could pursue his hobbies of hunting and fishing and allow his favorite dogs to roam. At first, the cabin had no modern conveniences such as central heat, indoor plumbing, or electricity. Initially, the Turners either brought food with them from Kansas City or relied on Dr. Turner's skills as a hunter and fisherman to sustain them. An active spring, perhaps one hundred yards from the cabin, provided fresh water and served as a storage place for perishable foods while the couple stayed at the cabin.[9]

From the very beginning, Turner intended to build a lake on the property. He clearly built his cabin at a point on a sloping south hillside that would give him a commanding and attractive vista of the lake. Turner, however, could not afford the cost of building a large dam. He began seeking federal support through the Works Progress Administration (WPA) for the construction of a dam sometime in late 1935 or early 1936.

The WPA had been established by executive order of President Roosevelt on May 6, 1935, with an initial appropriation of nearly five billion dollars. The money was to be spent for relief work: creating public works projects that would serve the common good (roads, schools, hospitals, parks, reservoirs, and so on) while employing millions of unemployed Americans. Workers spending their wages, government officials hoped, would help to stimulate the stagnant depression economy. The building of a dam on private property owned by Turner and Sojourner was construed to be a "public" project because, it was argued, if water supplies continued to be difficult to maintain in the drought-ridden years of the mid-1930s, the lake formed by building the dam could be opened to "the public."[10]

Each state employed an administrator for WPA projects within its borders. According to historian Robert H. Ferrell, "The choice of a state's WPA administrator lay with its senators." Missouri's senators, Bennett Champ Clark and Harry S. Truman, supported the appointment of Matthew S. Murray, a longtime loyal associate of notorious Kansas City boss Thomas J. Pendergast. As Ferrell points out, this placed Murray and, by extension, Pendergast, in control of eighty thousand jobs in Missouri.[11]

The Murray-Pendergast connection raises the intriguing but difficult-to-answer question of what role, if any, Pendergast played in helping Turner obtain WPA funds for construction of the dam. Contemporaries of Turner remember that the doctor and the boss knew each other well and sometimes did favors for each other. None, however, remembers a specific oral tradition overtly connecting Pendergast to the allocation of WPA funds to the Lake Placid project. A number of these contemporaries are inclined to think that Pendergast likely played a role in the building of the dam since the two men sometimes assisted each other. Also, Turner's desire to obtain federal support would have meshed with the boss's willingness to do favors for black leaders in the hope of securing black votes for his causes and candidates.[12]

Another important connection between Turner and Pendergast appears to have been Dr. William J. Thompkins, an African American doctor who preceded Turner as superintendent of General Hospital No. 2. A native of Jefferson City and a graduate of Lincoln Institute, Thompkins earned his medical degree from Howard University, Washington, DC, in 1905. He began the practice of medicine in Kansas City in 1906 and in 1915 was appointed the "first Negro superintendent of General Hospital No. 2." One of the most prominent African Americans in Kansas City during the first three decades of the twentieth century, Thompkins was also a businessman and a newspaper publisher who launched and edited the *Kansas City American* during the mid-1920s. According to Pendergast biographers Lawrence H. Larsen and Nancy J. Hulston, Pendergast helped to finance the newspaper's publication. In 1927 Thompkins was appointed assistant commissioner of health in the Department of Hygiene and Communicable Diseases in Kansas City. His high profile in the city's African American community made him a natural ally of political boss Tom Pendergast. By the early 1930s Thompkins had become widely known as a power broker among black Democrats throughout the Midwest. According to his obituary, "In the campaign of 1932 [Thompkins] had charge of the colored contingent for all states west of the Mississippi river for the Democratic party. The National Colored Democratic association, of which he was president[,] consists of clubs in Missouri, Oklahoma, Kansas, Nebraska, Colorado, Iowa, California, and 19 other states." Thompkins's active support of the Democratic Party led President Roosevelt to appoint him to the prestigious position of recorder of deeds for the District of Columbia in 1934. This position had previously been held by other prominent African Americans, including Frederick Douglass, Monroe Trotter, and Blanche K. Bruce. Thompkins's appointment came at the recommendation of Senator-elect Harry S. Truman, in recognition of the doctor's strong and active involvement in Democratic Party politics.[13] In a late 1980s reminiscence on the founding of Lake Placid, Girard T. Bryant, one of the early investors, wrote that he believed Thompkins had helped Turner obtain WPA funding for the Lake Placid dam.[14]

Even before construction of the dam commenced, other Kansas City African Americans began building cabins on the property. One of the first was veteran teacher H. O. Cook, who built a cabin southwest of Dr. Turner's cottage. Cook served as principal of Lincoln High School for more than twenty years. His wife, Myrtle, was a former teacher at Lincoln High School and an active member of the National Association of Colored Women.[15] Dr. Turner allowed one of his patients, Ketchum E. ("K. E.") Snell, to live in an old cabin at the property's entrance. Sent by the doctor to the lake to recuperate from an illness in the fresh Ozarks air, Snell helped build the Turner cabin. Snell liked the outdoors of Morgan County so well that he decided to stay, despite the fact that he had relatives, including a wife, in Kansas City. In addition to providing him with a cabin, Turner periodically purchased an old car for Snell's use and supplied him with clothing and food. Snell earned small amounts of money by doing maintenance work for cabin owners and occasionally charging hunters for their use of the property.[16]

Snell quickly became a fixture in the Stover area. A black person in Stover during the mid-1930s was a rarity. According to the federal census, only 236 African Americans lived in Morgan County in 1930, more than half of whom resided in the county seat of Versailles. The number of African Americans who called Morgan County home had dropped to 185 by 1940.[17]

Snell's Cabin (courtesy of the State Historical Society of Missouri)

One of the first local white families to befriend Snell were the Wrays, who lived several hundred yards south of his cabin. Although not one of the WPA workers, Jodie Wray had done contract work for the WPA on the Lake Placid dam. Snell sometimes purchased farm produce, including eggs, chickens, and garden vegetables, from the Wrays. Alice Wray Jones, an adolescent at the time, remembers Snell as a gentle, polite man who initially declined the Wrays' invitation to dine with them. He eventually accepted and came to be regarded as almost one of the family. He had a "place" at the family table and often ate with the Wrays multiple times a week. On many occasions, Alice and her sister, Betty, would either walk or ride their horse to Snell's cabin to visit. At an earlier point in his life, Snell had been a schoolteacher, and the Wray daughters found him to be a never-ending source of information. He always asked them about their schoolwork and encouraged them to do their best in school. Snell had also worked as a meat cutter, a job that made him a skilled assistant when it came time for the Wrays to butcher hogs, beef, or chickens.[18]

The Lake Placid dam was under construction by late 1936 or early 1937. An article in the May 21, 1937, *Stover Tri-County Republican* noted that "the J. F. Martin family spent Sunday visiting the Turner Dam which is under construction on the old Reed Blackman Place." The paper observed, "It is being constructed of native stone and cement and is worthy of the attention of the people of the surrounding country."[19] Emma Jean Clark, who as a young girl often visited the property with the Turners, recalls, "We took a great deal of pride as the dam was being built because this would enable us to have water. The older people were looking forward to being able to fish in the new lake."[20]

The dam was completed during the summer of 1937, and the lake quickly filled, covering approximately fifteen acres. By 1940 six cabins stood near the lake. In addition to the Turner, Cook, and Snell structures, Dr. Joe Houston Lewis had built a cabin he called "Jest-a-mere." A dentist, Lewis had graduated from Sumner High School in Kansas City, Kansas, the University of Minnesota, and Meharry Medical College.[21] Steve Blantyre, a Kansas City businessman, also built a cabin. Early in 1940, Girard T. Bryant's cabin was completed some distance from the water. Uninterested in hunting, fishing, or water sports, schoolteacher Bryant simply wanted a place where he could read in peace. During the first two summers that he owned a lake cabin, however, Bryant was forced to take jobs as a dining-car waiter on the Union Pacific Railway to supplement his meager teacher's salary. Thus, his wife, Louise, and daughters, Betty and Barbara, spent most of their time at Lake Placid without him.[22]

At least two of the early cabin owners at Lake Placid were druggists. Leonard Hughes, who ran a pharmacy at 2519 Tracy, had become acquainted with Turner through his business. Leonard's wife, Eva, operated a business known as Eva's Wardrobe Exchange. The Hugheses built one of the largest cabins at the lake, a place that would accommodate several families. Their former daughter-in-law, Mayme Hughes Rodgers, recalls that she and her husband, also named Leonard, spent their honeymoon at the lake in September 1949. More than a decade later, Rodgers purchased her own cabin at Lake Placid.[23]

William Houston, who operated a pharmacy at 2300 Vine Street in Kansas City, built an early cabin at the lake. An 1897 graduate of Lincoln High School, the very light-skinned Houston had "passed" for white as a University of Kansas student during the first decade of the twentieth century. Upon his graduation from college, Houston was licensed as a pharmacist by the state of Missouri. After Houston's death in May 1941, his cabin, which he had named "My Blue Heaven," passed on to his half-brother Arthur "Chic" Pullam.[24] Pullam was a longtime postal worker in Kansas City and a former player on the Kansas City Monarchs baseball team. Pullam's daughter, Barbara Pullam Thompson, recalls that "it was quite prestigious" to have a cabin at Lake Placid during the 1940s. One of her most vivid memories of Lake Placid while a teenager, however, is a negative one: an automobile accident en route to the lake with the Carlis Evans family (who operated a bakery at Twenty-fourth and Vine in Kansas City). Just south of Sedalia, their car rolled over three times before coming to rest on the driver's side. Barbara was holding a big pot of chili beans at the time, and the beans were strewn all over the car and its occupants. Although no one was seriously injured in the accident, all of the car's occupants received medical attention from the doctors when they finally arrived at the lake. After Chic Pullam's death, "My Blue Heaven" was passed to his son Richard, a former "Tuskegee airman," who lived year-round in retirement at Lake Placid until his death in August 1997.[25]

By late 1939 Turner and Sojourner decided to formalize their effort at creating what they envisioned as "a recreational center for colored people" in the Missouri Ozarks. In December they drafted articles of incorporation for Lake Placid Resort, Incorporated. According to the document, "the amount of capital" was $50,000, "divided into 50,000 shares of stock of the par value of One dollar, ($1.00), each." There were 27,500 shares of the stock divided among five stockholders: Dr. P. C. Turner (15,844 shares); J. M. Sojourner (6,000 shares); Mayme Turner (5,000 shares); K. E. Snell (500 shares); and Josephine Abbie Sojourner (156 shares). Presumably, the remaining 27,500 shares of stock were to be divided among future purchasers of Lake Placid property. The corporation subsequently hired Kansas City businessman and Lake Placid property owner Steve Blantyre as its agent to promote and sell lots. The lots were to range in price from $65 to $159 (although some would later be sold for as little as $30), the amount to be paid in cash or "on time," with financing arranged through the black-owned People's Finance Company, located on Vine Street in Kansas City. Turner was a principal stockowner in the People's Finance Company. On January 31, 1940, Missouri secretary of state Dwight H. Brown issued a "Certificate of Authority to Commence Business" to Lake Placid Resort, Incorporated.[26]

Later that same year, property owners organized the Lake Placid Lot Owners' Association, which initially met at the African American YMCA in Kansas City. The association, first presided over by Girard T. Bryant, assessed each lot owner a three-dollar fee "to provide funds for stocking the lake with fish, for upkeep of roads, and other necessary improvements." In addition, each cabin owner was assessed an annual five-dollar fee "for caretaker services." In September 1941 the association adopted "regulations for fishing," which prohibited "out-board motor boats" on the lake and declared: "Outsiders are forbidden on this private property." Guests who came to Lake Placid were stopped at the entrance, gained Snell's approval for entry, and signed a guest register kept by the caretaker. The guest register for the late 1930s and early 1940s documents a steady stream of visitors to the lake, mostly from the Kansas City area.[27]

Although the number of cabins increased during the early years of the 1940s, the growth was not as quick or as great as either Turner or the men he had purchased the land from had hoped. By 1942 with money still due for the purchase of the land, Blackman and Wiest sued Turner and the Lake Placid Resort, Incorporated, charging them with breach of contract and seeking to repossess the land, with its improvements, including the lake and the cabins. Turner and his associates employed Carl Johnson, a prominent black Kansas City attorney (and later judge), to argue the case in the Morgan County Circuit Court. Early in 1943, the court decided in favor of the defendants, arguing that Turner and Sojourner had not violated the original contract because no time period, other than "reasonable," had been set to achieve its terms.[28]

Lake Placid boomed during the post–World War II era. A rapidly expanding economy (in which a growing number of middle-class blacks shared) and a persistent white racial recalcitrance that hung on to Jim Crowism throughout Kansas City, Missouri, and the Midwest fueled the resort's growth. One of the people who began regularly visiting Lake Placid during the postwar period was Leonard Pryor, who first met Turner while dating the doctor's niece Maxine Turner. Pryor had grown up in Topeka, Kansas, with a father who was an avid outdoorsman. He met Maxine while attending Washburn College in Topeka. After a stint in the navy during World War II, Pryor married Maxine, and the two of them became like surrogate children to the childless Turners.[29]

Among Leonard Pryor's fondest memories is the excitement of preparing for a late Friday night trip to the lake. Pryor would try to have the car packed, filled with gas, and ready to go so that he and the Turners could leave immediately after Dr. Turner got off work. Sometimes it would be 10:00 P.M. before Turner finished his rounds at the hospital. Regardless of the time, Pryor recalls, when the doctor had fulfilled his responsibilities, the three of them would drive out of town on US Highway 50, leaving the bright city lights behind and heading for the quiet peace of the Missouri Ozarks. "You could not find this kind of place in the inner city," Pryor remembers. "You are with nature and if you love nature, you would love [Lake Placid]." The trio always traveled well dressed, hoping that wearing fine clothes would reduce trouble with whites they might encounter if their car broke down.[30]

At Sedalia, Pryor and Turner would turn south on US Highway 65 until they reached Missouri Highway 52, which took them east, through Cole Camp, to County Road FF. At County Road FF, they would stop the car, whereupon Turner or Pryor would get out, armed with a .410 shotgun, and lie across the right front fender with his feet resting on the running board. Ready to shoot any game (usually rabbits) that might cross the road, the Turners and Pryor proceeded the last few miles to the lake. By the time they reached the lake, Pryor recalls, they had always killed enough game for at least one meal.[31]

Word spread within and beyond Kansas City that Lake Placid provided recreational opportunities for African Americans. Church groups began to visit, as did fraternities and sororities. Many blacks from St. Louis, most of them teachers, began coming to Lake Placid after World War II. Among the St. Louisans who bought property at the lake was Andrew S. Jackson, G. T. Bryant's brother-in-law. Jackson taught at Sumner High School, the oldest high school for African Americans west of the Mississippi River. Affectionately known as "Papa Jack," Jackson had been born on December 4, 1900, in Decatur, Illinois. He originally aspired to become a doctor but decided to become a teacher when it became clear that his family could not afford to send him to medical school. He moved to St. Louis in 1926. Like the vast majority of Missouri's African Americans during the 1930s and 1940s, Jackson worked and lived in a segregated world. He lived in a St. Louis neighborhood known as "the Ville," with other African American teachers, doctors, lawyers, preachers, and middle-class residents.[32]

With limited access to public places of recreation, other African American Sumner teachers and Ville residents began to visit Lake Placid. Among them were a number of couples who had formed a group known as "The Travelers," a "couples club" whose members had vacationed together at Kentucky Lake prior to their discovery of Lake Placid. William Wyatt, known to the club as "Chink," was one of the first of the group to buy a cabin at Lake Placid. Clarice Dreer Davis, the daughter of prominent community leader Herman Dreer, lived across the street from "Papa Jack" in the Ville and also taught for a while at Sumner High School. She visited Lake Placid many years before she and her husband, John, also a teacher, purchased a cabin there. She still remembers Lake Placid as "our little island of paradise."[33] Vivian DeShields Rasberry, another member of the Travelers, also visited Lake Placid for many years before purchasing a cabin there. Rasberry liked to play cards (pinochle and poker), and she found in Lake Placid a place of peace, where she and her fellow Travelers could literally play cards all night long.[34]

Children and adults swam off a concrete dock just below Dr. Turner's cabin. Fishing and boating were also popular. Meals were taken communally, with all present gathering at Turner's cabin, called there by the ringing of a dinner bell that hung from a pole near the cabin's front door. During the evenings, prior to electricity arriving at the lake during the 1950s, adults sometimes danced to music provided by a local band brought in to add to the revelry. One of the favorite bands from the early years was known as the Whiskers Band, because all of its members wore artificial whiskers when they played. The Whiskers Band "played mostly 'Rag Time' music, but they could play any kind." Among the band members was Warren Cooper, who owned Cooper's Store in Stover, where many of the Lake Placid visitors bought groceries during their weekend trips. In later years, after the arrival of electricity, vacationers brought record players and their favorite records for listening and dancing. A flyer for a July 4, 1953, picnic at Lake Placid announced a full day of activities, including swimming, boating, dancing, fishing, card playing, singing, and "Clay Pidgeon Shooting."[35]

The annual Lot Owners' Association meeting, held on the third Sunday in August, provided another important gathering time. A barbecue capped the weekend's activity. Emma Jean Clark recalls a trip with Dr. and Mrs. Turner from Kansas City to the lake, during which she held a live lamb on her lap the entire way, unaware that the animal was to be slaughtered and barbecued at Lake Placid.[36]

Local whites were sometimes present when African Americans gathered at the lake. Occasionally, Jodie and Alta Wray and their daughters, Alice and Betty, came to the lake, always at the invitation of the Turners or K. E. Snell. Turner's providing medical treatment to Mrs. Wray and the couple's daughters sealed the friendship between the Wrays and the doctor.

During the late 1930s, Alta Wray began to experience gynecological problems that her family physician, the same Dr. Wiest from whom Turner had purchased the Lake Placid land, felt unable to treat adequately. Wiest recommended that she consult Turner during his next visit to the lake. She readily agreed. Subsequently, Dr. Turner visited the Wray home, examined Mrs. Wray, and encouraged her to be admitted to Wheatley-Provident Hospital in Kansas City, a privately operated hospital for African Americans established in 1914 by Dr. J. Edward Perry. The Turners transported Mrs. Wray to Kansas City in their car. Dr. Turner performed a hysterectomy on Mrs. Wray at Wheatley-Provident, then took her into his home for several weeks of recuperation before returning her to Morgan County. In December 1999, an ailing and frail Alta Wray, ninety-two years old, still smiled warmly at the mention of the Turners' names and remembered them as "good people—they were good people."[37]

When the Wrays' daughters, Alice and Betty, then teenagers, needed their tonsils removed a few years later, the family again turned to Dr. Turner. Alice and Betty remember that they had the utmost faith in Dr. Turner and found their stay at Wheatley-Provident to be a comfortable and reassuring experience. That pleasant experience notwithstanding, Betty developed complications from the surgery and became seriously ill. Turner cared for the young woman and nurtured her through a life-threatening illness. After Betty was discharged from the hospital, she and her mother stayed in the Turner home for months, so that the doctor could monitor her recovery.[38]

The Wrays are only three of many persons, both black and white, who remember the Turners with what can be described as adulation. Dr. Carl Peterson, a turn-of-the-century octogenarian, recalls being inspired by Turner's mentoring while serving a medical internship at General Hospital No. 2. He resolved to work for and with the man who treated him like a son. Not surprisingly, Dr. Turner often brought young doctors and nurses to Lake Placid for rest and recreation.[39]

Turner's involvement with Lake Placid diminished during the early 1960s. Plagued by health problems, he ended his active medical practice in 1963, after thirty-seven years in medicine. Dr. Turner's wife, Mayme, a longtime nurse at General Hospital No. 2, died in 1964. Friends and family members recall that her death left her husband dispirited and less interested in the lake. Dr. Turner died on January 19, 1966, at Wheatley-Provident Hospital, as the result of a spinal injury he had suffered two days earlier in an automobile accident at the intersection of Linwood and Benton in Kansas City. His last visit to Lake Placid had occurred one week prior to the accident.[40]

Lake Placid experienced a decline in prosperity during the early 1960s—a decline that paralleled Turner's decreased involvement with the resort. No doubt the absence of his forceful and charismatic personality had an impact. The successes of the civil rights movement in Kansas City and elsewhere also played a role. By the mid-1960s, the passage of public accommodations laws in the state and nation opened many public recreational places to African Americans. Mayme Hughes Rodgers recalls that her children often complained about being "required" to go to Lake Placid during this period, preferring instead the urban entertainments available to them.[41]

The lake area seemed to decline even further after K. E. Snell died in 1973 at the age of eighty-three. His death left the lake without a permanent resident and caretaker. Although elderly, Snell seemed to be in reasonably good health until his short, final illness. He was still a close friend of the Wray family. Although he had family members living in the Kansas City area, Snell chose to be buried in Morgan County. He had been a longtime member of Stover's First Baptist Church, but he asked that his final resting place be in the Methodists' Mount Pleasant Cemetery because it lay along the road to Lake Placid. He had said to many people that even in death he wanted to be where he could watch who came and went to "his" lake. Mrs. Wray and her daughters remember Snell fondly, as does Evelyn Cooper. She and her husband owned Cooper's Store in Stover where Snell did most of his shopping for nearly forty years. During an interview on January 19, 2000, Mrs. Cooper described Snell as "a very precious man. He traded with [us] and he had a wonderful personality. He was just good."[42]

The past two decades have witnessed renewed activity at Lake Placid with a newly energized commitment to carrying on the traditions begun there more than six decades ago. Second- and third-generation vacationers to the lake have picked up where their parents, grandparents, aunts, and uncles left off. Among the leaders in the revival of the lake has been Robert Wilson of Des Moines, Iowa, who served as president of the Lake Placid Lot Owners' Association through much of the 1990s. Wilson's father, Paul L., and his mother, Dorris D., also previously served as presidents of the association.

Robert Wilson recalls that he first visited Lake Placid during the early 1950s when his aunt Ione Coleman, a former school nurse at Lincoln High School in Kansas City, purchased a cabin at the lake. Wilson remembers: "I enjoyed extended weekends and long periods during the summer visiting my aunt. . . . In the old days kids dived and swam from Dr. Turner's pier, we had community meals, there were bells to call the kids to eat, there was a party line telephone system, kids from everywhere met kids from everywhere. If there was a utopian situation for the young this was as close as you might expect to get and still be among the living." In 1994 Wilson's parents deeded their lake property to him; he, in turn, carries on the Lake Placid tradition.[43]

Another Lake Placid property owner who carries on the tradition is Dr. Keith Turner, a psychiatrist who practices in Riverside, California. Dr. Turner's parents, L. C. ("Chris") and Mrs. Turner, have been coming to the lake since the 1940s. Chris Turner, whose father was Dr. P. C. Turner's brother, is a retired postal worker from Topeka, Kansas. In recent years Keith purchased a cabin next to the one owned by his parents; he has also recently bought some acreage adjoining the Lake Placid property and plays a leadership role among those trying to preserve the memory of the lake and its founders. In turn, his teenage son, Miles, has also taken an interest in Lake Placid.[44]

Among the younger persons to show a deep interest in Lake Placid are Craig Pryor and Renee Pryor Newton, the children of Leonard and Maxine Pryor. As a boy of five or six during the early 1970s, Craig would often accompany his parents and his sister to Lake Placid on summer weekends. He remembers it as being "always peaceful . . . being down there was timeless. There was no concern for what you had to do and when you had to do it and near the end of the weekend you hated to leave, but you knew you would come back again on another weekend." The young boy often rode his mini-bike, wandered through the woods, and played in the lake. "It was almost an unrestrictive 'Fantasy Land,'" he recalls. "Everyone was family down there, so you knew your neighbors and as a child my parents never worried about me running around the area because they knew everybody."[45]

Craig's sister, Renee, also fondly remembers Lake Placid, especially overnight trips there with friends from the Jack and Jills, a group formed in the pre–World War II period when African Americans did not have access to Kansas City's white YMCA facilities. Renee especially remembers the sounds of nature at Lake Placid—the frogs croaking and the summer night sound of nearby crickets. She now takes her adolescent daughter to the lake. Whatever happens to Lake Placid in the future, she hopes it will always be "a quiet place, so people [who] want to be there can enjoy nature and not feel the pressure of the world."[46]

Much has changed in American society since the day, more than sixty years ago, that Mr. Sojourner and Dr. Turner purchased land for their "recreational center for colored people" in Morgan County. Lake Placid no longer serves as the hub of summer activity; African Americans can now go to the Lake of the Ozarks or any other place of public accommodation that they choose. Still, it is important to remember the society that created Lake Placid and the paradoxical side effects of racial cooperation that flowed from its presence in the Missouri Ozarks. Lake Placid remains what, in a sense, it has always been: a place of beauty that stands as a silent reminder of the ugliness of American racism. It stands, too, as a testimony to the perseverance, energy, and creativity of multiple generations of African Americans who refused to allow Jim Crow to deny them the opportunity to find recreation in peace.

Chapter 13

William J. Thompkins

African American Physician, Politician, and Publisher

William J. Thompkins (courtesy of the Historical
Society of Washington, DC)

In 1931 Dr. William J. Thompkins, a late-middle-aged African American physician who practiced his profession in the Thompkins Building near the corner of East Eighteenth Street and Paseo Boulevard in Kansas City, sought an audience with Governor Franklin D. Roosevelt (FDR) of New York, the presumptive Democratic challenger to President Herbert Hoover in the 1932 election.[1] A supporter of Roosevelt since at least the fall of 1930, Thompkins apparently wanted to lay the groundwork for a federal patronage position in the event that FDR won the presidency.[2]

In his effort to meet with Roosevelt, Thompkins solicited the help of Frank P. Walsh, described by historian Franklin D. Mitchell as an "old Kansas City progressive residing in New York." Walsh, a Missouri-born labor lawyer heavily involved in state and national Democratic politics, wrote to Governor Roosevelt, indicating, "This [letter] will be handed to you by my old friend, Doctor William J. Thompkins." Walsh praised Thompkins as "the most consistent and loyal Democrat, at least whom I know, in the United States."[3]

Who was William J. Thompkins? And what had he done to warrant such an endorsement from a longtime Democratic Party activist at a time when the movement of African Americans away from the Grand Old Party of President Abraham Lincoln had barely begun?[4]

William James Thompkins was born in Jefferson City, Missouri, in 1879, the son of Marion and Eliza Thompkins. The family lived at 409 Madison Street, three blocks south of the Missouri Governor's Mansion. Marion Thompkins's name does not appear on the 1880 federal census taker's list of residents present in the family home that year. Eliza, a thirty-nine-year-old Missouri-born black woman, is described as a widow, "keeping house" for her children: Augusta (aged twelve), John (ten), Jennie (eight), and William (one). The census taker reported Eliza's inability to read and write and Augusta, John, and Jennie's being enrolled in school.[5] Although the Thompkins family lived on a block with white and black neighbors, the children attended a racially segregated school, as prescribed by Missouri law and local custom. The "colored school" and the town's two black churches lay within three blocks of the Thompkins home.[6]

Little is known of William Thompkins's childhood. In a biographical sketch included in a 1935 history of the Missouri Democratic Party "and its Representative members," Thompkins's early life commitment to the Democratic Party received emphasis along with the claim that his father had supported Democrats as far back as the Civil War. The Thompkins entry further announced his conviction "that the party of Jefferson and Jackson offered the best ethics for the welfare of the Negro race," failing to comment on the fact that both of those presidents had been slave owners. The entry also reported that Thompkins had first worked "as a bell boy in the old Madison Hotel," across the street from the Governor's Mansion. There, it noted, he "enjoyed the acquaintance and friendship of such men as [Congressman] Champ Clark, Governors [Alexander] Dockery, [William Joel] Stone and [Lon V.] Stephens," all Democrats.[7]

On September 5, 1892, Thompkins left the local black school for the Lincoln Institute Elementary Department. Located at the time on the outskirts of Missouri's capital city, Lincoln Institute served as the state's publicly supported normal school for African Americans. Thompkins remained at Lincoln for nearly a decade, until 1901. The school's catalog for 1900-1901 lists him as a "Class A" student in the normal department.[8]

Thompkins graduated from Lincoln Institute in 1901 and subsequently enrolled as a medical student at the University of Colorado in Boulder.[9] He completed his medical studies at all-black Howard University in Washington, DC.[10]

Historian Thomas J. Ward Jr. describes Howard Medical School as "the first school opened for the purpose of educating African American doctors." Howard began admitting medical students in November 1868. By the time Thompkins enrolled there, the school had tightened both its admissions and graduation requirements. Ward writes, "By 1900, both Meharry [in Nashville] and Howard had adopted the admission procedures of the Association of American Medical Colleges (AAMC), which required that each student either possess a high school diploma or pass an examination in English, arithmetic, algebra, physics, and Latin before admission."[11]

How Thompkins could afford to attend the University of Colorado or Howard University remains unclear. In a late-life interview, his daughter Marion Thompkins Ross recalled that her father often spoke of working on riverboats during the summers while he was a medical student. It is likely that he held one or more jobs during the school year as well. Ward quotes the so-called Flexner Report on medical education in the United States, completed toward the end of the first decade of the twentieth century, as saying "that most of Howard's medical students held outside employment while enrolled at the school." Indeed, Ward writes, "In the late nineteenth century Howard Medical School held classes only between 3:30 and 10 P.M., allowing its students to work at federal jobs in Washington."[12] Thompkins graduated from Howard in 1905 and served an internship at Howard's Freedmen's Hospital in Washington, DC, during the following year.

In 1906 Thompkins returned to Missouri and secured a license to practice medicine in his home state.[13] He moved to Kansas City to engage in medical practice. Why the young doctor chose Kansas City instead of his hometown remains unclear, although, likely, he did not think there were enough African Americans in the capital city to sustain a medical practice. Perhaps, too, he had learned from the experience of Dr. J. Edward Perry, an African American physician who had established a practice in Kansas City three years earlier. A native of Texas and a graduate of Meharry Medical College, Perry tried to open a business in Jefferson City in 1895, during the period when Thompkins was a Lincoln Institute student. According to his memoir, Perry was advised by the Lincoln president, Inman E. Page, that he "had not the money or experience to cope with the local situation." Presumably, this meant that Page thought the whites in Jefferson City would be hostile to the presence of a black doctor and that African Americans were neither numerous nor wealthy enough to sustain a practice by an African American physician. Perry summarized Page's counsel as follows: "He advised me to get out of town as quickly as possible."[14]

Information on Thompkins's first decade of residency and practice in Kansas City is scarce. As early as 1913, he sought to return to Washington, DC, as the "surgeon in chief of Freedm[e]n's Hospital," the same segregated facility where he had completed an internship the previous decade. Seeking to use the connection with Frank P. Walsh that he apparently had established even at that early date, he urged Walsh to contact US Secretary of the Interior Franklin K. Lane and recently elected President Woodrow Wilson on his behalf. In a letter to Secretary Lane, Walsh explained that Thompkins's desire "to have charge of the hospital of his race at Washington, at the bottom, comes from his desire to serve his people and humanity." Thompkins did not get the job.[15]

One year later, in 1914, Thompkins secured an appointment as the superintendent of Kansas City's General Hospital No. 2, a racially segregated public health facility located in the "Old City Hospital" at Twenty-second and Cherry Streets. The building had been vacated by whites in 1908, and between then and 1911, white doctors and nurses, exclusively, treated black patients in the facility. In 1911 four African American doctors and several black nurses joined the staff.[16]

Dr. Thompkins's appointment as superintendent marked the first time an African American physician had held that position. He served in that capacity from 1914 to 1916 and from 1918 to 1922. During his tenure, the hospital gained recognition by the American College of Surgeons, the

Kansas City General Hospital "Colored Division" (courtesy of the State Historical Society of Missouri)

American Medical Association, and the National Hospital Association. Dr. J. Edward Perry, Thompkins's contemporary, recalled in his memoir, "Dr. Thompkins proved an excellent executive and the work and management of the institution continued on a high plane of efficiency under his direction."[17]

In 1917 Thompkins made another attempt to return to Washington, DC, as "Surgeon-in-Chief" at the Freedmen's Hospital. This time he called upon Democrats who controlled the Missouri House of Representatives to endorse his application for the position to President Wilson. On January 18, 1917, the chief clerk of the Missouri House, R. E. L. Morris, and House Speaker Drake Watson wrote the Democratic president, who had been elected to his second term in office, in support of Thompkins's effort. Despite this political endorsement, Thompkins again failed to get the job.[18]

Thompkins's daughter Marion recalled that her father always thought of political activism as a way of achieving health goals for members of his race and, one might add, as a way of promoting his own career. Like a growing minority of other African Americans of his era, Thompkins thought that Republicans at both state and national levels took the African American vote for granted and did not offer enough patronage positions to blacks or enough support for African American causes. According to historian Sherry Lamb Schirmer, Thompkins gave respectability and prestige to a small group of Kansas City black Democrats known as the Negro Central League, which formed in 1900. Likewise, historian Larry Grothaus credits Thompkins with organizing "the Negro Democracy in Kansas City" into an "active and important group" by 1920.[19]

In 1919 Thompkins became involved in a national effort to assert African Americans' rights and privileges throughout the country. Like many blacks of the World War I era, including the famous intellectual and social activist Dr. W. E. B. DuBois, Thompkins recognized the incongruity that young black men were fighting and dying to make the world safe for democracy abroad while being denied access to freedom and equality in the land of their birth. In the wake of the November 1918 armistice that ended the war, Thompkins and scores of Kansas City blacks joined the National Negro Constitution League of America in petitioning Congress to end Jim Crow legislation in the country. Drawing strength from an "awakened sense of justice and freedom," members of the league, including Thompkins, urged Congress to "make inoperative, null and void, all such State Laws as conflict with, and make ineffective, the 14th and 15th Amendments to the Constitution of the United States."[20]

Not satisfied to leave the destiny of African Americans in the hands of disinterested or even hostile whites, Thompkins penned a column in the *Kansas City Sun* a few weeks later under the title "Race Loyalty." He urged African Americans to take greater control of their collective destiny by supporting legislative efforts to establish race-specific social service agencies and institutions that promised to care for, among others, "the Negro blind, deaf, dumb, feebleminded and tubercular." He urged blacks to support increased funding for all-black Lincoln Institute, the appointment of a "Negro deputy superintendent of public schools," and the creation of a "Negro industrial commission" that would "make the Negro people of Missouri self-supporting and a greater economic asset to the state."[21]

Thompkins took particular interest in the high rate of tuberculosis among Missouri blacks during the postwar years, a disease that he referred to as "the great white plague" in his 1919 newspaper call to action. The rate of death from tuberculosis for blacks was nearly four times that of whites during the years after the war. In 1926 the Kansas City Health Department commissioned Thompkins to study the disease among the city's black population. One consequence of that study was the creation of a tuberculosis hospital in the community of Leeds, located at the eastern edge of Kansas City.[22]

His lifelong support of and involvement with the Democratic Party put Thompkins into direct and repeated contact with Kansas City's leading Democrat, political boss Tom Pendergast. In the wake of his 1926 study on tuberculosis, Thompkins was appointed to the city's hygiene department, an appointment that Schirmer argues "represented an alliance between Pendergast forces and the old guard of black Democrats." Not long after his appointment, Thompkins undertook a study of the general health conditions of Kansas Citians, focusing especially on the sad state of sanitation and its consequences in the city's African American neighborhoods. He detailed his findings in a fifteen-page report to Dr. John Lavan, health commissioner of child hygiene and communicable diseases for the city.[23]

In his report Thompkins noted, "The health conditions of this city . . . as far as sanitation is concerned, are worse now than they have ever been." One reason for this, he asserted, was "the large influx of Colored population from the South, and the consequent practice of tenement-house owners of constructing cheap outhouses in conjunction with their poorly constructed homes." Cheap, quick construction occurred in response to the movement of African Americans from South to North and from rural to urban settings as part of what historians call the Great Migration during the era of World War I and the generation that followed it. Kansas City's African American population grew by more than seven thousand persons during the 1910s and by an additional nearly eight thousand during the 1920s.[24]

Thompkins cited other sources of poor sanitation in the black community, including the problem of rats and flies in "certain public meeting places" such as "pool-halls," "pastime or pleasure clubs," and "restaurant and lunch counters." Likewise, he noted, "Another great menace to the health of Negroes comes as a result of poor regulation and supervision of the barber-shops in Colored communities." Indeed, Thompkins's report was, more than anything, a call for new, more forceful government regulations aimed at improving the city's sanitation, especially in African American neighborhoods. Some African Americans in Kansas City objected to Thompkins's report, alleging that the portrayal of blacks as sickly would make whites less likely to hire them.[25]

Meanwhile, Thompkins and Felix Payne Sr., widely known as one of Tom Pendergast's "black associates," moved to establish a new method of recruiting African Americans in Kansas City into the Democratic Party.

In 1928 with the support of Pendergast and probably with his financial backing, they established a black newspaper, the *Kansas City American*. This paper, which tended to support the Democratic Party, offered an antidote to the Republican-leaning African American newspaper in the city, *The Call*, published by Chester A. Franklin. Thompkins emerged as the publisher and editor of the new paper.[26]

During the 1928 presidential election, Thompkins used the pages of the *Kansas City American* to criticize the Republican Party and its presidential candidate, Herbert Hoover. By contrast, he promoted the fortunes of Democratic presidential candidate Al Smith of New York, as well as other Democratic candidates at all levels. In addition, he served as the country's "Central Division" director of the Smith-for-President Colored League. Historian Samuel O'Dell has written that, under Thompkins's guidance, Missouri was "perhaps the best organized state . . . where Smith supporters formed twenty-nine local Smith-for-President clubs."[27]

Smith's loss to Hoover and the latter's four-year reign as president, marked by the onset of the Great Depression, further engaged Thompkins as a Republican critic. In 1932 he took to the campaign trail, making speeches on behalf of Democratic candidate Franklin D. Roosevelt and others of his party. He emerged as the president of a political action group known as the National Colored Democratic Association and used his position and the organization to persuade African Americans to vote the Democratic ticket. White political organizers recognized and sought his power and influence. On June 20, 1932, for example, an assistant to Missouri Democratic gubernatorial candidate Francis M. Wilson wrote to Thompkins, asking for his help in delivering the black vote in the Missouri Bootheel. The aide had learned that "there is a colored Democratic organization, with headquarters in Sikeston that has about three hundred members in this and New Madrid County, and who vote as a unit." He sought Thompkins's advice on making sure that those voters supported Wilson. Likewise, he asked Thompkins to rally the black vote in Kansas City on Wilson's behalf.[28] Meanwhile, Thompkins recalled in a letter to First Lady Eleanor Roosevelt in 1935, he responded to "the request of our National Committeeman, the Honorable W. T. Kemper," who instructed him "to get the Negro press and the Negro leaders into action" in support of "the Roosevelt cause."[29]

In addition to traveling and speaking for Roosevelt and other Democratic candidates during the 1932 campaign, Thompkins used the *Kansas City American* to attack President Hoover and other Republicans. In a hard-hitting editorial entitled "What Can Be Worse than Hoover," published on July 14, Thompkins condemned what he described as the president's "anti-Negro proclivities" and his tendency to support actions "positively inimical to what Negroes consider their best interest[s]."[30]

Roosevelt defeated Hoover in the 1932 election, a contest in which African Americans in the United States evidenced a growing willingness to abandon the Republican Party in an effort to promote their economic interests. Indeed, in Missouri, according to historian Larry Grothaus, "A majority of Blacks . . . voted for the Democratic party in 1932."[31]

Thompkins wasted no time in calling his contributions to this victory to the attention of Roosevelt and his advisers. On November 19, 1932, Thompkins wrote to Louis M. Howe, a close associate of the president-elect, and proclaimed himself to be someone who had spent "twenty-five years' work and devotion for the cause of the party and its ideals." Thompkins assured Howe of his "constancy and persistence," adding that *never once have I been off the range, nor have I been found sulking in my tent*" (emphasis in original). This last comment was likely a reference to such Republican-turned-Democrats as Arthur Wergs Mitchell of Chicago, with whom Thompkins later openly clashed at a meeting of "dominant black Democrats" called by Mitchell in January 1933.[32]

Thompkins hoped that his hard work on behalf of Roosevelt and the Democrats would result in his being appointed to an important patronage position. He spent a great deal of time over the next year trying to gain such an appointment. Especially interested in being named the governor of the Virgin Islands, he explained in a letter to a member of the House Committee on Insular Affairs, "For the President of the United States to name a Colored man Governor of the Virgin Islands would be the highest honor that has ever been recorded a race man in America, and would be the most outstanding stroke that could be made in the way of honoring the Negro race."[33]

Thompkins mustered considerable support from powerful Democrats for his effort to gain the Virgin Islands position. Among his supporters was Kansas City congressman Joseph B. Shannon. Congressman John J. Cochran, Shannon's cross-state colleague, also supported Thompkins's effort. In a letter to James A. Farley, FDR's postmaster general and chairman of the National Democratic Committee, Cochran asserted his belief that "if there is one place in the United States where the Negro is a Democrat it is in Kansas City, Missouri." Cochran credited Thompkins for this reality, adding, "Through the efforts of our good friend, Mr. Thomas Pendergast and others, the Colored man votes the Democratic ticket and is taken care of by the political organization."[34]

Thompkins even solicited the support of Eleanor Roosevelt in his effort to obtain the Virgin Islands position. In a more than eight-hundred-word letter to Mrs. Roosevelt, he outlined his contributions to the Democratic Party and his qualifications for the post. Recognizing the First Lady's empathy for children, he included that, if he received the gubernatorial post, one of his priorities would be to reduce infant mortality among residents of the Virgin Islands.[35]

In the end Thompkins failed to get the Virgin Islands post, and an African American was not appointed to the governorship of that American protectorate until 1946. What Thompkins failed to realize was that he was running up against FDR's so-called Southern strategy, the president's effort to avoid doing anything that would offend white southern congressional leaders, whose support he needed to enact his New Deal program.[36] The president did, however, nominate Thompkins to serve as recorder of deeds for the District of Columbia on March 19, 1934. This nomination came only five days after Farley, the party chairman, endorsed Thompkins's application to a top presidential assistant and assured him that "this appointment has the approval of William T. Kemper, National Committeeman for the State of Missouri, and [Missouri] Senator Bennett Champ Clark." Thompkins's appointment to the recorder's position was safe for the president, inasmuch as the recorder's job had been held by an African American for roughly fifty years, since Frederick Douglass first held it during the early 1880s. Thompkins was confirmed unanimously by the US Senate and assumed the duties of his new office on April 20, 1934, at a salary of $5,600 per year. Four months later, Thompkins wrote to Louis Howe, now secretary to Roosevelt, assuring Howe that he understood the president and his ideals, that he admired Roosevelt, and that he "firmly believe[d]" that "I can sell him to the colored race."[37]

The new job meant that Thompkins, then in his mid-fifties, would have to relocate his family from a home on Euclid Avenue in Kansas City to Washington, DC. Thompkins's Kentucky-born wife, Jessie, whom he had met in Kansas City while she worked as a teacher at Lincoln High School and married on June 17, 1913, was in her mid-forties in 1934. His daughter Helen was eighteen, and daughter Marion, the only family member to survive into the twenty-first century, was only six years old when the family left Kansas City. In a February 2006 interview, she recalled starting elementary school at W. W. Yates School in Kansas City and her family's regular attendance at Metropolitan AME Church. She also had fond memories of the neighborhood in which she grew up, the stories her father told her, and the frequent visits to the family home by her father's close friend and political and business associate, Felix Payne.[38]

Despite the move to Washington, DC, Thompkins remained in close touch with many people in Kansas City, especially Payne. Indeed, he hired Payne's son Felix Jr. to work in the DC recorder's office, as well as other Kansas City African Americans, among them William Dancy. Dancy recalled in a 2001 interview that his father had been an ally of Thompkins and that he had done "a lot of stomping throughout the little towns in Missouri for both Roosevelt and Truman" and that Thompkins had promised his father "that when I got old enough I would have a job." After Dancy graduated from Lincoln High School in Kansas City, he went to work for Thompkins in the District of Columbia's office of the record-er.[39] The Thompkins family returned frequently to Missouri so that Dr. Thompkins could check on his property and business interests in Kansas City and visit an aunt, Eva Carter, who lived in Jefferson City. Thompkins also attended Lincoln University board of curators' meetings in Jefferson City after his appointment to that institution's governing board in 1933.[40]

Thompkins also returned to Missouri during the 1934 political season to campaign for Democratic congressional candidates. In a letter to FDR aide Marvin Hunter McIntyre, Thompkins reported that he had "been in Missouri working in the 10th, 11th and 12th [congressional] districts" and that he had worked especially hard for "the Honorable Thomas C. Hennings, Jr.," who defeated incumbent Leonidas C. Dyer "with more than [a] 15,000 majority in a solid Negro district." Thompkins added, "I am confident that Mr. Hennings is going to make a successful Congress-man for the President and the Party." Thompkins also worked on behalf of a number of lower-profile Jackson County candidates, including Harry S. Truman.[41] In a 1963 interview, longtime Truman friend and associate Harry H. Vaughan confirmed that Thompkins was "a very enthusiastic Truman supporter," adding that Thompkins "was Mr. Truman's particu-lar connection—liaison with the Negro population."[42]

In addition to traveling to Missouri during the off-year election, Thompkins reported to McIntyre that he had gone to Nebraska on behalf of the Democrats. He wrote a booklet describing the benefits of the New Deal, "with special emphasis on the Negroes." Likewise, in a letter to Lou-is Howe, Thompkins itemized the cost to him of producing this booklet, indicating that he regarded the $350.48 he had spent as a "contribution to the success of the greatest Administration in the history of the Unit-ed States." Clearly, Thompkins was trying to let those who mattered in the party know that his appointment to a federal patronage position had been a good choice.[43]

Some months later, during the winter of 1935, Thompkins planned a self-described "Goodwill Tour . . . Through the Heart of the South Preaching the Doctrine of the New Deal." Before he departed, he circulated his proposed remarks to a number of people in the Roosevelt administration and the First Lady. On January 22, 1935, Eleanor Roosevelt responded to Thompkins, telling him, "I think your speech is excellent," although she urged him to emphasize that "the new measures . . . will benefit all and there will be no distinction as to color."[44] Weeks later, on the evening of February 13, Thompkins boarded "the aristocrat of winter trains, 'The Florida Special,'" and traveled to Jacksonville, Miami, St. Petersburg, St. Augustine, Daytona Beach, Palm Beach, and other Florida cities, endeavoring "to show not only what the New Deal has done for the nation, but for our group in particular."[45]

Thompkins's trip through Florida generated a great deal of publicity for himself, his cause, and the president. From Florida, Thompkins traveled through Alabama, making speeches in Mobile and Pascagoula. The *Mobile (AL) Press* quoted Thompkins as identifying Roosevelt as "the greatest humanitarian since Christ."[46] In Mississippi, Thompkins stopped at the Biloxi home of Jefferson Davis, former president of the Confederacy, before going on to Gulfport, Pass Christian, and Bay St. Louis. From Mississippi, he went to New Orleans, where he participated in Mardi Gras. Thompkins next motored to Montgomery, Alabama, and then to Birmingham. He visited Tuskegee Institute, where he found two women whom he had trained as nurses at Kansas City's General Hospital No. 2. He also spent time with the aging African American scientist George Washington Carver.[47]

Although he no longer lived in Kansas City, Thompkins maintained a financial and managerial interest in the *Kansas City American*, and he guided the newspaper's support of FDR and other Democrats. In a letter to the president in late 1935, he assured Roosevelt that he continued "to interpret to our many readers of the *Kansas City American* my conception of the ideals for which you have stood and now stand."[48]

The 1936 election season saw Thompkins traveling again throughout the Midwest and South in support of his party. Among the many speeches on behalf of the president that he delivered that year was one in late February at the Bishops Council of the African Methodist Episcopal Church of America, Africa, and the West Indies, held at the Ebenezer Church in Kansas City, Missouri. Thompkins took the occasion to applaud the president's "social justice program" and hailed his tendency "to recognize merit without regard to race[,] color[,] or conditions." He urged "our people" to support the president so that his administration could "keep open the door of hope" to all people.[49]

Whenever Thompkins spoke, letters of praise for his efforts poured in to Democratic Party leaders in an effort at adulation that one suspects the doctor had a hand in orchestrating. After speeches by Thompkins in Taft and Muskogee, Oklahoma, for example, he was praised by the superintendent of the Oklahoma State Hospital for Negro Insane as a "great leader" who could bring "one hundred thousand disciples" to the Democratic cause, if he could but "have a few more days to present the cause."[50] Sam Battles, the white Democratic State Central Committee chairman for Oklahoma, concurred, explaining in a letter to President Roosevelt that he had heard Thompkins deliver "a very logical report of the accomplishments of this administration," adding patronizingly, "He is one of the first Negroes that it has been my privilege to hear that appealed to logic rather than the emotions of the people." Battles concluded, "I consider his work very much worthwhile among his people."[51]

During the 1940 political campaign, Thompkins spent a considerable amount of time in Missouri, working on behalf of his old friend and political ally Harry S. Truman in the latter's race for the US Senate against Missouri governor Lloyd C. Stark. According to Truman scholar Robert H. Ferrell, Truman appointed Thompkins "general chairman of the Negro Division" for his campaign in Missouri. Thompkins traveled throughout the state on Truman's behalf and often gave the man from Independence advice. Indeed, Ferrell credits Thompkins with helping Truman to craft a speech in Sedalia during the campaign. The occasion was the dedication of a hospital for African Americans, and Truman, at the urging of Thompkins, pledged his belief "in the brotherhood of man, not merely the brotherhood of white men, but the brotherhood of all men before the law." As Ferrell writes, "It was an extraordinary thing to say in outstate Missouri, where southern ideas and ways dominated . . . [Truman] was making a bid for black support in a tight race."[52]

In addition to his work on Truman's behalf, Thompkins campaigned again for President Roosevelt's reelection, just as he had done in 1936. During the final days of the campaign, he chronicled his travels and speech-making on behalf of the president through West Virginia, Ohio, Indiana, Illinois, and Missouri in a series of letters to General Edwin M. Watson, secretary to the president. In back-to-back letters to Watson on October 28 and 29, 1940, he lamented the fact that the popular African American heavyweight boxer Joe Louis had endorsed Roosevelt's opponent, Wendell Willkie, but then reported to Watson that he had picked up the endorsement of Jessie Owens, the African American track star and hero of the 1936 Olympics. Thompkins explained to Watson that he believed "Owens would be the better in oratorical combat and the worse [*sic*] that could happen would be a stalemate contest." In one of the letters, Thompkins signed himself as "Just a private in the ranks without portfolio."[53]

Roosevelt won an unprecedented third-term victory in the 1940 election. Thompkins sent him a "victory ham," purchased in central Missouri, on November 5. Sending "victory hams" to celebrate political victories had become a tradition for Thompkins by this time.[54]

Thompkins was growing increasingly restive as a "private in the ranks" of the Democratic Party, however. On June 26, 1941, he wrote to Marvin H. McIntyre in an effort to help an old friend, Frederick S. Weaver of Missouri, obtain a patronage position. Thompkins began his letter by telling McIntyre, "For some time Negro Democrats have been trying to obtain jobs in the Federal Departments, and, as I have told you before, many of these Negro Democrats have become disillusioned because prominent positions have been filled by Negroes who have never worked for the Democratic Party." Clearly frustrated that he had not been consulted about the Department of Agriculture's intent to hire Sherman Briscoe of Chicago as "Negro writer" for the department, Thompkins lashed out at the appointment: "Mr. Briscoe is hardly a Democrat or I would have heard of him. He is hardly a competent newspaper man, or I would know something of his record in that regard, being an editor myself. I have contacted several prominent Negro writers and none have heard of him."[55]

Thompkins was not the only African American unhappy with the president and his party. This was the era in which labor leader A. Philip Randolph threatened the president with a march on Washington if the latter did not take steps to help African Americans obtain jobs in the growing defense industry. According to historian Thomas Lee Green, it was Thompkins who "alerted the administration to Brotherhood of Sleeping Car Porters president A. Philip Randolph's intention to stage a march on Washington."[56]

Despite his growing unhappiness with the Roosevelt administration, Thompkins continued serving as the recorder of deeds for the District of Columbia under the Democratic president. He also remained active as an organizer of African American voters for the Democratic Party and a promoter of Democratic causes throughout the country, although during the last year of his life, he grew increasingly disturbed with the president and the party for their failure to provide more patronage positions for

African Americans. Because of his prominence as a national spokesman for black Democrats, Thompkins often received letters from disenchanted African Americans throughout the country, some of whom threatened to abandon the Democratic Party and turn to the Republicans. Increasingly alienated from the Roosevelt administration, Thompkins grew critical of many African Americans who had gained favor with the president. In June 1943 he blasted Roosevelt's "Black Cabinet" as "political snobs," most of whom, he argued, "partake of political largess as if it were their due, and never lift a finger to further the interests of the Democratic party."[57]

Two months later, as talk about a Roosevelt fourth term grew louder, Thompkins wrote to James L. Houghteling, director of the National Organization Section of the US Treasury Department, warning that the Democrats were in trouble with African Americans. Thompkins enclosed a list of names of seventy-six African Americans from nineteen states who, he asserted, "have been ignored or overlooked." He urged that the men and women whose names appeared on the list be rewarded for their work on behalf of the Democratic Party and the president, explaining in the folksy way that he sometimes employed, "The mule who plows the corn should eat some of the corn."[58]

Dr. William J. Thompkins did not live to see Roosevelt's election to a fourth term. He died three months before the 1944 election, on August 4. Among his mourners was the president of the United States, who sent Jessie Thompkins a telegram the next day, expressing his "heartfelt sympathy" in the wake of her husband's passing. Had Thompkins lived just nine more months, he would have witnessed his old friend Harry S. Truman's advancement to the presidency. Marion Thompkins Ross, Thompkins's younger daughter, recalled that her mother often commented that if Thompkins had lived to see a Truman presidency, he could have gotten any position he wanted from the man from Missouri. Alas, he did not. He left behind, however, a remarkable legacy of loyalty to the Democratic Party, to his profession, and to his people, as a "race man" of great talent and energy.[59]

Chapter 14

The Abraham Lincoln Legacy
in Missouri

In late spring of 1955 the famous artist Thomas Hart Benton, who was born in Newton County, Missouri, in 1889, stood before a large audience in Inman E. Page Library on the Lincoln University campus in Jefferson City.[1] He was there to unveil and dedicate his recently completed mural that he had donated to the university, a painting honoring President Abraham Lincoln and his legacy. In the dedicatory address, Benton described Lincoln as:

> the symbol of something even greater than his place in the clash of events. He has come to stand for a universal and eternal impulse of the human soul, valid not only in a grim period of our own history but valid in all periods of all history. That is the impulse to be free, free not only from some particular bondage, but from all bondage, from all tyranny, from all injustice, and from all the inherited misfortunes that an historical fate may have imposed, or that some doctrinal fanaticism may try to impose.[2]

As a symbol of the aspiration toward freedom, President Abraham Lincoln was a controversial figure in Missouri during the 1860 presidential election. Many Missourians, especially those who owned slaves or who traced their ancestry to the South, perceived Lincoln, the candidate of the less-than-a-decade-old Republican Party, as an extremist who was in the company of abolitionists.

Four presidential candidates appeared on the ballot in Missouri in November 1860. Stephen A. Douglas, the "popular sovereignty" candidate from Illinois, carried the state by 429 votes out of more than 165,000 cast. Senator John Bell, the "old-line Whig from Tennessee" and a moderate, ran second. The pro-Southern candidate, Vice President John C. Breckenridge, ran a poor third, receiving 31,317 votes. Lincoln came in a distant fourth, garnering only 17,028 votes, or roughly 10 percent of the total. Thus, as a symbol of freedom in a state where more than a hundred thousand slaves resided, the Illinoisan attracted little support.[3]

Lincoln took office in March 1861. By that time, seven Southern states had seceded from the Union and created the Confederate States of America. Fearing that other slave states, including Missouri, would soon join the rebellious seven, the new president moved cautiously and tentatively, trying not to offend border-state slave owners.[4]

In August 1861 Lincoln was appalled by what he regarded as the dangerous and precipitous action of General John C. Fremont who announced his intent to confiscate "the property of those who had taken up arms against the Union." General Fremont made it clear that "property" included slaves, who would subsequently be freed. Fearing that Fremont's action would cause the border states, particularly Kentucky and Missouri, to side with the Confederacy, the president directed the general to rescind his order. When Fremont refused to do so, Lincoln removed him from command and rescinded the order himself. This action caused Missourians to divide even more firmly in their attitudes toward the president. Residents of the slaveholding Boonslick counties along the Missouri River applauded Lincoln's decision, while opponents of slavery, such as the editor of the *St. Louis Missouri Democrat* and the German press throughout the state, criticized it.[5]

A year later, pressure from the Radicals within his party prompted the president to contemplate taking the action that history would come to know as the Emancipation Proclamation. Issued in its final form in January 1863, the proclamation freed all slaves residing in states in official rebellion against the Union. Since Missouri was not officially in rebellion, the slaves of Missourians were not freed by the Emancipation Proclamation. Indeed, Missouri slaves would not be formally freed until January 11, 1865, when a state constitutional convention meeting in St. Louis voted to abolish the institution forthwith.[6]

In subsequent years, Missouri blacks celebrated the anniversary of their emancipation on a variety of dates. Sometimes the January 11 date was chosen. At other times, emancipation commemorations were held in September, on or around the date that President Lincoln announced his intention to free Southern slaves in 1862. The most enduring Emancipation Day celebration in Missouri, however, came on or around August 4 each year. Oral tradition in the black community suggests that this date was chosen in part because all slaves were emancipated in the British Empire on August 1, 1834, but also because August 4 was a month after America's Independence Day, a metaphorical acknowledgment of the delay African Americans experienced in achieving their freedom. As one elderly man explained in a late-life interview, "White folks had their day for celebrating freedom [July 4]; black folks wanted their own day, too." Fielding Draffen of Kansas City summed up the significance of August 4 for black people when he was growing up in Saline County during the decade of the 1930s: "When I was a kid . . . the fourth of August was sacred to African American people. By the threat of death you didn't even go to work on that day. You celebrated on that day . . . people would talk about it coming up. . . . It was considered a day [on which] you kind of reflected on what your ancestors came through and [you] just kind of enjoyed the day."[7]

Although Lincoln's Emancipation Proclamation did not directly impact Missouri slaves, it did establish the principle that emancipation was a goal of the Civil War. Consequently, it emboldened many Missouri slaves to abandon their masters and seek a life of freedom elsewhere, especially if Union soldiers were operating in their communities. Examples of this phenomenon are plentiful, including in the writings and reports of Brigadier General Clinton B. Fisk, commander of the Department of North Missouri. In a report to Major General William Rosecrans, Department of the Missouri commander, for example, General Fisk noted, "Two negro men, the property of James I. Hickman, of Boone County, in the month of February, 1863, ran away from their owner and sought refuge within our lines at Jefferson City." Likewise, in early March 1865, General Fisk, writing from Macon, Missouri, reported, "There are many negroes with their families seeking homes, fleeing from their old masters and from fear of assassination by guer[r]illas."[8] In January 1864 the *Howard County Advertiser*, published in Fayette, reported, "We learn that negro men, women and children are crossing [the Missouri River] in considerable numbers on the ice, from this county, en route for Tipton."[9]

Yet another of Lincoln's actions caused a number of Missouri slaves to seek to abandon their masters. Although Lincoln opposed the arming of African Americans for the Union cause early in the war, by the early spring of 1863, after a series of setbacks for his army in the field, the president became an unabashed proponent of using what he referred to as "the Sable Arm." Writing in March 1863 to Andrew Johnson, governor of Tennessee, Lincoln described "the colored population [as] the great *available* and yet *unavailed of* force for restoring the Union." The president added, "The bare sight of 50,000 armed and drilled black soldiers upon the banks of the Mississippi would end the rebellion at once."[10]

Toward that end, and with the support of the president and legal authorization from Congress, Union officers began recruiting black soldiers, especially in the border states, including Missouri, by the fall of 1863. This created quite a controversy in the state, even after it was agreed that loyal owners whose slaves enlisted would be compensated three hundred dollars for each slave lost. At least some slave owners and other Southern sympathizers, especially in central Missouri, resisted the recruitment of black soldiers with violence.[11] According to historian John Blassingame, "In such counties as Monroe and Macon, patrols of slave owners and guer[r]illas blocked attempts of the slaves to enlist. In several instances in Callaway County a band of owners followed companies of Negroes going to enlist, 'shooting among them, killing and wounding some,' and carrying back to slavery all they could capture."[12] General Fisk reported to Major J. W. Barnes, assistant adjutant general of the Department of the Missouri, "[Guerrilla] Jim Jackson and company are roaming through Boone, Callaway, and Howard Counties. They are chiefly engaged in plundering and murdering negroes. They have hung two negroes in Boone and one in Callaway County within the last few days."[13]

The recruitment of black soldiers in Missouri and the associated violence and threat of violence against black men had at least two profound and long-lasting impacts on African American life in the state. The first was a tendency of African Americans to move from the rural countryside into cities and towns, especially towns where Federal troops were garrisoned such as Cape Girardeau, Ironton, Rolla, Springfield, and Jefferson City. This was dramatically clear in Cole County, the seat of Missouri state government, where antislavery state and local politicians gained increased power as the war wore on and where large numbers of Federal soldiers were stationed throughout the conflict. In August 1864 a member of the City of Jefferson's Board of Aldermen called that body's attention "to the very annoying condition of the city d[e]riving from the great increase of Colored people who are everyday congregating from other parts of the country."[14] In January 1865 the Cole County sheriff conducted a special census of the capital city's black population and discovered that it had grown from 333 persons in 1860 to 565 at the time of the census, an increase of 70 percent.[15]

A corollary to this demographic shift is that many African Americans, especially black males of military age, left the state altogether in an effort to escape bushwhacker violence. General Fisk took note of this reality in

March 1865 when he commented that he was helping "the poor blacks" who were fleeing the violence to find homes "in Northwest Missouri, Kansas, Illinois, and Iowa."[16]

Large slave-owning counties such as Boone, Howard, Cooper, and Saline in the Missouri River valley actually lost black population between 1860 and 1870. Despite the fact that the *counties* lost African American residents during that period, however, towns in those counties tended to gain in population. Boone County, for example, fell from 5,766 blacks in 1860 to 5,097 in 1870; yet the town of Columbia grew from 541 blacks in 1860 to 798 in 1870.[17] So, one aspect of Lincoln's legacy in Missouri is that the Civil War and President Lincoln's policies contributed to the urbanization of Missouri's black population decades before the state as a whole became more urban than rural.[18]

A second point that needs to be made about the mobility of African Americans during the Civil War years is the tendency toward gender imbalance in many of Missouri's black communities during the generation after the war, and extending through the remainder of the century. In the Cooper County town of Boonville, for example, "black" and "mulatto" women outnumbered men 52 to 48 percent in 1870 and 55 to 45 percent in 1880. As late as 1890, African American women still outnumbered men, 588 to 502.[19]

Similarly, in Boone County's Columbia, African American females outnumbered males 56 to 44 percent in 1870 and 55 to 45 percent in 1880. Twenty-five years after war's end, in 1890, black females in Columbia outnumbered males 902 to 692. Marshall, in Saline County, witnessed a transformation from a slave population in 1860 that was 55 percent male to a freedmen population in 1870 that was 52 percent female. By 1890 African American females still outnumbered males 420 to 336. Although the cause of this imbalance remains unclear and insufficiently researched, it may be that black males of the Civil War era felt more threatened than black females did and, thus, decided to leave the area.[20]

One consequence of this gender imbalance was that black women were forced to enter the paid labor force in larger numbers and far earlier than white women. Black educators such as Josephine Silone Yates, who came to Missouri to teach at Lincoln Institute in Jefferson City in 1881, focused on training young black women to develop breadwinners' skills so that they could become "self-sustaining, independent, [and] self-reliant." The survival of black women, Yates and others argued, hinged upon their ability to learn "cooking, sewing and other useful employments."[21]

The penchant of African Americans to congregate in groups in towns and cities carried over into the countryside, with blacks creating self-sufficient and interdependent communities all over the state during the generation following the Civil War. Pennytown, south of the Saline County seat of Marshall, Missouri, is one such example. The community's namesake, Joseph Penny, was a middle-aged freedman from Kentucky who moved to the county during the late 1860s. Penny spent several years as a tenant farmer until in March 1871 he had accumulated enough money to buy eight acres of land from a white landowner for $160. This was marginal agricultural land "on the edge of Saline's great rolling prairie and within the timbered breaks of [the] Blackwater River drainage."[22]

During the next several years, a number of other enterprising blacks bought property adjacent to Penny's, and a freedmen's hamlet emerged. By 1879 this communal group of settlers owned almost sixty-four acres in tracts ranging from one and one-fourth to twenty acres. In 1880 there were twenty-six all-black households in Saline County's Salt Fork Township, and an additional twelve white households with black occupants. The agricultural census for that year suggests a division of labor and sharing within the black settlement. Of eleven landowners, three had some machinery, eight had a horse or two, six had milk cows (although only four produced butter), seven had swine, three raised wheat, seven raised corn, two raised tobacco, three raised Irish potatoes, three raised apple trees, six cultivated peach trees, apparently all had poultry and eggs, six produced molasses, seven cut cordwood, and three had built some fencing. These figures and the community's oral tradition help define a domestic environment of communal living in part-time gardening, farming, hunting, fishing, and working out for neighboring white commercial agriculturalists.[23]

Island communities of African Americans like Pennytown emerged all over the state of Missouri during the generation after the Civil War, including in the rural Ozarks. More than seven decades ago, the great African American scholar W. E. B. DuBois, writing in a now-classic book titled *Black Reconstruction in America*, noted that first and foremost freedmen wanted "land which they could own and work for their own crops. . . . They wanted little farms which would make them independent."[24]

African Americans fleeing racial repression in the South during the 1870s found land literally for the taking in the rural Missouri Ozarks. This land was available because of the passage of the Homestead Act, a law supported by President Lincoln and enacted by Congress in 1862.

The legislation went into effect in January 1863, the same month and year that the Emancipation Proclamation became law. The Homestead Act "offered . . . settlers free title to 160 acres . . . [of land] after they had established residence and improved the land for five years."[25]

By the mid- to late 1870s, the "good land" in Missouri had been gobbled up by entrepreneurial farmers, most of them white. But there was still some unclaimed, rocky, hilly land in the Ozarks. Despite the poor quality, it was still land, and African Americans moved to claim it. The federal census of 1870 reveals only 26 African Americans in the Ozark county of Wright in that year. A decade later, in 1880, an influx of black Exodusters from the South, most of them from Tennessee, had increased the county's African American population tenfold, to 260 persons.[26] These black residents tilled the soil, raised their families, and created social and cultural institutions that sustained them during the awful and trying Jim Crow years. They built homes, schools, and churches that formed the core of their existence until, a generation or more later, another set of historical circumstances caused their migration from the Ozarks to urban centers such as Kansas City, St. Louis, Chicago, and Detroit.[27]

Another black settlement in the rural Ozarks that emerged during this period was the community of Eldridge, located in Laclede County about midway between Camdenton and Lebanon. Laclede County's African American population almost tripled between 1870 and 1880. There has not been an African American living in Eldridge, however, since Eunice Kenoly Winfrey's family moved away in 1941. Yet the town is named for a black man and was once a predominantly black town.[28]

Alfred Eldridge came to Missouri from Tennessee during the late 1870s. He homesteaded a quarter section of land (160 acres) in Township 36, Section 27, of Hooker (later Eldridge) Township. Apparently other Exodusters coming through followed Eldridge's example and settled on unclaimed land as well. A black community emerged, served by a general store operated by Eldridge. By the early twentieth century, a Laclede County newspaper (the *Sentinel*) had taken to referring to this part of the county as "Little Africa."[29] There were at least three other black neighborhoods in Missouri during the late nineteenth century that were also known as Little Africa: one each in Hickory, Howard, and Pike Counties. Butler County had a post–Civil War African American hamlet east of Poplar Bluff named Morocco by whites.[30]

In addition to land, one of the things freedmen craved most in the immediate postwar period was access to education. W. E. B. DuBois, writing in the 1935 book referenced earlier, *Black Reconstruction*, had this to say about the freedmen's yearning for educational opportunities: "They [the freedmen] wanted to know; they wanted to be able to interpret the cabalistic letters and figures which were the key to more. They were consumed with curiosity at the meaning of the world. . . . [As a consequence] they were consumed with desire for schools. The uprising of the black man, and the pouring of himself into organized effort for education, in those years between 1861 and 1871, was one of the marvelous occurrences of the modern world; almost without parallel in the history of civilization."[31]

In this regard, the former slaves' hunger for education reflected the aspiration for freedom referred to by Thomas Hart Benton in his 1955 address, in this case the desire to escape the ignorance that white society tried to impose on slaves during the antebellum period. This makes perfect sense, given the fact that African Americans had been denied access to education as slaves. An 1847 Missouri law made it illegal even for masters to teach their own slaves to read and write.[32]

Not surprisingly, President Lincoln's role as the Great Emancipator was memorialized by the naming for him of many schools for blacks established in Missouri after the Civil War. Indeed, there were schools named for the sixteenth president throughout the state, and the practice continued into the middle of the twentieth century. Throughout this period, Missouri law required black and white students to be educated in racially separate schools.[33]

In Saline County, where Abraham Lincoln was anything but popular and where pro-Confederacy sentiment continued after the war, the name of the slain president appeared on multiple school buildings for African Americans. In the county seat of Marshall, for example, the black school was called Lincoln, and in the small village of Arrow Rock (once home to the rabidly secessionist governor Claiborne Fox Jackson, an owner of many slaves), a black school was named for the Great Emancipator. Likewise, the Saline county communities of Gilliam, Blackburn, Miami, and Mount Leonard also had Lincoln schools that continued to provide educational opportunities for former slaves and their descendants until school desegregation occurred in the late 1950s.[34]

In Howard County, the county with the second-largest number of slaves in the state on the eve of the Civil War, the town of Fayette had a Lincoln School for blacks that operated for decades. One of the many interesting people associated with this school was Fannie Marie Tolson, who attended the school during the 1920s and 1930s and then came back to teach there until integration closed its doors in the mid-1950s.[35] Adjacent Chariton

Lincoln School, Fayette, Missouri (courtesy of the Fannie Marie Tolson Collection, the State Historical Society of Missouri)

County had African American schools named for President Lincoln in Salisbury and in the county seat of Keytesville.

Southwest of Keytesville, in Pettis County's Sedalia, black students attended a Lincoln School, established in 1868 in a frame building north of the railroad tracks. The school was located in an all-black section of town set aside for African Americans by town founder George R. Smith after the Civil War. The neighborhood, known as Lincolnville, served as yet another lasting tribute to the martyred president.[36]

West of Sedalia, the Johnson County town of Holden had a Lincoln School. Still farther west, in Kansas City, a school for African Americans was established in 1867. Located at modern-day Tenth and McGee Streets, the school soon became known as the Lincoln School and began offering high school classes in 1882. In 1902 a new Lincoln High School was built at Nineteenth and Tracy, where it remained until 1936, when a larger facility was erected at Twenty-first and Woodland.[37]

Lincoln High School, Kansas City (courtesy of the Irene Whitley Marcus Collection, the State Historical Society of Missouri)

In neighboring Clay County, Excelsior Springs had a Lincoln School for many years, a facility that served the community's rather large black population, which was drawn to the town because of jobs associated with the spas and bathhouses for which the city was famous. A Lincoln School for African American students also existed in St. Joseph (Buchanan County). Nearby, in the Caldwell County town of Hamilton, there was another Lincoln School. Four counties south, in Henry County, a Lincoln School emerged in Clinton in a two-story frame building formerly used by white students. After this building was destroyed by fire during the 1890s, it was replaced by a much larger Italianate structure designed to accommodate the influx of African Americans into the town during the last decade of the nineteenth century.

In southwest Missouri, the mining towns of Joplin and Carthage had African American schools named for President Lincoln. The same was true in the Newton County town of Neosho, where a succession of black schools named for Lincoln existed, the last one built in 1940. In Springfield the "colored" school became known as the Lincoln School soon after the Civil War. There was also a Lincoln School in nearby Ash Grove, about twenty miles northwest of Springfield.

The Howell County town of West Plains also had a Lincoln School. One of the oldest extant Lincoln School buildings remaining in Missouri is in the Phelps County town of Rolla. Built in 1882, this Lincoln School continued to serve black students until the early 1950s.

Lincoln Schools in the Bootheel were located in Charleston and Sikeston. Following the Mississippi River north, one could find schools named for the president in Ste. Genevieve and St. Mary. Pike County had Lincoln Schools in Bowling Green and in Louisiana. Moving toward the interior of the state, Lincoln Schools existed in the Adair County town of Kirksville and in Shelby County's Shelbina, a railroad town with a large community of freedmen after the Civil War.

Unquestionably, the most famous of the Missouri schools named for the sixteenth president of the United States was Lincoln Institute, located in Jefferson City and since 1921 known as Lincoln University. Lincoln Institute was the brainchild of black Missouri soldiers who enlisted to serve the Union cause during the Civil War. According to Richard Baxter Foster, a white officer with the Sixty-second US Colored Infantry, the men of his unit were sitting around a campfire at Fort McIntosh, Texas, in January 1866 when conversation turned to the topic of what could be done to establish a school for freedmen in Missouri. These soldiers had been taught to read and write by their white officers, including the abolitionist Foster, and they resolved to pass on this legacy of learning to their fellow Missourians back home.[38]

The men of the Sixty-second began to collect money and pledges of money for the venture—roughly five thousand dollars in all. They pooled their money with the nearly fourteen hundred dollars raised by the Sixty-fifth US Colored Infantry, also a unit composed of black Missourians.[39]

The soldiers entrusted their money to Lieutenant Foster and sent him to Missouri to open a school for blacks. After an unsuccessful attempt at establishing the school in St. Louis, Foster decided to try to launch the venture in Jefferson City, the state capital. Although he did not address the issue directly, it seems likely that Foster chose Jefferson City because he knew the Radical Republicans were in power in Missouri, and he hoped they would support his aborning school. He was right. The first board of trustees, organized in Jefferson City, included Radical governor Thomas C. Fletcher, state superintendent of schools Thomas A. Parker, and federal district judge Arnold Krekel. Begun as a private subscription school in 1866, Lincoln received its first state support in 1870 after black political leader James Milton Turner delivered twenty thousand black votes to the Republican Party in Missouri in exchange for a five-thousand-dollar state appropriation. Lincoln soon became the state's training school for black teachers. The 1870 election marked the first of many such contests in which African Americans would support the political party of the Great Emancipator. Indeed, part of the Lincoln legacy in Missouri was that African Americans in the Show-Me State overwhelmingly supported the Republican Party at the polls from 1870 until 1932.[40]

Throughout the late nineteenth and early twentieth centuries, Lincoln Institute was the only state-supported institution of higher education in Missouri that admitted African Americans. In the wake of World War I and the contributions made by black soldiers to the war effort, many African Americans in Missouri began to speak out in favor of an end to Jim Crow restrictions, including the practice of excluding blacks from the University of Missouri. Rather than open the university in Columbia to blacks, the legislature in 1921 renamed Lincoln Institute so that it would henceforth be known as Lincoln University. They also increased Lincoln's budget somewhat so that better-qualified faculty could be hired. Beginning in the early 1920s, the newly designated university recruited talented African Americans from reputable schools, including Harvard, Cornell, and Columbia Universities. Lincoln University, named for the sixteenth president of the United States, thus became widely known for a generation as the "Black Harvard of the Midwest." In those days, when a black student sought a course of study unavailable at Lincoln, the procedure they followed was to apply to the University of Missouri, be rejected, and then take their letter of rejection to the Missouri legislature, which would then appropriate money to send them to an out-of-state institution.[41]

In the 1938 landmark case known as *Gaines v. Missouri*, the US Supreme Court ordered the state of Missouri either to admit African American students to the University Of Missouri School of Law or to provide a separate law school for black students. Consistent with its record to date, the state created a Lincoln University School of Law for African American students.[42]

The name of Abraham Lincoln continues to resonate with African Americans throughout the state and the nation, even in the twenty-first century. In a 2006 interview, an elderly black playwright and former Lincoln University professor, born in Mississippi and reared in Virginia, remarked that even though he had lived through Franklin Roosevelt's New Deal, John Kennedy's New Frontier, and Lyndon Johnson's Great

Society, he could not bring himself to support the Democratic Party because, to him, "Democrats are a party of segregation." To this man, the memory of President Lincoln's role as the Great Emancipator was more important than all of the civil rights efforts promoted by Democrats during the post–World War II era.[43] The sixteenth president, as this man understands, and as Thomas Hart Benton understood a half century ago, "has come to stand for a universal . . . impulse of the human soul . . . the impulse to be free." It is a lasting legacy, worthy of remembrance and celebration as we commemorate the bicentennial of the birth of President Abraham Lincoln.

Epilogue

New Sources and Directions for Research on the African American Experience in Missouri

An abundance of relatively new and often easily accessible sources are available to twenty-first-century scholars of the African American experience in Missouri. In the Prologue to this anthology, I commented on the "cultural resource survey" as a new way of doing African American history. There are two large bodies of cultural-resource-related research records available online that can be accessed through the website of the State Historic Preservation Office (SHPO) at the Missouri Department of Natural Resources.

The first link (http://www.dnr.mo.gov/shpo/mnrlist.htm) takes a researcher to a large body of National Register nominations arranged by Missouri counties. These nominations provide in-depth research on specific structures still standing in Missouri, along with supportive data that document why those buildings are deemed eligible for inclusion in the National Register of Historic Places. Clicking on the Audrain County link, for example, allows researchers to access a footnoted narrative about the history of the Lincoln School for African Americans, a building that still stands in the city of Vandalia, Missouri. The Boone County link takes researchers to information about a number of African American historic sites, including four key social and cultural institutions of the City of Columbia: the John W. "Blind" Boone House, residence of the famous ragtime pianist; the Frederick Douglass School, which served the city's African American community for decades; and, two important African American churches, St. Paul's AME Church and the Second Baptist Church. The Cole County link provides access to information about the Jefferson City Community Center on East Dunklin Street, a structure that served as a principal gathering place for the capital city's

African American population from the time it was built in 1942 until the mid-1960s and beyond, when the City of Jefferson finally opened public places of accommodation to African American citizens. Additionally, the Cole County site features the nomination for the Lincoln University Hilltop Historic District. Lincoln University was Missouri's only public institution of higher education for African Americans for more than a half century after the Civil War. Likewise, the Saline County link takes a researcher to the nomination for the Freewill Baptist Church of Pennytown, south of Marshall, Missouri. This church is the only remaining structure in what was once a vibrant post–Civil War African American community. Information about scores of buildings that hold the key to vast amounts of African American history in Missouri can be accessed through these National Register nominations.

In addition, another link available from the SHPO/DNR website (http: www.dnr.mo.gov/shop/survey-eg.htm) provides access to "A Sampling of Architectural Surveys." Among these surveys is one titled "African American Schools in Rural and Small Town Missouri." The purpose of this survey, conducted by historians Gary R. Kremer and Brett Rogers, was to identify and describe buildings still standing in the state that once housed segregated African American schools. The survey, funded jointly by William Woods University and the Missouri State Historic Preservation Office, includes hundreds of pages of narrative, photographs, maps, and summations of oral histories collected and produced between 1999 and 2002. The full text of the survey may be accessed at the following websites:

> http://www.dnr.mo.gov/shpo/survey/SWAS021-R.pdf
> http://www.dnr.mo.gov/shpo/survey/SWAS2022-R.pdf
> http://www.dnr.mo.gov/shpo/survey/SWAS2023-R.pdf
> http://www.dnr.mo.gov/shpo/survey/SWAS024-R.pdf

Beyond the online sources available from the SHPO/DNR website, an additional body of cultural-resource-survey work can be accessed in original hard copy at the archives of the State Historic Preservation Office, located at the headquarters of the Missouri Department of Natural Resources in the Lewis and Clark State Office Building in Jefferson City, Missouri. It is worth noting that the African Americans who attended segregated schools and frequented segregated businesses prior to court-ordered integration during the mid- to late 1950s are reaching advanced age. Researchers interested in recording their stories should make taking their oral histories a priority.

Arguably, the most significant "new" research materials available to scholars of African American history in Missouri are the countless local public records housed in the state's courthouses and city halls. Always present but not widely accessible until the emergence of the Missouri State Archives' Local Records Program during the early 1990s, this material has been unearthed, rescued, and made available by local records archivists who work in this program.

Among the most visible results of the local records program has been the St. Louis Circuit Court Historical Records Project. This project, jointly engaged in by the State Archives, the St. Louis Circuit Court, and the American Culture Studies Program at Washington University, St. Louis, has produced the "Freedom Suit Case Files, 1814–1860" (http://stl-courtrecords.wustl.edu/about-freedom-suits-series.php). These case files include, not surprisingly, the most famous freedom suit of all, that of the slave Dred Scott, but they also include more than three hundred others, among them the case of *Winny v. Phebe Whitesides*, an early nineteenth-century case begun in 1819, two years before Missouri statehood. The Dred Scott opinion rendered by the Missouri Supreme Court, along with many other race-related Missouri Supreme Court cases, can be accessed at the Missouri State Archives' "Supreme Court of Missouri Historical Records" website (http://www.sos.mo.gov/archives/judiciary/supremecourt/default.asp).

Bob Moore at the Jefferson National Expansion Memorial in St. Louis, in conjunction with Missouri State Archives local records archivist Mike Everman and a bevy of interns, has developed a website titled "African American Life in St. Louis, 1804–1865" (http://www.nps.gov/jeff/historyculture/african-american-life-in-saint-louis-1804-through-1865.htm). Among the items on this site are lists of the freedom suits, lists of emancipations through the circuit courts, lists/database of free Negro licenses through the county court, and lists/database of slave auctions through the St. Louis Probate Court.

The vast majority of circuit court case records remain undigitized and are housed in courthouses in the counties in which the cases originally occurred. These cases are as diverse as they are fascinating; they provide a great deal of insight into every era of Missouri history.

The Callaway County case of *State of Missouri v. Celia* is an exception. This case, which documents the circumstances surrounding the

1850s instance of a young slave woman (Celia) who killed her master after being sexually abused by him for years, was recently digitized and can be found online (http://law2.umkc.edu/faculty/projects/ftrials/celia/celiahome.html). Ultimately Celia was executed, after a judge refused to accept her attorney's effort at a self-defense plea and after an all-white jury, half of whose members were slave owners, found her guilty of capital murder. This circuit court case served as the foundation and principal source of Melton A. McLaurin's highly acclaimed 1991 book, *Celia: A Slave.*

A Cooper County, Missouri, circuit court case, *Hickam v. Hickam*, documents the case of a Cooper County slave who alleged that she was not informed of her emancipation until twenty-four years after slavery officially ended in Missouri. Eda Hickam claimed that the Hickam family of Moniteau and later Cooper Counties continued to enslave her until after the family patriarch, Joseph Hickam, died in the summer of 1889. This case was the focal point of an essay by Rebecca Weber Bowen titled "Her Will against Theirs: Eda Hickam and the Ambiguity of Freedom in Postbellum Missouri" (in *Women in Missouri History: In Search of Power and Influence*, ed. LeeAnn Whites et al. (2004).

Jackson County Circuit Court cases include an extraordinary number (more than seventy) involving the free black man Hiram Young, an Independence wagon maker who provided wagons and oxen yokes for the antebellum Santa Fe Trail trade. Platte County Circuit Court cases include the complicated case of a young black man named Armstrong who in 1900 was found guilty of raping a young white girl and sentenced to be hanged. The sentence was carried out, despite serious questions of irregularities during the trial. St. Charles County Circuit Court case files shed considerable light on the life and activities of a free woman of color, Sina Simonds, who purchased her freedom in 1817 and engaged in numerous property transactions over the course of the next four decades. Historian Diane Mutti Burke used circuit court records to document the extensive hiring out of slaves in Missouri in her important book *On Slavery's Border: Missouri's Small Slaveholding Households, 1815–1865* (2010). Much remains to be done on this topic, including in the state's metropolitan areas.

In 1950 the circuit courts of Cole and Boone Counties heard legal challenges from "next friends" of Elmer Bell Jr., George Everett Horne, and Gus T. Ridgel, all African American minors, to the University of Missouri's practice of prohibiting African American students from attending the University of Missouri. Ultimately, the courts sided with the young men and ordered the University of Missouri to open its doors to African Americans. The 1950s cases overturned the more famous Gaines case of 1936, in which the Boone County Circuit Court sided with segregation. Circuit court cases challenging segregation were filed in a number of other Missouri counties during the middle decades of the twentieth century.

Most probate court records, likewise, have not been digitized and require researchers to visit the county courthouses in the counties in which cases originated. Still, delving into them can be extremely rewarding for researchers. It is very common, for example, to find posters in these records advertising the sale of slaves, including in some cases children as young as one and two years old. The May 1861 case of Benjamin W. Smithson of Cedar County, for example, lists two African American girls on the estate inventory and documents that Mr. Smithson's widow gave Colonel James Johnson power of attorney to hire out a slave named Mariah. Likewise, Franklin County Probate Court Records document what happened to the thirteen slaves of Valentine Hunter, who died in 1850.

The Missouri State Archives' Local Records Program has also brought to light city records that can be enormously useful to researchers. Minutes of city councils and boards of aldermen, for example, sometimes provide insight into a community's attitudes toward African Americans. A board of aldermen meeting in August 1864 in Jefferson City, for example, revealed the board taking up the "annoying condition" of large numbers of freedmen fleeing into the capital city to escape bushwhackers. Records as obscure as "Coroners' Inquests," likewise, can provide insight into important historical events. Although the record is not available online, one can access a coroner's inquest database at the State Archives website (http://www.sos.mo.gov/archives/resources/coroners/#searchDB). Using the name William Lyons, a researcher can find information that will take him or her to Case No. 738, a case in which William Shelton (aka Stagger Lee) killed Billie Lyons in December 1895. The coroner's report of this case closely parallels the narrative that formed the foundation for the American classic, the "Ballad of Stagger Lee." The Missouri State Archives has also digitized the minutes for the governing boards of St. Louis County and Jackson County for the nineteenth-century, although those digital files have not yet been placed online.

There are a number of state records groups available in their original hard-copy format in the Missouri State Archives' Government Documents Collection. These include the reports to the legislature of the Missouri Negro Industrial Commission, a state agency created in February 1918 by Governor Frederick D. Gardner. The commission originally came into being at the request of African American leaders in Missouri who wanted to empower the state's black population to contribute to the war effort by buying and selling war bonds. They also wanted to improve agricultural production and food conservation among African American farmers and consumers.

The commission's first chair was Nathaniel C. Bruce, an alumnus of Tuskegee Institute in Alabama and the founder of a Chariton County, Missouri, school for African Americans known as the Dalton Vocational School. The Missouri Negro Industrial Commission continued in existence until 1928 when it died from lack of state financial support. Although this commission was short-lived, it was, as historian Tom Baker has pointed out, the first state agency to be primarily concerned with the welfare of African Americans in Missouri. A complete history of that commission remains to be written.

Another early twentieth-century state record group that is not yet available online is that which contains the biennial reports to the legislature of the Missouri Industrial Home for Negro Girls. This state-owned and operated facility, located in Moniteau County, just north of Tipton, housed female African American juveniles, primarily because Missourians did not want to house young black girls who had run afoul of the law together with white female juvenile delinquents.

The Missouri Industrial Home for Negro Girls housed approximately one thousand young girls during its forty-year history. During that period, the institution was headed by an African American "matron," making that position the principal patronage job in the state for black women.

Yet another state record group available at the Missouri State Archives is the collection of papers associated with the Missouri Human Rights Commission, established in 1957 at the urging of Missouri governor James T. Blair Jr. The records of the Human Rights Commission document the struggle for civil rights that has occurred over the past half century and more in the state of Missouri. Additionally, records of the Urban League of St. Louis (1910–1985), and the Kansas City Urban League (1920–1998) are available at the State Archives in Jefferson City.

A number of federal records have become available recently that provide exciting possibilities for adding to our understanding of the African American experience in Missouri. One such collection is the "Union Provost Marshal Papers, 1861–1866," now partially available through the Missouri Digital Heritage Initiative website (http://www.sos.mo.gov/archives/provost/). In particular, these records provide glimpses into such topics as the recruitment of African Americans into the Union Army, the treatment of "Contrabands" (that is, slaves captured by Union soldiers), the theft and confiscation of slaves, and the physical treatment (or mistreatment) of slaves. Historian Michael Fellman was among the first students of Missouri history to make use of these records in any significant way in his pioneering work, *Inside War: The Guerrilla Conflict in Missouri during the American Civil War* (1990). Fellman was forced to use the Provost Marshal Papers at the National Archives in Washington, DC. Now, thanks to the work of the Missouri State Archives, those records can be accessed on microfilm at the Kirkpatrick State Information Center in Jefferson City, and many can be accessed through the Missouri Digital Heritage Initiative (MDHI) website online. Included in this latter group are the following: "Descriptive Recruitment Lists of Volunteers for the United States Colored Troops for the State of Missouri, 1863–1865" (http://www.slcl.org/content/descriptive-recruitment-lists-volunteers-united-states-colored-troops-state-missouri-1863-18) and "Union Provost Marshals' File of Papers Relating to Two or More Civilians" (http://www.sos.mo.gov/archives/provost/provostPDF.asp).

Another federal record group that holds great promise for scholars of Missouri's black history, especially African American women's history, is the collection of pension records compiled by the federal government in the wake of post–Civil War congressional action aimed at ensuring "that the widows and children of colored soldiers" receive pensions earned by the roughly hundred thousand African American soldiers who served in the Union cause during the Civil War. As historian Noralee Frankel pointed out in a 1997 article in *Prologue*, "It was the complicated procedures involved in documenting nonlegal slave marriages that make these pension records so rich for women's and family history" (http://www.archives.gov/publications/prologue/1997/summer/slave-women.html). Historian Dianne Mutti Burke pointed the way for Missouri scholars in the use of these records in her aforementioned book, *On Slavery's Border*.

Oral histories pertaining to the African American experience in Missouri are more available than ever before. The "Political History" project of the State Historical Society of Missouri (SHSMO) contains scores of interviews that date to the mid-1990s. In many instances, these interviews deal with topics of racial history, including struggles over civil rights legislation. Many of these interviews have been transcribed and can be accessed online (http://statehistoricalsocietyofmissouri.org/cdm/landing-page/collection/ohc).

Among the interviews in this collection is one with State Representative Elbert Walton Jr. from St. Louis. The collection also includes interviews with brothers Roy Cooper Jr. and Alex Cooper, two members of one of the most prominent and well-known African American families of the southeastern Missouri delta.

Oral histories held by the SHSMO but which are not available digitally include the Kansas City Monarchs Oral History Collection (1978–1981). This collection contains oral history interviews and related correspondence with eighteen individuals who played with or were associated with the Kansas City Monarchs of the Negro National League. Likewise, the Kansas City Jazz Oral History Collection contains audio recordings and transcriptions of interviews with jazz musicians who played in Kansas City during the "Golden Age of Jazz," roughly the mid-1920s to the mid-1940s.

The SHSMO holds scores of other important collections pertinent to the study of nineteenth- and twentieth-century African American history in Missouri, although these collections are not yet available online. The SHSMO website provides a list of collections pertaining to African Americans in Missouri (http://shs.umsystem.edu/manuscripts/descriptions/desc-afam.html). The David M. Grant Papers, for example, document the career of an important St. Louis–area civil rights attorney and community leader during a forty-year span stretching from the mid-1930s into the 1970s. The Ernest Calloway Papers cover the period from the mid-1930s into the 1970s and document Calloway's activities as president of the St. Louis NAACP, his work with Teamsters' Local 688, and his role as a political activist in St. Louis. The DeVerne Calloway Papers document the career of Missouri's first black female General Assembly member, DeVerne Lee Calloway, as well as her work on behalf of civil rights with (among other groups) the Missouri Commission on Human Rights.

Other important collections held by the SHSMO include the Herman Dreer Papers (1933–1976). This collection includes the research, writings, and correspondence of an African American scholar and teacher at Sumner High School and Harris-Stowe College in St. Louis. The William L. Fambrough Sr. Photograph Collection (1940s–1970s) includes negatives and prints recording events and people by a Kansas City African American who worked for years as a professional photographer.

African American newspapers are extremely helpful and important sources of African American history in Missouri. Although the majority of these papers are not yet available online, there are at least some black Missouri newspapers that can be accessed digitally. They include *The [Columbia, Mo.] Professional World* (1901–1903), the *Kansas City*

Rising Son (1903–1907), and the *Lincoln University Clarion* (1935–1975), all of which can be accessed online (http://shs.umsystem.edu/newspaper/mdnp/mdnptable.shtml). Unquestionably, the SHSMO will continue to digitize newspapers pertaining to the African American experience in Missouri. In addition to these online sources, the SHSMO holds more than two dozen titles of African American newspapers published in Missouri. A list of those titles can be accessed online (http://shs.umsystem.edu/newspaper/guides/africanamericannews.shtml).

The Missouri History Museum in St. Louis is an important repository of materials pertaining to the state's African American history. The museum's Slaves and Slavery Collection, 1722–1950 (http://mohistory.org/files/archives_guides/SlaveryCollection.pdf) contains nearly a hundred items, including receipts for sales of slaves, deeds of emancipation, personal correspondence, and broadsides advertising rewards for the capture and return of runaway slaves. Likewise, the "Guide to Civil War Manuscripts in the Missouri Historical Society Archives" (http://mohistory.org/files/archives_guides/CivilWarManuscriptsGuide.pdf) evidences the presence of a number of documents pertaining to African American soldiers from Missouri during the Civil War. The Charles Turner Scrapbooks (1886–1918) contain newspaper clippings, political flyers and handbills, business cards, and photographs of late nineteenth- and early twentieth-century African American life in St. Louis. This collection is especially strong in materials pertaining to what was known as the Market Street Black Business District.

The St. Louis County Libraries hold the Julius K. Hunter and Friends African American Research Collection. Although this collection contains much material beyond the borders of Missouri, it is still useful for students of Missouri history. This collection was created in 2000 and can be accessed online (http://www.slcl.org/content/julius-k-hunter-and-friends-african-american-research-collection).

The Black Archives of Mid-America, located in Kansas City, Missouri, has a number of collections that document that city's rich African American heritage. With the exception of some photographs (http://www.blackarchives.org/collections), the bulk of these materials are not available online, however. One of the largest of the collections housed at the Black Archives—and arguably, one of the most important—is the one that contains the papers of Chester A. and Ada Crogman Franklin, longtime owners and publishers of *The Call*, Kansas City's important African American newspaper. The Franklins published this newspaper from 1919 until Ada Franklin died in 1983.

The Kansas City Public Library's Missouri Valley Special Collections houses the John Ramos Collection, another valuable source of materials pertaining to the African American experience in Kansas City. The origins of this collection date to 1926 when W. R. Howell, a history teacher at the all-black Lincoln High School in Kansas City, and Priscilla Hurd, a librarian at the Kansas City Library's Lincoln Branch, began to assemble material by and about Kansas City African Americans. The Lincoln Branch closed in 1971 and the collection moved to the Kansas City Public Library. Subsequently, the collection was named in honor of Dr. John Ramos Jr., the first African American elected (1961) to serve on the Kansas City Board of Education.

Another important source of information on African American life in Kansas City that can be accessed at the Kansas City Public Library is the Black Archives Oral History Collection (http://www.kchistory.org/cdm4/item_viewer.php?CISOROOT=/Local&CISOPTR=37109). The material in this collection was produced through a grant-funded collaboration between the Kansas City Public Library and the Black Archives of Mid-America. It features oral histories with fifty-six individuals, primarily African Americans, whose stories shed light on the black experience in Kansas City during the mid-twentieth century. The interviews were conducted in 1975 and 1976.

Among the many topics for further research that needs to be undertaken is the life of African Americans in communities where African Americans once lived in relatively large numbers, but from which they moved, especially during the era of the so-called Great Migration, extending roughly from the second decade of the twentieth century down to the post–World War II era. Federal census returns are extremely helpful in documenting black life in these communities, especially the 1940 federal census, which lists, among other things, the occupations of individuals, as well as the amount of money they had earned over the previous twelve months. This census also indicates whether individuals listed had changed residences over the previous five years.

Many people listed in the 1940 census are still alive, although they are reaching advanced ages. Researchers who want to record their recollections of life during the Great Depression and the era of the Second World War have a limited time to do so. One direction for future inquiry is suggested by a recent work authored by Katherine van Wormer et al, *The Maid Narratives: Black Domestics and White Families in the Jim Crow South* (Baton Rouge: Louisiana State University Press, 2012). No comparable work on African American women who worked as domestics for white Missouri families exists. Likewise, an interpretative history of the 1950s and 1960s civil rights movement in Missouri from the perspective of participants remains to be written. A 2009 publication by the University of Illinois Press entitled *Foot Soldiers for Democracy: The Men, Women, and Children of the Birmingham Civil Rights Movement,* edited by Horace Huntley and John McKerley, could serve as a model for such an undertaking.

Taken together, the repositories and collections listed above provide an abundance of sources for researchers to launch their own efforts to add to the rich existing literature on the African American experience in Missouri. There have never been more sources available than there are now.

Notes

Prologue
Race and Meaning in Missouri History

1. Donald J. Kemper, "Catholic Integration in St. Louis, 1935–1947," *Missouri Historical Review* 73 (October 1978): 1–22.

2. Lorenzo J. Greene, *Working with Carter G. Woodson, the Father of Black History: A Diary, 1928–1930,* ed. and introduction by Arvarh E. Strickland (Baton Rouge: Louisiana State University Press, 1989), 463.

3. In 1985, both Aptheker and Meier wrote letters to the author praising both Greene and the *Midwest Journal.* August Meier to author, 23 September 1985, and Herbert Aptheker to author, 24 December 1985, both letters in possession of author. See also Gary R. Kremer, "Lincoln University's *Midwest Journal: A Magazine of Research and Creative Writing, 1948–1956,*" paper delivered at the 2012 Missouri Conference on History, Columbia, Missouri, 29 March 2012.

4. I taught classes at the Missouri State Penitentiary for ten years. The level of racial mistrust quickly diminished. A few years after I began teaching at the prison, one of my early students evidenced the absence of mistrust when he wrote in a letter to me: "You know, in talking with you over the years and you having been around so long[,] I guess I assume that you already know certain things. Sometimes we talk like 'con to con.'" C.D. to author, 27 July 1983, letter in possession of author.

5. Constance M. Greiff, ed., *Lost America: From the Mississippi to the Pacific* (Princeton, NJ: Pyne Press, 1972), viii. See also my essay "The Cultural Resource Survey: A New Way of Doing Black History," *Gateway Heritage* (October 1985): 20–27.

6. A description of this early effort is in Donald H. Ewalt, Jr., and Gary R. Kremer, "The Historian as Preservationist: A Missouri Case Study," *The Public Historian* 3 (Fall 1981): 5–22.

7. John Michael Vlach, "The Shotgun House: An African Architectural Legacy," part 1, *Pioneer America* 8 (January 1976): 47–56; Part 2 (July 1976): 57–70.

8. William Lynwood Montell, *The Saga of Coe Ridge: A Study in Oral History* (Knoxville: University of Tennessee Press, 1970).

9. *Sixth Annual Report of the Superintendent of Public Schools of the State of Missouri* (Jefferson City, MO: James F. Regan and John N. Edwards, 1872), 93.

10. A peer reviewer of an early version of my 1991 book, *James Milton Turner and the Promise of America: The Public Life of a Post–Civil War Black Leader,* attacked my lack of criticism of Turner (describing my manuscript as having "Too much gee whiz") and encouraged me to revise the manuscript so as to avoid "gushing like a schoolboy over Turner's genius." "Reader's Report," in possession of author.

11. Gary R. Kremer, *George Washington Carver: A Biography* (Santa Barbara, CA: Greenwood/ABC-CLIO, 2011), 71.

12. Leon F. Litwack, *Been in the Storm So Long: The Aftermath of Slavery* (New York: Vintage Books, 1980). The essay on Pennytown, in particular, helped me to move beyond thinking of the period from 1877 to 1918 as the "nadir" of African American life in post-slavery America, as described in Rayford W. Logan, *The Betrayal of the Negro: From Rutherford B. Hayes to Woodrow Wilson* (New York: Collier Books, 1972; originally *The Negro in American Life and Thought: The Nadir, 1877–1901* [New York: Dial Press, 1954]).

13. Gary R. Kremer, ed., *George Washington Carver: In His Own Words* (Columbia: University of Missouri Press, 1987), 1.

14. Louis R. Harlan, *Booker T. Washington: The Making of a Black Leader, 1856–1901* (New York: Oxford University Press, 1972), 277.

15. Gary R. Kremer, *George Washington Carver: A Biography* (Santa Barbara, CA: Greenwood, ABC-CLIO, 2011).

16. *Hartville Wright County Republican*, 2 September 1911.

17. Elizabeth Clark-Lewis, *Living In, Living Out: African American Domestics and the Great Migration* (New York: Kodansha, 1996; originally *Living In, Living Out: African American Domestics in Washington, D.C., 1910–1940* [Washington, DC: Smithsonian Institution, 1994]).

18. Andrew Billingsley, *Climbing Jacob's Ladder: The Enduring Legacy of African-American Families* (New York: Simon and Schuster, 1992); Ira Berlin, *The Making of African America: The Four Great Migrations* (New York: Penguin Books, 2010).

19. Timothy E. Baumann, "'Because That's Where My Roots Are': Searching for Patterns of African American Ethnicity in Arrow Rock, Missouri" (PhD diss., Department of Anthropology, University of Tennessee–Knoxville, 2001).

20. Robin D. G. Kelley, *Race Rebels: Culture, Politics, and the Black Working Class* (New York: Free Press, 1996).

21. The homecoming celebration occurred on 18 August 2000.

22. David W. Blight, *Race and Reunion: The Civil War in American Memory* (Cambridge, MA: Belknap Press of Harvard University Press, 2001).

Chapter 1
"Some Aspects of Black Education in Reconstruction Missouri: An Address by Richard B. Foster"

1. This annotated document originally appeared in the January 1976 issue of the *Missouri Historical Review* and was coedited with Antonio F. Holland. It is reprinted with the permission of the State Historical Society of Missouri.

2. Carter G. Woodson, *The Mis-education of the Negro* (Washington, DC: Associated Publishers, 1933), 26.

3. Henry Bullock, *A History of Negro Education in the South* (New York: Praeger, 1970). 24.

4. W. Sherman Savage, *The History of Lincoln University* (Jefferson City, MO: Lincoln University, 1939), 7–10; William E. Parrish, *Missouri Under Radical Rule, 1865–1870* (Columbia: University of Missouri Press, 1965), 128–32.

5. Words introduced in brackets in the text of this document represent editorial interpolations added where the original manuscript was illegible.

6. Foster's estimate of five thousand seems conservative when compared with a study done by a Freedmen's Bureau agent in 1869. The agent reported that by fall of 1869 there were 114 Negro schools, mostly public, with 6,240 pupils in attendance

throughout the state. The census of 1870 revealed an enrollment of 9,080 black students. Professor William Parrish estimates that the potential Negro student group of the entire state contained approximately 42,000 children. Parrish, *Missouri Under Radical Rule*, 123.

7. For example, in 1873 average salaries ranged from $46.70 monthly for a male teacher in a colored school to $82.72 monthly in white schools. Women were grossly underpaid in both cases: $40 monthly average in black schools; $46.64 monthly in white schools. Ibid., 128.

8. St. Joseph had started its first black school in 1866. By 1871 St. Joseph had two one-room schools for blacks and by 1874, 386 of the 651 blacks enumerated in the city were enrolled under four teachers. Robert Irving Brigham, "The Education of the Negro in Missouri" (unpublished PhD diss., University of Missouri, 1946), 84.

9. St. Louis had more schools for blacks at this time than any other community in the state. The state legislature had granted power to the city to establish separate schools for blacks in 1865. In 1866 three schools were established for blacks, one in the north, one in the south, and one in the central part of the city. By 1868 there were five black schools. In 1871 a sixth school was established, and by 1875 there were twelve black schools. Ibid., 90–91.

10. The school was located on a lot known as Hobo Hill, fronting on Miller Street, between Miller and McCarty (then called Van Buren), and Marshall and Jackson. It was the site of the first public school land to be purchased by Jefferson City, also the first site of Lincoln University, and, currently, the site of Simonsen Junior High School. Jerena East Giffen, *The House on Hobo Hill: The History of the Jefferson City Public Schools* (Jefferson City, MO: Jefferson City Public Schools, 1964), 14, 58.

11. Another example of the kind of schools about which Foster is speaking includes a school established in St. Louis by Hiram Revels in 1856. Revels later became the first Negro to sit in the US Senate. In Hannibal, Tom Henderson, a free black man who had become a Methodist minister, held classes at the Second Baptist Church before the Civil War. When war came, he turned the job over to Blanche K. Bruce, who later also became a US senator. In Columbia, the board of education opened a combination school-church in the fall of 1866. In 1865 the Western Sanitary Commission at St. Louis was operating a high school for about fifty or sixty black people in the basement of one of the churches. In 1869 one of the three black elementary schools in St. Louis was being conducted by two teachers in the basement of the Chambers Street Baptist Church, corner of Tenth and Chambers Streets. Parrish, *Missouri Under Radical Rule*, 118–20, 124; J. W. Evans, "A Brief Sketch of the Development of Negro Education in St. Louis, Missouri," *Journal of Negro Education* 7 (October 1938): 548–52.

12. Foster's assistant was Fannie Payne, and the school she was conducting was located in the Colored Baptist Church, which at the time was itself housed in an old frame building once used for a stable. It stood near the present site of the railroad depot. Ms. Payne's brother, W. H. Payne, was the second principal of the school (after Foster), and the first black principal. He was educated at Adrian College in Michigan. Savage, *The History of Lincoln University*, 8, 12, 16–17, 198.

13. Despite State Superintendent T. A. Parker's efforts to advance the cause of black education in Missouri, progress along those lines was handicapped by the general unwillingness of Missouri school boards to go along with his plans. The ground rules for the establishment of black schools had been laid in 1866 by the Twenty-third General Assembly, which stipulated that separate schools were to be established by

a township in which there were twenty blacks of school age enumerated. In such localities as had less than twenty blacks of school age, the money raised for their schooling was to be used for their education in such ways as local school boards saw fit. However, as late as 1867, the superintendent of Missouri schools pointed out that there was no effective way of enforcing such laws in the state of Missouri. The 1868 legislature tried to remedy this situation by giving the state superintendent the power to establish schools for blacks should local school boards refuse to do so. Additional legislation, passed in 1871, made school officials who failed to live up to this specific duty liable to a fine of from fifty to five hundred dollars. Brigham, "Education of the Negro in Missouri," 83–84.

14. Subscription schools were simply schools in which the pupils were charged a fee to cover the cost of the teacher's services and the facilities used. They received no state support. Both black and white subscription schools were common during this period.

15. Ebenezer Bassett was a Connecticut-born high school principal who had studied at Yale. He was appointed to the Haitian ministership by President Ulysses S. Grant and served during Grant's entire tenure in office. Benjamin Quarles, *Frederick Douglass* (New York: Atheneum, 1968), 321, 323.

16. James Milton Turner was born a slave in St. Louis County in 1839. After serving in the Civil War, he returned to Missouri and became involved in efforts to advance the cause of black education in particular and civil rights generally. In the process, he became recognized as a spokesman for blacks not only in Missouri but throughout the country. Though, as Foster reports in this speech, Turner did not receive the ministership to Liberia when he first applied in 1869, he was appointed to that position by President Grant early in 1871. Gary R. Kremer, "James Milton Turner: The Hopeful Years, 1868–1875" (unpublished essay written in the US History Seminar at The American University, Washington, DC, Spring 1975), 7–12; a revised version of this essay was subsequently published as "Background to Apostasy: James Milton Turner and the Republican Party," *Missouri Historical Review* 70 (January 1976): 184–98.

17. Again, this was the school that was being conducted in the Colored Baptist Church. W. H. Payne and Charles A. Beal, both of whom had been students at Adrian College in Michigan, had dedicated their lives to Negro education and had sent letters to the governors of former slave states inquiring about the possibility of gaining teaching positions in black schools. Their letter to Governor Thomas Fletcher was passed on to Richard B. Foster who immediately solicited Beal's and Payne's assistance. Payne came as a teacher and was made principal, and Beal was made field agent. Lincoln Institute did not have enough money to pay Payne a salary and he was asked to provide his own remuneration. He was able to get the American Missionary Association to contribute four hundred dollars toward that end. Savage, *The History of Lincoln University*, 8, 12, 16, 198.

18. In 1869 a bill was offered in the legislature by Representative L. A. Thompson of Montgomery County to enlarge the University of the State of Missouri by establishing the Department of Agriculture and Mechanic Arts. This bill included a proposal that would have given Lincoln Institute 10 percent of the income from the agricultural college land grants provided by the federal government. When the bill was finally passed, the part about Lincoln Institute had been dropped. It was not until 1870, after a mass demonstration by black citizens from all parts of the state in Jefferson City, that Lincoln Institute was allocated state funds to continue its educational programs. In that year, the general assembly, in an attempt at compro-

mise, offered a resolution, introduced by J. B. Harper of Putnam County, granting five thousand dollars annually in state aid to Lincoln if its trustees would consent to convert the school into one designed for the training of Negro teachers for public schools. Savage, *The History of Lincoln University*, 12–14; Parrish, *Missouri Under Radical Rule*, 131–32.

19. A normal school had as its primary purpose the training of persons to become teachers. An agricultural college, on the other hand, was less academic and more vocational, training its students to become scientific farmers and practitioners of the mechanical arts.

20. The next biennial report of the State Auditor did, of course, reflect the newly appropriated $5,000 specifically earmarked for Lincoln Institute. By 1879 the state of Missouri had taken over complete operation of the school. Parrish, *Missouri Under Radical Rule*, 132.

21. Cyrus Trigg apparently gained his freedom sometime prior to or during 1855. He appeared before the Cole County Court in that year and asked the court to grant him a "free license" to remain in the state. His descendants, among them Lincoln University professor Joseph Trigg, still live in Jefferson City. Gary R. Kremer, "Cole County, Missouri Freedmen, 1865–1880]" (unpublished master's thesis, Lincoln University, Jefferson City, MO, 1972), 15–16.

Chapter 2
"Pennytown: A Freedmen's Hamlet, 1871–1945"

1. This essay originally appeared in the 1989–1990 issue of the *Missouri Folklore Society Journal* and is reprinted with the permission of the Missouri Folklore Society. It was coauthored with Lynn Morrow. Versions of this essay were presented at the annual meeting of the Missouri Folklore Society Conference in Jefferson City, Missouri, in September 1987, and the National Council for Geographic Education, Springfield, Missouri, in October 1987. The genesis of this paper was Morrow's nomination of the Pennytown Free Will Baptist Church to the National Register of Historic Places, 3 October 1986; the church has subsequently been enrolled in the Register. Rayford W. Logan, *The Betrayal of the Negro: From Rutherford B. Hayes to Woodrow Wilson* (New York: Collier Books, 1965; originally *The Negro in American Life and Thought: The Nadir, 1877–1901* [New York: Macmillan, 1954]).

2. Leon L. Litwack, *Been in the Storm So Long: The Aftermath of Slavery* (New York: Alfred A. Knopf, 1979), 401. For the importance of landownership to blacks and for white southerners' efforts to deny blacks property, see also Roger L. Ransom and Richard Sutch, *One Kind of Freedom: The Economic Consequences of Emancipation* (New York: Cambridge University Press, 1977), 81–87.

3. Saline County Courthouse, Recorder of Deeds, book 13, page 202; *Saline County Atlas, 1876*, 43.

4. Compilations by Morrow from abstract books for Section 24, Township 49, Range 21 in Saline County, Van Dyke Abstract Office, Marshall, Missouri.

5. A. H. Orr, "Penelope's Freedom" (n.d., n.p.), a pamphlet by the president of the Saline County Historical Society honoring Penelope Lewis, a daughter of a pioneer Pennytown family.

6. See "The South" in J. B. Jackson, *American Space: The Centennial Years, 1865–1876* (New York: W. W. Norton, 1972), 137–66. In keeping with the irony of southern history, Pennytown grew on the north slope of Blackwater River valley while, to the

southeast, on the south slope of the valley lived W. B. Napton on his great Elk Hill estate. Napton is credited with the authorship of Missouri's classic states' rights declaration of 1849, the Jackson Resolutions.

7. In 1880, the three remaining black adults in the township were from North Carolina, Tennessee, and Mississippi. Interviews by authors with Mrs. Josephine Lawrence on 13 and 27 August 1986, and Morrow's compilations from Salt Fork Township, the 1880 census, and the subsequent 1900 census. Most of the social history related in this article comes from several interviews with Mrs. Lawrence and from her life-long collection of Pennytown memorabilia. In her youth at Pennytown, Mrs. Lawrence regularly traveled from house to house reading mail, newspapers, and sale bills to her semiliterate and illiterate friends and neighbors. Later she commonly wrote obituaries for the Pennytown dead.

8. This paper omitted statistics from the 1910 census due to both its illegibility and Morrow's questions as to its inclusiveness. Note that in the 1870s the Saline County Court created Salt Fork Township from land formerly in Blackwater Township.

9. George Frederickson, "On Herbert G. Gutman's 'The Black Family in Slavery and Freedom, 1750–1925,'" in Allen Weinstein et al., *American Negro Slavery* (New York: Oxford University Press, 1979), 279.

10. C. L. Lawrence, Sr., "Richard Lawrence Sr., My Paternal Ancestor, the Man We Called Grandpy," typed manuscript in Mrs. Lawrence's Papers, dated 8 March 1975. For regional comparisons to Pennytown, see Peter C. Smith and Karl B. Raitz, "Negro Hamlets and Agricultural Estates in Kentucky's Inner Bluegrass," *Geographical Review* (1947): 217–34; Suzanna Maria Grenz, "The Black Community in Boone County, Missouri, 1850–1900" (PhD diss., University of Missouri–Columbia, 1979).

11. Interview by Morrow with Rufus and Louis Brown in Slater, Missouri, 11 September 1986.

12. Interview by Morrow and Kremer with Mrs. Sam Mote, Spring 1983, summarized by Gary Kremer, "A New Way of Doing Black History: The Cultural Resource Survey," *Gateway Heritage* (Spring 1985): 24.

13. See Jack and Olivia Solomon, *Cracklin Bread and Asfidity: Folk Recipes and Remedies* (Montgomery: University of Alabama Press, 1979).

14. Saline County Courthouse, Recorder of Deeds, book 76, page 616. Although it is unclear, the institutional origins of the Free Will Baptist Church may be tied to one of the older black churches in the county such as Bethel Baptist or Zoar Baptist. See Gaston Wamble, "Negroes and Missouri Protestant Churches before and after the Civil War," *Missouri Historical Review* 61(April 1967): 340–42.

15. Saline County Courthouse, Recorder of Deeds, book 69, page 134; Grand Lodge United Brothers of Friendship (UBF) and Sisters of Mysterious Ten (SMT), *Proceedings* (Kansas City, MO, 1905), 12.

16. See Loretta J. Williams, *Black Freemasonry and Middle-Class Realities* (Columbia: University of Missouri Press, 1980), 79; UBF and SMT, *Proceedings* (St. Joseph, MO, 1924), 100, 183. The *Proceedings* lists all the members by name.

17. Contract, 15 April 1933, between Ada Wheeler and Nellie Jackson, Lawrence Papers.

18. Agreement between Mrs. Finley and Francis Spears, 12 October 1938, Lawrence Papers.

19. The origin of the Thornlea School is unclear, but descendants think it was some time after the 1886 Free Will Baptist Church was built. Joe Penny descendants remember it as part of District 93, which the county formed in 1909. See W. G. Durrett, Clerk

of Saline County Court, *Common School Districts: Renumbered as Provided by the Law of 1909.*

20. Frank Brown to Nellie Jackson, n.d., Lawrence Papers.

21. David Lowenthal, "Past Time, Present Place: Landscape and Memory," *Geographical Review* (1975): 1, 7.

22. Carl Schmidt, "Pennytown Was an Experiment," in A. H. Orr et al., *History of Saline County* (Marceline, MO: Walsworth Publishing, 1967), 254. By 1945 everyone had left Pennytown save Francis and Willa Spears. Francis became the last Pennytown resident, selling his land to M. F. A. Petroleum Company in 1977.

23. William H. Wiggins, Jr., described the phenomenon of diverse black American festivals in *O Freedom! Afro-American Emancipation Celebrations* (Knoxville: University of Tennessee Press, 1987).

24. From 1978 to 1984 Kremer directed the Missouri Black Historic Sites Project, funded by Lincoln University and the Missouri Department of Natural Resources. Kremer's findings are contained in a four-volume monograph series entitled *Missouri Black Historic Sites,* available at the Office of Historic Preservation, Missouri Department of Natural Resources, Jefferson City, Missouri.

25. See discussion by Donald Ewalt and Gary Kremer, "The Historian as Preservationist: A Missouri Case Study," *The Public Historian* (Fall 1981): 5–22. In addition, a 1960s Housing and Urban Development project dramatically changed Marshall's historic *Africa* settlement by the imposition of modern housing.

Chapter 3
"'Yours for the Race': The Life and Work of Josephine Silone Yates"

1. This essay originally appeared in the January 1996 issue of the *Missouri Historical Review* and is reprinted with the permission of the State Historical Society of Missouri. It was coauthored with Cindy M. Mackey, then an undergraduate student working with Gary R. Kremer in the William Woods University honors program.

2. See Sharon Harley, "Mary Church Terrell: Genteel Militant," in *Black Leaders of the Nineteenth Century*, ed. Leon Litwack and August Meier (Urbana: University of Illinois Press, 1988), 307–22; Willard B. Gatewood, *Aristocrats of Color: The Black Elite, 1880–1920* (Bloomington: Indiana University Press, 1990); Evelyn Brooks Higginbotham, *Righteous Discontent: The Women's Movement in the Black Baptist Church, 1880–1920* (Cambridge, MA: Harvard University Press, 1993); Alfreda M. Duster, ed., *Crusade for Justice: The Autobiography of Ida B. Wells* (Chicago: University of Chicago Press, 1970); and Mildred I. Thompson, *Ida B. Wells-Barnett: An Exploratory Study of an American Black Woman, 1893–1930* (Brooklyn, NY: Carlson Publishing, 1990). The motto of the National Association of Colored Women (NACW) was "Lifting as We Climb."

3. Gatewood, *Aristocrats of Color*, 243.

4. Lawson Scruggs, *Women of Distinction* (Raleigh, NC: L. A. Scruggs, 1893), 40; Wilson J. Moses, *The Golden Age of Black Nationalism, 1850–1925* (Hamden, CT: Archon Books, 1978), 114; Hallie Q. Brown, *Homespun Heroines and Other Women of Distinction* (Xenia, OH: Aldrine Publishing, 1926), 178.

5. For example, see Leon Litwack, *Been in the Storm So Long: The Aftermath of Slavery* (New York: Alfred A. Knopf, 1979). Litwack writes: "Some blacks who had been free before the war resented being called 'freedmen' and tried in every way to

dissociate themselves from the former slaves" (513). In the 1900 census, Yates listed the birthplace of her father as Africa. "Population Schedule," Twelfth Census of the United States, 1900, Jackson County, Missouri, 837.

6. Scruggs, *Women of Distinction*, 40–41.

7. Ibid., 41.

8. Linda M. Perkins, "Fanny Jackson Coppin," in *Black Women in America: An Historical Encyclopedia*, ed. Darlene Clark Hine (Brooklyn, NY: Carlson Publishing, 1993), 1:282.

9. Scruggs, *Women of Distinction*, 46; Robert L. Johns, "Josephine Silone Yates," in *Notable Black American Women*, ed. Jessie Carney Smith (Detroit: Gale Research, 1992), 1286.

10. Savage, *The History of Lincoln University*, 42.

11. Ibid., 42–44; Minutes, Lincoln Institute Board of Regents, June 1881 (Office of the President, Lincoln University, Jefferson City, Missouri), 132–36.

12. Minutes, Lincoln Institute Board of Regents, June 1881, 132, and 15 May 1885, 163.

13. Savage, *The History of Lincoln University*, 47.

14. Minutes, Lincoln Institute Board of Regents, 4 February 1881, 34.

15. Josephine Silone Yates, "The Equipment of the Teacher," *The Voice of the Negro* 1 (June 1904): 248–52.

16. Ibid., 250–51.

17. Ibid., 248.

18. Ibid.

19. Scruggs, *Women of Distinction*, 45; Savage, *The History of Lincoln University*, 50.

20. Yates, "The Equipment of the Teacher," 248.

21. Johns, "Josephine Silone Yates," 1286–87; J. Silone Yates Probate File, Case No. 12155, Book 13, 546, filed 2 November 1912, Jackson County Probate Court, Kansas City, Missouri; "Population Schedule," Twelfth Census of the United States, 1900, Jackson County, 837.

22. Jan Gleiter, "Josephine Silone Yates," in Hine, *Black Women in America*, 2:1297; Moses, *The Golden Age*, 117.

23. A captioned photograph of this home is part of a "Black Kansas City" exhibit at the Black Archives of Mid-America, Kansas City. Unfortunately, the building's image is not clear enough for reproduction.

24. US Bureau of the Census, Special Reports, *Occupations at the Twelfth Census* (Washington, DC: GPO, 1904), 322–24. There were 3,106,665 people in Missouri in 1900, and 161,234 (5.1 percent) of them were black. US Bureau of the Census, *Twelfth Census of the United States*, Population, part 1 (Washington, DC: US Census Office, 1901), xxii, table VII; 546, table 19.

25. Gatewood, *Aristocrats of Color*, 240, 242.

26. Charles Harris Wesley, *The History of the National Association of Colored Women* (Washington, DC: NACW, 1984), 26; Dorothy Salem, "National Association of Colored Women," in Hine, *Black Women in America*, 2:843.

27. Josephine Silone Yates, correspondence, *Woman's Era* 1 (August 1894): 5.

28. Beverly W. Jones, "Mary Church Terrell and the National Association of Colored Women, 1896 to 1901," *Journal of Negro History* 67 (Spring 1982): 22–23. See also Salem, "National Association of Colored Women," 2:845.

29. Quoted in Jones, "Mary Church Terrell," 24.

30. Wesley, *The History of the National Association of Colored Women*, 43.

31. Herbert Aptheker, *A Documentary History of the Negro People in the United States* (Secaucus, NJ: Citadel Press, 1951; 6th paperback edition, 1972), 2:776–77.

32. *Washington, D.C. Colored American*, 27 July 1901; Louis R. Harlan and Raymond W. Smock, eds., *The Booker T. Washington Papers*, vol. 6, *1901–1902* (Urbana: University of Illinois Press, 1977), 178–79.

33. Duster, *Crusade for Justice*, 267–68.

34. Josephine Silone Yates, "The National Association of Colored Women," *The Voice of the Negro* 1 (July 1904): 284.

35. Wesley, *The History of the National Association of Colored Women*, 60–62; Elizabeth Carter-Brooks, "Josephine Silone Yates, Second President of the N.A.C.W.," in Elizabeth L. Davis, *Lifting as They Climb* (Washington, DC: NACW, 1933), 167–68.

36. Comments contained in W. E. B. DuBois, ed., *Efforts for Social Betterment among Negro Americans*, Atlanta University Publications, no. 14 (Atlanta: Atlanta University Press, 1909), 47, 49.

37. Josephine Silone Yates to Margaret Murray Washington, 13 May 1902, NACW Papers, microfilm copy, University of North Carolina, Chapel Hill. The authors are indebted to Patrick J. Huber for discovering and sharing the Yates–Washington correspondence. *The (Indianapolis) Freeman*, 28 February, 2 May 1903.

38. Yates, "The National Association of Colored Women," 283; *The (Indianapolis) Freeman*, 5 December 1903, 24 June 1899. For more on ragtime see Susan Curtis, *Dancing to a Black Man's Tune: A Life of Scott Joplin* (Columbia: University of Missouri Press, 1994).

39. Yates, "The National Association of Colored Women," 284.

40. Minutes, Lincoln Institute Board of Regents, 18 May 1885, 164. The Lincoln Board of Regents' minutes for 4 June 1901 (250), list the total enrollment for 1901 at 256. Savage writes in *The History of Lincoln University* that enrollment had reached 240 by the 1902 fall term (108). Josephine Silone Yates, "Educational Work at Lincoln Institute," *Southern Workman* 1 (June 1905): 350–52.

41. Savage, *The History of Lincoln University*, 105.

42. Ibid., 107.

43. *Kansas City Rising Son*, 17 November 1905.

44. Ibid., 23 September 1904. On the value of landownership in the Jim Crow South, Jimmie Lewis Franklin has recently written, "Work on the land and its products played a significant part in an individual's view of personal worth and identity." Jimmie Lewis Franklin, "Black Southerners, Shared Experience, and Place: A Reflection," *Journal of Southern History* 60 (February 1994): 11.

45. *Thirty-eighth Annual Catalogue of Lincoln Institute*, 1909–1910 (Jefferson City, MO: Cole County Democrat Printing Company, 1909), 2.

46. *Kansas City Rising Son*, 28 October 1904. For more on the Olive Branch see *The (Indianapolis) Freeman*, 28 February 1903.

47. Henry Gates, Jr., refers to Cooper as "a prototypical black feminist." See the introduction in *Reading Black, Reading Feminist: A Critical Anthology*, ed. Henry Louis Gates, Jr. (New York: Penguin Books, 1990), 1.

48. *The (Indianapolis) Freeman*, 29 July 1899.

49. The Lincoln Institute Board of Regents Minutes for 11 June 1908 (318) state that Anna J. Cooper was reelected chair of languages; presumably, this means that she had been at the institute for all or part of the 1906–1907 academic year.

50. Death Certificate of Josephine Silone Yates, Missouri Department of Vital Statistics, Jefferson City.

51. *The (Indianapolis) Freeman*, 21 September 1912. See also *The (Chicago) Broad-ax*, 14 September 1912, and *The Washington, D.C. Bee*, 21 September 1912.

Chapter 4
"The World of Make-Believe:
James Milton Turner and Black Masonry"

1. This article originally appeared in the October 1979 issue of the *Missouri Historical Review* and is reprinted with the permission of the State Historical Society of Missouri.

2. Testimony of C. H. Tandy, Case No. 2884, Circuit Court of St. Louis, June Term, 1916, Records of the Circuit Court, Division 2, Civil Courts Building, St. Louis, Missouri.

3. Gary R. Kremer, "A Biography of James Milton Turner" (unpublished PhD diss., The American University, Washington, DC, 1978). This dissertation was published in revised form as *James Milton Turner and the Promise of America: The Public Life of a Post–Civil War Black Leader* (Columbia: University of Missouri Press, 1991).

4. There is an increasing amount of evidence to suggest that free blacks such as Turner viewed the former slaves' life as quite alien to their own. They did not share the same values or goals. They criticized the freedmen's work habits, religious worship, and general social conduct. Indeed, as one historian has written, many educated free blacks "saw the freedmen as a primitive social class in need of rehabilitation." William Toll, "Free Men, Freedmen, and Race: Black Social Theory in the Gilded Age," *Journal of Southern History* 44 (November 1978): 572. For an extensive discussion of the free blacks' perception of slaves, see Leon F. Litwack, *Been in the Storm So Long: The Aftermath of Slavery* (New York: Alfred A. Knopf, 1979), particularly 454, 513–14. Perhaps Turner's clearest expression of dissatisfaction with the freedmen came in 1879, during the black Exodus to Kansas, when he labeled the former slaves as "improvident" and "spendthrifts," who were "without frugal habits" and who reminded him "more of grown up children than of persons of mature mind." Turner, letter to the editor, *St. Louis Globe-Democrat*, 23 March 1879.

5. Helpful articles on various aspects of Turner's life include the following: Irving Dilliard, "James Milton Turner: A Little Known Benefactor of His People," *Journal of Negro History* 19 (October 1934): 372–411; Noah Webster Moore, "James Milton Turner, Diplomat, Educator, and Defender of Rights, 1840–1915," *Missouri Historical Society Bulletin* 27 (April 1971): 194–201; Lawrence O. Christensen, "J. Milton Turner: An Appraisal," *Missouri Historical Review* 70 (October 1975): 1–19; Gary R. Kremer, "Background to Apostasy: James Milton Turner and the Republican Party," *Missouri Historical Review* 71 (October 1976): 59–75. These articles offer no information about Turner's Masonic career.

6. For Frazier's concept of "the world of make-believe," see his *Black Bourgeoisie: The Rise of a New Middle Class* (Chicago: Free Press, 1957; reprint, New York: Collier Books, 1962), 153–238.

7. William A. Muraskin, *Middle-Class Blacks in a White Society: Prince Hall Freemasonry in America* (Berkeley: University of California Press, 1975).

8. Ibid., 74.

9. Frazier, *Black Bourgeoisie*, 60–85.

10. Kremer, "A Biography of James Milton Turner," chapter 1; J. Milton Turner to F. A. Seely, 28 February 1870, in Letters Received, A–F, January–December 1870,

Freedmen's Bureau Records, (National Archives, Washington, DC), Educational Division, microfilm publication no. 803, roll 10, frames 428–34.

11. Kremer, "Background to Apostasy," 59–75.

12. *(Columbia) Missouri Statesman*, 20 May 1870.

13. *(Jefferson City) People's Tribune*, 17 May 1871. This article summarized Turner's reception by blacks and whites alike throughout the campaign.

14. Dispatch No. 4, 25 May 1872, "Despatches From United States Ministers to Liberia, 1863–1906" (National Archives, Washington, DC), microcopy no. 170, vol. 2, 24 October 1869–24 January 1872.

15. J. Milton Turner to Blanche K. Bruce, 12 March 1877, in Blanche K. Bruce Papers, Moorland-Spingarn Research Center, Howard University, Washington, DC.

16. *Report and Testimony of the Select Committee of the United States to Investigate the Causes of the Removal of the Negroes from the Southern States to the Northern States*, US 46th Cong., 2nd sess., Senate Report 693 (1880), pt. 2, 120–21.

17. Christensen, "J. Milton Turner: An Appraisal," 1–19; Kremer, "A Biography of James Milton Turner," chaps. 6–7. The most recent study of the Cherokee freedmen, including Turner's role, is Daniel F. Littlefield, Jr., *The Cherokee Freedmen: From Emancipation to American Citizenship* (Westport, CT: Greenwood Press, 1978).

18. The best single example of this is the controversy Turner created when he called together a convention of black Independents and Democrats in Indianapolis in 1888. Kremer, "A Biography of James Milton Turner," 254–66.

19. *Official Proceedings of the Fourteenth Annual Communication of the Most Worshipful Grand Lodge, A.F. & A.M.* (Hannibal, MO: Most Worshipful Grand Lodge, A.F. and A.M. of Missouri, 1880), 27–38 (hereafter cited as *Official Proceedings*).

20. For a discussion of the membership of Prince Hall Freemansory, see Muraskin, *Middle-Class Blacks in a White Society*, 43–85.

21. *Official Proceedings* (1890), 87.

22. Ibid. (1893), 107.

23. Muraskin, *Middle-Class Blacks in a White Society*, 132.

24. *Official Proceedings* (1894), 10, 73, 111.

25. Ibid., 37, 39–40.

26. Muraskin, *Middle-Class Blacks in a White Society*, 196–97.

27. *Official Proceedings* (1894), 33. This resolution also called for Brooks's photograph to appear in the same edition of the *Proceedings*.

28. Ibid., 34–35. Mrs. E. A. Stadler, archivist of the Missouri Historical Society, St. Louis, informed the author in an interview on 5 July 1977 that those records never were made a part of the society's holdings. She checked the society's minutes for that period, in my presence, and could find no reference to black Masons, Turner, or W. P. Brooks. She said that in her judgment there were only two possible explanations: (1) the black Masons changed their minds, and decided not to turn over the material; (2) the Society rejected the offer since it was making no effort to collect black materials at that time. It also should be noted that this was not the first time that Turner showed an interest in preserving an account of black historical contributions. In 1882 he delivered a eulogy of Dred Scott upon the occasion of the presentation of a portrait of the latter to the Missouri Historical Society. Turner noted at that time that:

> the Negro has been with us in felling forests, in redeeming lagoons, and in building cities where there were waste places. And, I may add, that his toil in our fields of plenteous harvest has aided the ramifications of our substantial

commerce. The Negro has been with us from the very beginning of the history of our State, and, indeed, of the nation itself. Surely he must somewhere, at some time and somehow have carved his humble niche in the temple of time.

Irving Dilliard, ed., "Dred Scott Eulogized by James Milton Turner," *Journal of Negro History* 26 (January 1941): 9. For the original, handwritten version of this eulogy, see Dred Scott Papers, Missouri Historical Society, St. Louis, Missouri.

29. *Official Proceedings* (1895), 117.

30. Ibid., 46, 60–61.

31. Ibid., 14–15. For Turner's parliamentary maneuvers on behalf of the measure, see ibid., 39, 44, 45–46, 51.

32. Ibid., 52–54.

33. Muraskin, *Middle-Class Blacks in a White Society*, 151.

34. *Official Proceedings* (1896), 66, 99.

35. Ibid., 25.

36. Ibid., 42, 45.

37. Ibid., 41.

38. Ibid., 42.

39. *Official Proceedings* (1897), 9, 21–23.

40. Ibid., 23.

41. Ibid., 28–29.

42. *Official Proceedings* (1898), 11; ibid. (1899), 91.

43. *St. Louis Post-Dispatch*, 6 March 1898.

44. *Official Proceedings* (1902), 36–37, 93.

45. Ibid., 47.

46. *Official Proceedings* (1903), 8–9.

47. Ibid., illustration between 20 and 21.

48. Ibid., 8–9, 18, 20–22, 42.

49. "State of the Country," ibid., 49-53.

50. Dispatch no. 273, 3 September 1877, "Despatches From United States Ministers to Liberia, 1863–1906" (National Archives, Washington, DC), microcopy no. 170, vol. 6.

51. "State of the Country," *Official Proceedings* (1903), 50.

52. Ibid., 51.

53. Ibid., 51–52.

54. *Official Proceedings* (1905), 10, 48.

55. Ibid., 4.

56. Ibid., 7. Turner had served on similar committees in 1897 and 1903. See *Official Proceedings* (1897), 37; ibid. (1903), 18. For the importance of committees such as these in Prince Hall Freemasonry, see Muraskin, *Middle-Class Blacks in a White Society*, 125–26.

57. *Official Proceedings* (1905), 31–32.

58. Ibid. (1908), illustration between 124 and 125.

59. Ibid., illustration between 24 and 25.

60. Ibid., 18–19.

61. Ibid., 23.

62. Ibid., 38, 55–56.

63. Ibid., 40.

64. Ibid., 10, 59–60.

65. Ibid., 177.

66. Will of J. Milton Turner, Will No. 45591, St. Louis Probate Court, Civil Courts Building. St. Louis, Missouri.

67. *Official Proceedings* (1916), 18. See also *St. Louis Argus*, 5, 12, 19, 26 November, 5, 10 December 1915.

68. *Official Proceedings* (1917), 60–61.

Chapter 5
"George Washington Carver's Missouri"

1. An early version of this essay was delivered as a paper at the George Washington Carver Symposium at Missouri State University, Springfield, in 2008. A revised version of this essay appeared as a chapter in the author's *George Washington Carver: A Biography* (Santa Barbara, CA: Greenwood/ABC-CLIO, 2011), and is reprinted with the permission of ABC-CLIO.

2. Quoted in Gary R. Kremer, ed., *George Washington Carver: In His Own Words* (Columbia: University of Missouri Press, 1987), 20.

3. Ibid., 23.

4. Linda O. McMurry, *George Washington Carver: Scientist & Symbol* (New York: Oxford University Press, 1981), 5. The 1860 slave schedule for Newton County, Missouri, may be accessed through Ancestry.com.

5. Kremer, *George Washington Carver*, 23.

6. Edward C. Bearss, "The Army of the Frontier's First Campaign: The Confederates Win at Newtonia," *Missouri Historical Review* 60 (April 1966): 283–319.

7. Kremer, *George Washington Carver*, 23.

8. Robert P. Fuller and Merrill J. Mattes, "The Early Life of George Washington Carver" (unpublished manuscript, George Washington Carver National Monument, Diamond, Missouri, November 1957), 29; Kremer, *George Washington Carver*, 20.

9. Kremer, *George Washington Carver*, 31.

10. Quoted in Kremer, *George Washington Carver*, 39–41.

11. Ibid., 20.

12. Ibid.

13. McMurry, *George Washington Carver*, 18.

14. Kremer, *George Washington Carver*, 20, 23.

15. Ibid., 23.

16. McMurry, *George Washington Carver*, 20–21.

17. These figures are gleaned from federal census returns that can be accessed through Ancestry.com.

18. W. E. B. DuBois, *Black Reconstruction in America*, rev. ed., introduction by David Levering Lewis (New York: Oxford University Press, 2007), 99-100.

19. McMurry, *George Washington Carver*, 20, 27.

20. George Washington Carver to Isabelle Coleman, 24 July 1931, GWC roll 12, frames 1264–65. GWC Papers, microfilm edition, compiled and filmed by the National Historical Publication Commission, 1975, Inman E. Page Library, Lincoln University, Jefferson City, MO. The original GWC Papers are housed at the Tuskegee Institute Archives in Alabama.

21. Fuller and Mattes, "Early Life of George Washington Carver," 27.

22. Ibid.

23. The most famous retelling of this story appears in Glenn Clark, *The Man Who Talks with the Flowers: The Life Story of Dr. George Washington Carver* (Austin, MN: Macalester Park Publishing, 1939), 22.

24. McMurry, *George Washington Carver*, 20–21.

25. The best source on the so-called Exodus remains Nell Irvin Painter, *Exodus: Black Migration to Kansas after Reconstruction* (New York: Alfred A. Knopf, 1977).

Chapter 6
"Nathaniel C. Bruce, Black Education, and the 'Tuskegee of the Midwest'"

1. This essay originally appeared in the October 1991 issue of the *Missouri Historical Review* and is reprinted with the permission of the State Historical Society of Missouri. It was coauthored with Patrick J. Huber, then a graduate student in the Department of History, University of Missouri–Columbia.

2. The classic study of black education remains Henry A. Bullock, *A History of Negro Education in the South; from 1619 to the Present* (Cambridge, MA: Harvard University Press, 1967).

3. Booker T. Washington, *Up from Slavery: An Autobiography* (New York: Bantam Books, 1959), 155.

4. W. E. B. DuBois, *The Souls of Black Folk* (New York: Fawcett Publications, 1961), 39.

5. "Brief History of the B[artlett] A[gricultural] & I[ndustrial] School," unpaginated, Dalton Vocational School file, Inman E. Page Library, Lincoln University, Jefferson City, Missouri. Copies of these documents are housed at the Missouri State Archives, Jefferson City, Missouri (hereafter cited as Dalton File).

6. Like the origins of many early twentieth-century black leaders, Bruce's date of birth remains obscure. A document on Bruce in the Dalton Vocational School file gives his date of birth as 6 December 1868. In contrast, Bruce's death certificate states he was about eighty-four years old at the time of his death in 1942, placing his birth either in 1857 or 1858. However, the 1910 federal census for Chariton County records forty-two as his age for that year, making 1867 or 1868 his date of birth. The authors have trusted the latter source. An untitled document on Bruce's life, unpaginated, Dalton File; death certificate of Nathaniel C. Bruce, Bureau of Vital Records, Missouri Division of Health, Jefferson City, Missouri; US Census, 13th Report, 1910, "Chariton County, Missouri," roll 776, sheet 86, A–B.

7. "Briefs of the Life of N. C. Bruce," unpaginated, Dalton File.

8. John Francis Case, "Where Black Folks Made Good," *Missouri Ruralist* (20 July 1920): 5.

9. Ibid.

10. V. N. Jones, "History of the Dalton Vocational School," *Dalton Vocational School Digest* (November 1954). A reprint of this article appeared in *History of Dalton, Missouri and Bowling Green Township: 120 Years* (Dalton, MO: Dalton, Bowling Green Township History Committee, 1988), 53–54. "Brief History of the B. A. & I. School"; *State of Missouri Official Manual, 1923–1924* (Jefferson City, MO: Hugh Stephens Press, 1923), 856–57.

11. Case, "Where Black Folks Made Good," 5; Jones, "History of Dalton Vocational School."

12. N. C. Bruce, "The Champion Acre Yield," *Missouri Ruralist* (20 February 1914): 26.

13. "History of Dalton Vocational High School, Dalton, Missouri," unpaginated, Dalton File; John F. Case, "A Black Man Champion," *Missouri Ruralist* (5 December 1915): 18.

14. Case, "A Black Man Champion," 18.

15. *Boonville Weekly Advertiser*, 6 February 1914.

16. Case, "Where Black Folks Made Good," 5.

17. Ibid.

18. Ibid., 5, 17.

19. For Missouri's notorious indifference to and lack of support for black education, see Brigham, "Education of the Negro in Missouri."

20. "Report of Negro Industrial Commission," *Appendix to the House and Senate Journals of the Fiftieth General Assembly, State of Missouri* (1919), 2:3.

21. Ibid., 2:2.

22. Ibid., 2:8–9.

23. "Biennial Report of the Missouri Negro Industrial Commission," *Appendix to the House and Senate Journals of the Fifty-second General Assembly, State of Missouri* (1923), 2:40.

24. "Brief History of the B. A. & I. School"; *Laws of Missouri, Fifty-second General Assembly* (Jefferson City, 1923), 49.

25. "Where Negroes Go to School," *Missouri Ruralist* (1 October 1924): 9; "The Dalton Vocational School," unpaginated, Dalton File.

26. "Great Day for Negroes," *Missouri Ruralist* (1 September 1924); "Where Negroes Go to School," 9.

27. *Keytesville Chariton Courier*, 5 September 1924.

28. "Where Negroes Go to School," 9.

29. N. C. Bruce to J. D. Elliff, 9 March 1918, Elliff to Bruce, 11 March 1918, in Joseph D. Elliff Papers, Western Historical Manuscript Collection, University of Missouri–Columbia; Antonio F. Holland, "Nathan B. Young and the Development of Black Higher Education" (PhD diss., University of Missouri–Columbia, 1984), 203; Savage, *The History of Lincoln University*, 150–53. Holland's dissertation was subsequently published as *Nathan B. Young and the Struggle over Black Higher Education* (Columbia: University of Missouri Press, 2006).

30. Holland, "Nathan B. Young," 203.

31. "Brief History of B. A. & I. School"; an untitled document on Bruce's life; Jones, "History of Dalton Vocational School."

32. Holland, "Nathan B. Young," 203; Raymond Wolters, *The New Negro on Campus* (Princeton, NJ: Princeton University Press, 1975), 212–13; *Moberly Monitor-Index*, 4 June 1926.

33. Wolters, *The New Negro on Campus*, 212–13; Roy Wilkins with Tom Mathews, *Standing Fast: The Autobiography of Roy Wilkins* (New York: Viking Press, 1982), 74; *Kansas City Call*, 11 June 1926.

34. *Kansas City Call*, 2 December 1927. After resigning as inspector, Bruce occupied a number of educational or agricultural governmental positions. In 1928 and 1929, he served as temporary US farm agent for the flooded cotton counties of southeast Missouri. In the early 1930s, he was appointed director of black education in the state's prison system, and he served in that position for almost a decade.

Bruce died on 27 June 1942, in Chariton County, "within a short distance of the institution he loved so well." The *Kansas City Call* mourned his passing: "[He] spent many of his best years at [the Dalton Vocational School] and inspired the lives of many young people." *Kansas City Call*, 10 July 1942. See also "Briefs of the Life of N. C. Bruce"; and *State of Missouri Official Manual (1933–1934)*: 786, *(1935–1936)*: 797, *(1937–1938)*: 737, *(1939–1940)*: 725.

35. *Laws of Missouri, Fifty-fifth General Assembly* (Jefferson City, 1929), 286–87.

36. Ibid., 387; "Briefs of the Life of N. C. Bruce"; "Brief History of B. A. & I. School."

37. Jones, "History of Dalton Vocational School"; "Dalton Vocational School," *Missouri High School Reports*, 1942–1943.

38. "Dalton Vocational School," *Missouri High School Reports*, 1931–1932, 1940–1941, 1942–1943.

39. Jones, "History of Dalton Vocational School."

40. "Biennial Report of the Board of Curators, Lincoln University," *Appendix to the House and Senate Journals of the Sixtieth General Assembly, State of Missouri* (1939), 1:15; "Cornerstone Laying Dalton Vocational School," unpaginated, dated 21 May 1938, Dalton File.

41. "Dalton Vocational School: Total Amounts Requested and Appropriated by the Legislature in Last Ten Years, 1937–1938–1947–1948," unpaginated, Dalton File; "Dalton Vocational School," *Missouri High School Reports*, 1938–1939; Jones, "History of Dalton Vocational School."

42. Sherman D. Scruggs to members of the board of curators of Lincoln University, 13 September 1951, Dalton File, 3. The letter that recommended increased funding for the Dalton School was sent to the governor as well as twelve state senators and representatives.

43. Ibid., 2, 3.

44. Eliot F. Battle, interview with Patrick Huber, Columbia, Missouri, 14 October 1989; Jones, "History of Dalton Vocational School"; annual average salaries for Missouri teachers taken from *One Hundred and Fourth Report of the Public Schools of the State of Missouri (1954)*, 297–99; *State of Missouri Official Manual, 1955–1956*, 483.

45. "Dalton Vocational School," *Missouri High School Reports*, 1929–1930, 1944–1945, 1932–1933, 1934–1935.

46. "Report and Recommendations of the President of the University to the Board of Curators of Lincoln University, Jefferson City, Missouri," 11 April 1969, Dalton File, 3.

47. "Report and Recommendations," 3–4; letter from Earl E. Dawson, acting president of Lincoln University, to Virgil V. Bachtel, Superintendent Salisbury School District R-4, 6 August 1955.

48. "Report and Recommendations," 4.

49. Ibid.

50. Ibid., 5. General Warranty Deed from Board of Curators, Lincoln University of Missouri, to Roland L. Hughes and Rosia L. Hughes, 2 July 1971.

Chapter 7
"'The Black People Did the Work': African American Life in Arrow Rock, Missouri, 1850–1960"

1. This essay originally appeared in the July 2012 issue of the *Missouri Historical Review* and is reprinted with the permission of the State Historical Society of Missouri.

Quotation is from Michael Dickey, *Arrow Rock Crossroads of the Missouri Frontier* (Arrow Rock, MO: Friends of Arrow Rock, 2004), 95.

2. "By 1910 nearly 67 percent of Missouri's blacks lived in the cities, almost three times the national average." Lorenzo J. Greene, Gary R. Kremer, and Antonio F. Holland, *Missouri's Black Heritage,* rev. ed. (Columbia: University of Missouri Press, 1993), 113.

3. Miles W. Eaton, "The Development and Later Decline of the Hemp Industry in Missouri," *Missouri Historical Review* 43 (July 1949): 349.

4. R. Douglas Hurt, *Agriculture and Slavery in Missouri's Little Dixie* (Columbia: University of Missouri Press, 1992), 74.

5. William Barclay Napton, *Past and Present of Saline County Missouri* (Indianapolis: Bowen, 1910), 134.

6. "Your ob't servant" to "Messrs. Yeatman, Pittman & Co.," 13 February 1850, in *Jefferson Inquirer,* 9 March 1850.

7. Dickey, *Arrow Rock,* 226.

8. *Jefferson City Jefferson Inquirer,* 23 July 1859; *Liberty Weekly Tribune,* 29 July 1859; Thomas G. Dyer, "'A Most Unexampled Exhibition of Madness and Brutality': Judge Lynch in Saline County, Missouri, 1859," pt. 1, *Missouri Historical Review* 89 (April 1995): 282–83.

9. Fisk to James E. Yeatman, 25 March 1865, in *The War of the Rebellion: A Compilation of the Official Records of the Union and Confederate Armies* (Washington, DC: GPO, 1888–1901), ser. 1, vol. 48, pt. 1, 1257.

10. *Ninth Census of the United States,* 1870, *Population Schedule,* Saline County, Missouri (National Archives Microfilm Publication M593), roll 804. Arrow Rock Township covers pages 1–81.

11. T. C. Rainey, *Along the Old Trail: Pioneer Sketches of Arrow Rock and Vicinity* (Marshall, MO: Marshall Chapter, Daughters of the American Revolution, 1914), 1:34.

12. Christopher Phillips and Jason L. Pendleton, eds., *The Union on Trial: The Political Journals of Judge William Barclay Napton, 1829–1883* (Columbia: University of Missouri Press, 2005), 235.

13. Rainey, *Along the Old Trail,* 65–66.

14. *Tenth Census of the United States,* 1880, *Population Schedule,* Saline County, Missouri (National Archives Microfilm Publication T9), roll 716. Arrow Rock Township appears on pages 573A–598B. The "Town of Arrow Rock" appears on pages 587A–590A. Tippin and Switzler families appear on page 588B. The 1880 census is the first federal census in which the "Town of Arrow Rock" is identified separately from the larger Arrow Rock Township.

15. Clark-Lewis, *Living In, Living Out.*

16. W. E. B. DuBois, *Black Reconstruction in America,* rev. ed., introduction by David Levering Lewis (New York: Oxford University Press, 2007), 99–100.

17. *Laws of the State of Missouri* (1866), 177.

18. Turner to F. A. Seely (chief disbursing officer for the Freedmen's Bureau in Missouri), 9, 12 November 1869, as quoted in Gary R. Kremer, *James Milton Turner and the Promise of America: The Public Life of a Post–Civil War Black Leader* (Columbia: University of Missouri Press, 1991), 33–34.

19. Ibid.

20. *Ninth Census of the United States,* 1870, Saline County, roll 804, 1–81.

21. Saline County Register of Teachers, 1873–1901, Arrow Rock State Historic Site,

Arrow Rock, MO; *Ninth Census of the United States,* 1870, Saline County, roll 804, 1–81; *History of Saline County, Missouri* (St. Louis: Missouri Historical Co., 1881), 528.

22. Saline County Register of Teachers; John Thomas Trigg, death certificate 42768, Missouri Death Certificates, 1910–1961, accessed 11 May 2012, at www.sos.mo.gov/images/archives/death-certs/1932/1932_00043658.pdf.

23. Warranty Deed, Record Book 18, 160–61, Recorder's Office, Saline County Courthouse, Marshall, MO.

24. *Ninth Census of the United States,* 1870, Saline County, roll 804, 3A, 8B; *Tenth Census of the United States,* 1880, Saline County, roll 716, 586A–586B.

25. Deed to church property, Friends of Arrow Rock Archives, Arrow Rock, MO; Dennis Banks, interview by Mary Burge, 1986. Notes from this interview are available at Friends of Arrow Rock Archives.

26. Robin D. G. Kelley, *Race Rebels: Culture, Politics, and the Black Working Class* (New York: Free Press, 1994), 38.

27. *Official Proceedings of the Fourteenth Annual Communication of the Most Worshipful Grand Lodge, A.F. & A.M.* (1880), 105 (hereafter cited as *Official Proceedings*).

28. Leslie Schwalm, *Emancipation's Diaspora: Race and Reconstruction in the Upper Midwest* (Chapel Hill: University of North Carolina Press, 2009), 161.

29. Muraskin, *Middle-Class Blacks in a White Society,* 196–98.

30. *Arrow Rock Statesman,* 24 December 1915.

31. *Official Proceedings* (1888), 62; *Official Proceedings* (1889), 61.

32. *Tenth Census of the United States,* 1880, Saline County, roll 716, 573B.

33. Ibid., 585B.

34. *Arrow Rock Enterprise,* 28 July 1893.

35. Abstract of Block No. 30 of the Town of Arrow Rock, Friends of Arrow Rock Archives.

36. Edward S. Lewis to Elizabeth Taylor, 23 May 1927, ibid. In addition to the Masons and the Odd Fellows, Arrow Rock also had two other black lodges during this period: the Sherman Lodge No. 17 of Lincoln Sons and Daughters of Freedom, and the United Brothers of Friendship. Sherman Lodge Ledger, kept by lodge member Dennis Banks, was donated to the Friends of Arrow Rock by his niece Teresa Habernal and can be accessed at the Friends of Arrow Rock Archives. The C. R. Smith Lodge No. 170 of the United Brothers of Friendship was established in Arrow Rock in 1911. A 1911 program from a statewide annual meeting in Kansas City identifies nine members of this lodge and nineteen members of its women's auxiliary, Edwards Temple No. 197 of the Sisters of the Mysterious Ten. *Proceedings, Forty-first Annual Grand Session of the Grand Lodge, United Brothers of Friendship* (Kansas City, MO: Grand Lodge United Brothers of Friendship and Sisters of the Mysterious Ten, 1911), 133, 243.

37. Herbert Blumer, "Race Prejudice as a Sense of Group Position," *Pacific Sociological Review* 1 (Spring 1958): 3–7.

38. *Arrow Rock Enterprise,* 20 May 1892.

39. Ibid., 25 March 1892.

40. Ibid., 28 July 1893.

41. *Twelfth Census of the United States,* 1900, *Population, Schedule,* Saline County, Missouri (National Archives Microfilm Publication T623), roll 901, 12A–15B.

42. *Arrow Rock Enterprise,* 5 August 1892.

43. Dorothy Kruger, interview by Pam Parsons and Kathy Borgman, 18 February 1997, Friends of Arrow Rock Archives.

44. *Thirteenth Census of the United States,* 1910, *Population Schedule,* Saline County, Missouri (National Archives Microfilm Publication T624), roll 823. "Arrow Rock Village" extends from page IA through page 4A.

45. *Arrow Rock Enterprise,* 25 August 1893.

46. Marvin Henry Williams, interview by Gary R. Kremer and Pam Parsons, 19 September 1996, Friends of Arrow Rock Archives.

47. Fielding Draffen, quoted in transcript of public meeting conducted by Gary Kremer, 4 May 1997, Friends of Arrow Rock Archives.

48. Ibid.; Williams, interview.

49. It seems likely that this quarry was opened as a consequence of an effort in 1928 to improve the Missouri River, championed by James A. Reed, US senator from Missouri. *Report of the Secretary of War to the President, 1929* (Washington, DC: GPO, 1929), 29; *War Department Appropriation Bill, 1929, Nonmilitary Activities, Hearings before the Subcommittee of House Committee on Appropriations,* 70th Cong., 1st sess. (1928), 456–57; *Sixteenth Census of the United States,* 1940, *Population Schedule,* Saline County, Missouri, Ancestry.com. The town of Arrow Rock appears in Enumeration District 98-1, 1A–4A.

50. *Sixteenth Census,* 1940, Saline County, 2A.

51. Williams, interview.

52. Pearl Adams, interview by Gary R. Kremer and Pam Parsons, 27 October 1996, Friends of Arrow Rock Archives.

53. *Sixteenth Census,* 1940, Saline County, 1A–4A.

54. Ibid.

55. Ibid.

56. Thelma Conway and Teresa Habernal, interview by Gary R. Kremer, 17 June 1997, Friends of Arrow Rock Archives.

57. Betty Banks Finley, interview by Authorene Phillips and Pam Parsons, 3 January 1997, notes, ibid.

58. Quoted in Howard W. Marshall, *Play Me Something Quick and Devilish: Old-Time Fiddlers in Missouri* (Columbia: University of Missouri Press, 2013), 171.

59. Mary Lou Pearson, interview by Pam Parsons and Kathy Borgman, 18 February 1997, Friends of Arrow Rock Archives.

60. Ibid.

61. Ibid.

62. Hortense Nichols, interview by Gary R. Kremer and Pam Parsons, 27 October 1996, Friends of Arrow Rock Archives.

63. Nichols, interview.

64. Andrew Billingsley, *Climbing Jacob's Ladder: The Enduring Legacy of African-American Families* (New York: Simon and Schuster, 1992), 352.

65. Quoted in ibid., 354.

66. Adams, interview.

67. Rainey, *Along the Old Trail,* 82.

68. Mary Burge, interview by Pam Parsons and Kathy Borgman, 18 February 1997, Friends of Arrow Rock Archives.

69. Ruth Wilson Banks Perry, interview by Authorene Phillips, 25 September 1996, ibid.

70. The author's thinking about this topic has been significantly influenced by Ira Berlin's book *The Making of African America: The Four Great Migrations* (New York: Penguin Books, 2010).

Chapter 8
"'Just like the Garden of Eden': African American Community Life in Kansas City's Leeds"

1. This essay first appeared in the January 2004 issue of the *Missouri Historical Review* and is reprinted with the permission of the State Historical Society of Missouri. For a good summary of much of this research, see Leon F. Litwack, *Trouble in Mind: Black Southerners in the Age of Jim Crow* (New York: Vintage Books, 1999).

2. The term "Jim Crow era," as used here, refers to the period from the end of Reconstruction during the 1870s to the beginning of the modern-day civil rights movement during the mid-1950s.

3. Sherry Lamb Schirmer, *A City Divided: The Racial Landscape of Kansas City, 1900–1960* (Columbia: University of Missouri Press, 2002), 29.

4. Lorenzo J. Greene, Gary R. Kremer, and Antonio F. Holland, *Missouri's Black Heritage*, rev. ed. (Columbia: University of Missouri Press, 1993), 107–13.

5. Schirmer, *City Divided*, 39–41.

6. Ibid., 42–45.

7. Plat for Couch's 1st Addition, County Recorder's Office, Jackson County Courthouse, Kansas City, Missouri.

8. Plat for Hollie Addition, ibid. Although the legal name was "Hollie Addition," named for the owner, Hollie B. Allen, Leeds residents referred to it as "Allen's Addition."

9. "Leeds" vertical file, Missouri Valley Room, Kansas City Public Library.

10. Interview with Dolly Mosby Malone, 14 November 2001. All interviews cited in this article were conducted by the author. Tapes and transcripts of the interviews are housed at the State Historical Society of Missouri Research Center-Columbia.

11. Leon F. Litwack documents this intense desire on the part of African Americans to own land. In addition to his book *Trouble in Mind*, see his *Been in the Storm So Long: The Aftermath of Slavery* (New York: Knopf, 1979).

12. US Census, Fourteenth Report, 1920, *Population Schedules*, "Jackson County, Kaw Township, Ward 14, District No. 238."

13. Malone, interview.

14. Interview with Gertrude Gillum, 10 May 2001.

15. Interview with Kenneth E. Ray, 16 May 2001.

16. Interview with Vivienne Starks Smith, 24 July 2002.

17. Interview with Mary Garth, 24 May 2001.

18. Interview with Delores Louise Ray, 24 May 2001; Gertrude Gillum, interview; Kenneth Ray, interview.

19. US Census, Fourteenth Report, 1920, *Population Schedules*.

20. Interviews with Clara Horne Walker, 28 June 2001; Rosa Mae Gillespie, 19 April 2001; Lois Kinney, 16 August 2001; Isola Richardson, 19 April 2001; Kenneth Ray, interview.

21. Gillespie, interview.

22. Interview with Easter Hubley, 10 May 2001.

23. Garth, interview.

24. Interview with Charles Jones, 16 August 2001.

25. Ibid.; Charles Ward also remembered his family relying on wild game; interview with Charles Ward, 17 October 2001.

26. Interview with Thomas McCormick, 12 December 2001; Richardson, interview.

27. Smith, interviews, 13 April 2001, 24 July 2002.

28. Interview with Ruby M. Robinson, 25 April 2001; Smith, interview, 24 July 2002.

29. US Census, Fourteenth Report, 1920, *Population Schedules*.

30. Gertrude Gillum, interview.

31. Interview with Lella Jo Birks, 15 August 2001.

32. Telephone interview with Lawrence Jackson, 11 October 2002.

33. Smith, interview, 24 July 2002.

34. Interview with Hazel Nicholson, 31 May 2001; Robinson, interview.

35. Garth, interview.

36. Robinson, interview.

37. Kenneth Ray, interview; "The History of Gilbert Memorial A.M.E. Church, Kansas City, MO," Missouri State Museum.

38. "Pilgrim's Rest Baptist Church History," Missouri State Museum; *Kansas City Missouri City Directory* (Kansas City: Gate City Directory Company, 1918), 1101.

39. *Kansas City Call*, 7 January 1922.

40. Nicholson, interview.

41. Interview with Betty Holt, 7 June 2001; Nicholson, interview.

42. Robinson, interview.

43. Malone, interview; Whitfield Ross, "History of Dunbar School," Missouri State Museum.

44. McCormick, interview.

45. Ross, "History of Dunbar School."

46. Malone, interview

47. Ross, "History of Dunbar School."

48. Interview with Ronald Gillum, 10 May 2001; interview with Yvonne Brooks Bullock, 2 May 2001; quote is from Kenneth Ray, interview.

49. Kenneth Ray, interview; McCormick, interview; Richardson, interview

50. Malone interview, McCormick interview; Delores Louise Ray interview; quote is from Birks, interview.

51. McCormick, interview.

52. *Kansas City Call*, 24 June 1922.

53. Gertrude Gillum, interview; Delores Louise Ray interview; Jackson, interview.

54. *Kansas City Call*, 17, 24, June 1922.

55. Kenneth Ray, interview; Ward, interview; Jones, interview.

56. Ward interview; interview with Dora Horn Craven, 24 July 2002.

57. Gillespie, interview; Kenneth Ray, interview.

58. *Kansas City American*, 23 May 1929.

59. Craven, interview.

60. Nicholson, interview; interview with Yvonne Starks Wilson, 16 August 2001; Delores Louise Ray, interview.

61. Malone, interview.

62. Wilson, interview.

63. Maya Angelou, *I Know Why the Caged Bird Sings* (New York: Bantam Books, 1971), 111–12.

64. Dora May Craven, interview, 24 July 2002.

65. Malone, interview; interview with Mary Woods, 31 May 2001; interviews with Gertrude and Ronald Gillum, 10 May 2001. The Kansas City Municipal Farm was established in 1909 as a "progressive" institution where "vagrants, mendicants, and petty criminals" could be reformed. *Kansas City Times*, 19 January 1909. Kristine Stilwell, "'If You Don't Slip': The Hobo Life, 1911–1916" (PhD diss., University of Missouri–Columbia, 2004).

66. Malone, interview; McCormick, interview.

67. Malone, interview.

68. Ronald Gillum, interview.

69. McCormick, interview.

70. Craven, interview.

71. Lawrence H. Larsen and Nancy J. Hulston, *Pendergast!* (Columbia: University of Missouri Press, 1997), 103–5. Larsen and Hulston document Pendergast's efforts to bring African Americans into the Democratic Party.

72. Richardson, interview; Malone, interview; Jackson, interview. Isola Richardson and Darie Richardson are not related.

73. Malone interview; interview with Lynthia V. Ponder, 16 August 2001; Garth, interview; interview with Alvin Brooks, 28 June 2001; Craven, interview.

74. Larsen and Hulston, *Pendergast!* 117.

75. Ward, interview; Robinson, interview; Hubley, interview.

76. Interview with Robert L. White, 10 May 2001; Richardson, interview.

77. Yvonne Brooks Bullock, interview, 2 May 2001.

78. Ibid.; Jones, interview; Craven, interview.

79. Walker, interview; White, interview.

80. Bullock, interview; Kenneth Ray, interview.

Chapter 9
"The Whitley Sisters Remember:
Living with Segregation in Kansas City, Missouri"

1. This essay originally appeared in the August 1999 issue of *Kawsmouth: A Journal of Regional History* and is reprinted with permission of the University of Missouri–Kansas City. It was coauthored with Trina Philpot, then an undergraduate student working with Gary R. Kremer in the William Woods University honors program.

2. Sherry Lamb Schirmer, "Landscape of Denial: Space, Status, and Gender in the Construction of Racial Perceptions among White Kansas Citians, 1900–1958" (PhD diss., University of Kansas, 1995), 184. This dissertation was published as *A City Divided: The Racial Landscape of Kansas City, 1900–1960* (Columbia: University of Missouri Press, 2002).

3. The major source for this paper has been a series of interviews with the Whitley sisters (Gertrude Whitley Bardwell, Geneva Whitley Carple, and Irene Whitley Marcus) over the course of more than a year. Copies of these taped interviews and their transcriptions are in the possession of the authors.

4. Gary R. Kremer and Jennifer Kane, "African American Community Life in the Ozarks: Hartville, Missouri, 1870–1940," a paper presented at the 1996 Missouri Conference on History, April 1996, Jefferson City, Missouri. Frank Whitley, a self-proclaimed "Black Historian," talked of his parents' lives as slaves and their migration to Tennessee as part of the Exodus of 1879–1880 in several late-life interviews. See, for example, the *News and Leader* [Springfield, Mo.], 15 October 1977 and

27 March 1983. For a general source on the Exodus, see Nell Irvin Painter, *Exodusters: Black Migration to Kansas after Reconstruction* (New York: Alfred A. Knopf, 1976).

5. Interview with Gertrude Whitley Bardwell and Irene Whitley Marcus, 12 December 1997, in the home of Irene Whitley Marcus, Kansas City, Missouri.

6. Ibid.; Asa Martin, *Our Negro Population: A Sociological Study of the Negroes of Kansas City, Missouri*, (Kansas City: Franklin Hudson Publishing, 1913), 90. Martin described the boundaries of the Bowery in 1912 as Twenty-fifth Street on the south, Seventeenth Street on the north, Troost on the west, and Woodland Avenue on the east. Those boundaries, only slightly expanded, are very close to those used by the Whitley sisters to describe their neighborhood during the 1920s and 1930s, although neither they nor any other African Americans we interviewed remember their neighborhood being referred to as "The Bowery." The term seems to have been a pejorative one developed by the sociologist Asa Martin.

7. Fourteenth Population Schedule of the United States (1920), Jackson County and Kansas City, Enumeration District 173, sheet 5, line 85.

8. Interview with Gertrude Whitley Bardwell, Geneva Whitley Carple, and Irene Whitley Marcus, 5 August 1998.

9. Interview with Gertrude Whitley Bardwell and Irene Whitley Marcus, 12 December 1997.

10. Interview with Gertrude Whitley Bardwell, Geneva Whitley Carple, and Irene Whitley Marcus, 6 October 1998. (One of the sisters, Gertrude, is now deceased.)

11. Ibid., 5 August 1998; "Bethel African Methodist Episcopal Church through the Years," in "The Ninety-fifth Session of the Northwest Missouri Conference, African Methodist Episcopal Church," 5–10 October 1976.

12. Interviews with Gertrude Whitley Bardwell and Irene Whitley Marcus, 12 December 1997; interview with Gertrude Whitley Bardwell, Geneva Whitley Carple, and Irene Whitley Marcus, 5 August 1998. "The History of the Daughters of Bethel, 1942–1981 and Ongoing," typescript copy in Irene Marcus Collection.

13. W. R. Howell, "The Colored Schools of Kansas City, Missouri," in William H. Young and Nathan B. Young Jr., *Your Kansas City and Mine* (Kansas City: William H. Young, 1950), 21, 156.

14. Interview with Gertrude Whitley Bardwell, Geneva Whitley Carple, and Irene Whitley Marcus, 6 October 1998, 12 January 1999.

15. W. R. Howell, "The Colored Schools of Kansas City, Missouri," in Young and Young, *Your Kansas City and Mine*, 21, 156.

16. Interview with Gertrude Whitley Bardwell and Irene Whitley Marcus, 12 December 1997.

17. Interview with Irene Whitley Marcus, 6 October 1998.

18. "History of the Paseo YWCA," in Young and Young, *Your Kansas City and Mine*, 20, 153.

19. Interview with Gertrude Whitley Bardwell and Irene Whitley Marcus, 30 November 1997. Another woman warmly remembered by the Whitley sisters is Mrs. Frances Hayden, who replaced Ms. Mountain as executive director of the YWCA. She served in that position from 1943 to 1963. Mrs. Hayden lived with her husband, a dentist, in the Whitleys' neighborhood and was also a "Daughter of Bethel." Obituary of Mrs. Frances Hayden, *Kansas City Call*, undated clipping in Irene Marcus Collection.

20. Interview with Gertrude Whitley Bardwell and Irene Whitley Marcus, 30 November 1997.

21. Ibid.; Young and Young, *Your Kansas City and Mine*, 105–6.

22. Joel Litvin, "The Urban League of Kansas City: 25 Years of Progress," a study done for the Urban League, 1963 (Urban League Archives, Kansas City, Missouri); Thomas A. Webster, "Salute to the Urban League," *Kansas City Globe* 8, no. 39 (16–23 October, 1980): 3–11.

23. Interview with Barbara Thompson Pullam, Jefferson City, Missouri. According to historian Janet Bruce, *The Kansas City Monarchs: Champions of Black Baseball* (Lawrence: University of Kansas, 1985), 50–51, the behavior of fans at Monarchs' games was a subject of controversy: "The crowds at Negro-league baseball games were loud and lively in support of the home team, The ball-park behavior of many of the newly arrived southerners . . . sometimes offended the sensibilities of middle-class blacks. They saw this boisterous 'rowdyism' (including everything from drinking and gambling to harassing the umpires, throwing seat cushions, and fighting) as an embarrassment for the race."

24. Bardwell, Carple, and Marcus interviews; Young and Young, *Your Kansas City and Mine*, 129.

25. Interview with Gertrude Whitley Bardwell, Geneva Whitley Carple, and Irene Whitley Marcus, 3 December 1998.

26. Ibid.

27. Ibid.

28. Ibid.

29. Ibid.

30. Ibid., 12 January 1999.

31. Ibid., 3 December 1998.

32. Ibid., 5 August 1998.

33. Ibid., 9 September 1998.

34. Ibid.; Fiftieth Anniversary Program, The Twin Citian Club, copy in Irene Marcus Collection.

35. Interview with Gertrude Whitley Bardwell, Geneva Whitley Carple, and Irene Whitley Marcus, 5 August 1998. For more on the Reverend D. A. Holmes, see Young and Young, *Your Kansas City and Mine*, 33, 152.

Chapter 10
"The Missouri Industrial Home
for Negro Girls: The 1930s"

1. This essay originally appeared in the fall 1983 issue of *American Studies* and was coauthored with Linda Rea Gibbens. It is reprinted with the permission of *American Studies*.

2. This essay draws heavily upon the conceptual framework provided by David J. Rothman in *Conscience and Convenience: The Asylum and Its Alternatives in Progressive America* (Boston: Little, Brown, 1980). For additional background on the philosophies behind early twentieth-century juvenile asylums and the importance of children to Progressives, see Steven L. Schlossman, *Love and the American Delinquent: The Theory and Practice of "Progressive" Juvenile Justice, 1825–1920* (Chicago: University of Chicago Press, 1977), and Anthony Platt, *The Child Savers* (Chicago: University of Chicago Press, 1969).

3. Rothman, *Conscience and Convenience*, 207.

4. Ibid., 262.

5. Ibid., 286.

6. The only history of the Missouri Industrial Home for Negro Girls at the time this essay was written was Nancy Ellen Cole's "Missouri Industrial Home for Negro Girls, Tipton, Missouri, 1909–1944" (MA thesis, Washington University, 1946). The authors wish to express their gratitude to Mrs. Cole for granting them access to her thesis and for helping in the preparation of this article.

7. According to Cole, "the control by the Governor over the State Industrial Home for Negro Girls had the most disastrous results throughout its history. Almost without exception . . . appointments were apparently made solely on the basis of political loyalty." Ibid., 30.

8. For the role of Missouri blacks in the 1932 election, see Larry H. Grothaus, "The Negro in Missouri Politics, 1890–1941" (PhD diss., University of Missouri–Columbia, 1970), chapter 4.

9. Mrs. A. G. Gordon to Governor Park, 12 June 1933. For a similar sentiment about the prestige of the Tipton position, see Casimir J. Welch to Sam O. Hargus, 17 June 1933, Guy B. Park Papers, Western Historical Manuscripts, the State Historical Society of Missouri, Columbia. The authors wish to thank Mrs. Henrietta Park Krause for allowing them access to the Park Papers.

10. William L. Igoe to Governor Park, 20 March 1933; C. S. McClellan, D. M. Grant, William A. Swanson, to William I. Igoe, 28 March 1933, Park Papers. Traditionally, a woman was appointed superintendent and her husband manager of the institution. In Bowles's case, there was some concern about her husband, Daniel, who was a St. Louis lawyer, formerly having been a Republican. At the time of Mrs. Bowles's application, her husband described himself as an Independent. He appears in the *Official Manual* of the State of Missouri as a Democrat. Missouri, *Official Manual, 1933–1934*, 795.

11. Biographical sketches of Ethel and Daniel Bowles; Enclosure, William I. Igoe to Governor Park, 30 March 1933, Park Papers.

12. Cole, "Missouri Industrial Home for Negro Girls," 10–13.

13. Ibid.; "Report of Commission for State Industrial School for Negro Girls," Forty-seventh General Assembly (1913), Missouri, House and Senate *Journals, Appendix*, 2:4.

14. *Laws of Missouri* (1913), 139–40. The law that applied to white girls was identical to the law for blacks, except that it did not include the word "Negro." The 1913 statute was revised in 1919 and 1923. The 1923 law limited the ages of white girls from twelve to twenty-one and black girls from ten to twenty-one. *Laws of Missouri* (1923), 127–28.

15. "Biennial Report of the State Industrial Home for Negro Girls, 1915–1916," Forty-ninth General Assembly (1917) Missouri, House and Senate *Journals, Appendix*, 6 (hereafter cited as Biennial Report).

16. Ibid.

17. Ibid.

18. August Meier, *Negro Thought in America, 1880–1915: Racial Ideologies in the Age of Booker T. Washington* (Ann Arbor: University of Michigan Press, 1963). Missouri blacks were heavily influenced during these years by a state-supported Missouri Negro Industrial Commission, led initially by N. C. Bruce, one of Booker T. Washington's students. The commission, formed in 1918, resolved to urge and stimulate "our race's old time loyalty, fidelity and hearty, persistent labor." "Report of Negro Industrial Commission," Fiftieth General Assembly (1919), Missouri, House and Senate *Journals, Appendix*, 4. See also subsequent biennial reports of the commission for the

1920s and 1930s.

19. Commenting on early twentieth-century women in the workforce, historian Peter Filene has written: "For very few of these women was employment anything like a glorious adventure. The great majority labored long, menially, and patiently in domestic service (36 percent), manufacturing (24 percent), and agriculture (15 percent). . . . Most worked because they had to, not because they wanted to. . . . The young, single wage earner might enjoy the chance to be away from home and to spend her income on new dresses, but she was awaiting a husband to rescue her from the factory, the department store, or someone else's kitchen." Peter Gabriel Filene, *Him/Her/Self: Sex Roles in Modern America* (New York: Mentor, 1976), 26.

20. "Biennial Report (1935)," 435–36.

21. Ibid., 437.

22. Ibid., 443; Cole, "Missouri Industrial Home for Negro Girls," 139–40.

23. There were eighty-two girls in the Tipton Home on 31 December 1932. The daily average number of girls for 1932 was 82.3. "Biennial Report (1933)," 452; Cole, "Missouri Industrial Home for Negro Girls," 22.

24. Cole, "Missouri Industrial Home for Negro Girls," 78.

25. According to Rothman, virtually all early twentieth-century "training schools" for juvenile delinquents followed "a merit and demerit system." Rothman, *Conscience and Convenience,* 277.

26. "Biennial Report (1935)," 436.

27. Ibid.

28. Quoted in Cole, "Missouri Industrial Home for Negro Girls," 149.

29. Case File No. 723, Case Files of Girls Incarcerated in the Missouri Industrial Home for Negro Girls, Record Group No. 213, Missouri State Archives, Jefferson City, Missouri (hereafter cited as Case Files).

30. Case File No. 626.

31. Case File No. 658.

32. Case File No. 653.

33. Case File No. 723.

34. Case File No. 652.

35. Case File No. 660.

36. Case File No. 626.

37. Quoted in Cole, "Missouri Industrial Home for Negro Girls," 157.

38. "Biennial Report (1933)," 434.

39. Quoted in Cole, "Missouri Industrial Home for Negro Girls," 158.

40. Ethel Bowles to Col. J. E. Mathews, 14 July 1938, Case File No. 725.

41. Rothman, *Conscience and Convenience,* 276–77.

42. See in particular Case File Nos. 681, 725.

43. Case File No. 594.

44. Ibid.

45. Ibid.

46. Case File No. 341.

47. Case File No. 660, undated letter from P. W. to "Dear Mother."

48. Case File No. 677.

49. Cole, "Missouri Industrial Home for Negro Girls," 196.

50. Case File No. 704. Just how much Lucille's compliments of Bowles were designed to get money out of the superintendent would be impossible to say. If, as it appears, Bowles sent her no money, it is significant that she continued the corre-

spondence for four years.

51. Ibid.

52. Ethel Bowles to Miss Sarah Young, 22 May 1935, Case File No. 626.

53. H.S. to "My Dear Mother," 5 October 1935, ibid.

54. Ibid., 8 December 1936.

55. "Your Mother" to "My dear Hattie," 15 December 1936, ibid.

56. I.D. to Ethel Bowles, 15 April 1935, Case File No. 596.

57. B.S. to Ethel Bowles, 15 April 1935, ibid.

58. Ibid., 24 July 1935.

Chapter 11
"Black Culture Mecca of the Midwest:
Lincoln University, 1921–1955"

1. This essay was originally presented at a "Black Heartland" symposium at Washington University in 1992. The proceedings of that symposium, including this essay, were published in two series of "Occasional Papers," both under the title *Black Heartland: African American Life, the Middle West, and the Meaning of American Regionalism,* ed. Gerald Early (St. Louis, MO: Washington University. Volume 1, Number 1, was published in 1996; Volume 1, Number 2, which carried my essay, was published in 1997. This essay is reprinted with the permission of Gerald Early.

2. Nathan B. Young to Dr. and Mrs. J. P. Wragg, 15 January 1927, quoted in Savage, *The History of Lincoln University,* 202. See Appendix A for a copy of a map drawn by Young to illustrate his point.

3. *Laws of Missouri* (1921), 86. Savage's history, though dated, remains the only book-length history of Lincoln University. For the "new Negro movement" on black campuses, see Raymond Wolters, *The New Negro on Campus: Black College Rebellions of the 1920s* (Princeton, NJ: Princeton University Press, 1975).

4. For Young's career at both Florida A&M and Lincoln University, see Antonio F. Holland, "Nathan B. Young and the Development of Black Higher Education" (PhD diss., University of Missouri–Columbia, 1984). This dissertation was subsequently published under the title *Nathan B. Young and the Struggle over Black Higher Education* (Columbia: University of Missouri Press, 2006).

5. W. E. B. DuBois, "Nathan B. Young," *Crisis* 26 (September 1923): 226–27; Wolters, *The New Negro on Campus,* 202–4.

6. W. Sherman Savage File, Faculty Files, Inman E. Page Library, Lincoln University, Jefferson City, Missouri (hereafter cited as Faculty Files, Page Library). For Savage's contribution to the study of black history, see August Meier and Elliott Rudwick, *Black History and the Historical Profession, 1915–1980,* Blacks in the New World Series (Urbana and Chicago: University of Illinois Press, 1986), 74, 83–84, 106.

7. Joanne V. Gabbin, *Sterling H. Brown: Building the Black Aesthetic Tradition,* Contributions in Afro-American and African Studies No. 86 (Westport, CT: Greenwood Press, 1985).

8. Ibid., 35–36; telephone interview with Thomas D. Pawley III, 13 December 1990; "Checkers," *The Collected Poems of Sterling A. Brown,* selected by Michael S. Harper (New York: Harper and Row, 1983), 71–72.

9. James D. Parks File, Faculty Files, Page Library; *News & Tribune* (Jefferson City, MO), 10 December 1969.

10. Thomas D. Pawley III, eulogy of Cecil A. Blue, 5 June 1983; Sterling Brown, Ar-

thur P. Davis, and Ulysses S. Lee, eds., *The Negro Caravan* (New York: Dryden Press, 1941), 74–86; Arthur P. Davis, "Ulysses Lee," *Dictionary of American Negro Biography*, ed. Rayford W. Logan and Michael Winston (New York: W. W. Norton, 1982).

11. Interview with Lorenzo J. Greene, 25 November 1981.

12. The author worked as Greene's research assistant during the late 1960s and early 1970s. For a concise and helpful biographical sketch of Lorenzo J. Greene, see Arvarh E. Strickland's "Introduction" to Lorenzo J. Greene, *Working with Carter G. Woodson, the Father of Black History: A Diary, 1928–1930*, ed. Arvarh E. Strickland (Baton Rouge: Louisiana State University Press, 1989), xvii–xxxii. For Greene's status among scholars of African American history, see Meier and Rudwick, *Black History and the Historical Profession, 1915–1980*, 79–83.

13. Lorenzo J. Greene, "The Black Experience in Missouri: A Personal View," in Lorenzo J. Greene, Gary R. Kremer, and Antonio F. Holland, *Missouri's Black Heritage* (St. Louis: Forum Press, 1980; rev. ed., Gary R. Kremer and Antonio F. Holland [Columbia: University of Missouri Press, 1993]), 3.

14. Lorenzo J. Greene spoke often to the author about the activities of this early debate club, the challenges it faced, and the successes it enjoyed. A copy of a letter dated 11 January 1934 prepared by Greene to be sent to potential debate team competitors outlines the year's proposed topics. The letter is signed by "Lorenzo J. Greene, Corresponding Secretary, Debating Committee." Copy of letter in possession of author.

15. For the Gaines and Bluford cases and their effect on education in Missouri, see Robert M. Sawyer, "The Gaines Case: Its Background and Influence on the University of Missouri and Lincoln University" (PhD diss., University of Missouri–Columbia, 1966); Armistead S. Pride File, Faculty Files, Page Library.

16. Interview with Thomas D. Pawley III, 8 May 1984.

17. Ibid.

18. Ibid. Although she taught dance and physical education, not drama, Myrtle Smith Livingston preceded both Teabeau and Pawley at Lincoln. Mrs. Livingston, who came to Lincoln in 1928, won third prize in a *Crisis* contest in 1926 for her play "For Unborn Children." Myrtle Smith Livingston File, Faculty Files, Page Library.

19. For Fuller's career at Lincoln, see Steven Houser, "O. Anderson Fuller, the First Black Doctor of Philosophy in Music in America, and His Development of the Music Education Curriculum at Lincoln University" (PhD diss., University of Missouri–Columbia, 1982).

20. Nancy Grant, "From Showboat to Symphony: A Study of Black Classical Musicians in St. Louis, 1920–1980," in Early, *Black Heartland*, vol. 1, no. 1 (1996), 14–25.

21. *Chicago Defender*, 2 December 1939.

22. *St. Louis Argus*, 27 November 1942; *Kansas City Call*, 4 December 1942.

23. *St. Louis Argus*, 24 January 1947.

24. Walter C. Daniel, "W. E. B. DuBois at Lincoln University: Founders' Day Address, 1941," *Missouri Historical Review* 74 (April 1980): 343–55.

25. Ibid., 352.

26. "Lincoln's Noted *Midwest Journal* Preserves Century of Black History," *Harambee* 1 (February 1972): 1–2.

27. August Meier to Gary R. Kremer, 23 September 1985, letter in possession of author.

28. *Midwest Journal* 1 (Winter 1948).

29. *Midwest Journal* 1 (Summer 1949): 25–26.

30. Shu-yi Yang, "Role of Students in China's Struggle," *Midwest Journal* 1 (Sum-

mer 1949): 89–94; W. E. B. DuBois, "The Freedom to Learn," *Midwest Journal* 1 (Winter 1949): 9–11.

31. Interview with Lorenzo J. Greene, 25 November 1981; *Midwest Journal* File, US Department of Justice, Washington, DC (copy of file in possession of author).

32. Herbert M. Hunter and Sameer Y. Abraham, eds., *Race, Class, and the World System: The Sociology of Oliver C. Cox* (New York: Monthly Review Press, 1987).

33. Oliver Cromwell Cox File, US Department of Justice, Washington, DC (copy in possession of author).

34. Program, "Lincoln University of Missouri Dedicates the Inman Page Library," 19–20 May 1950, Page Library File, Inman E. Page Library.

35. "LU Loses Two Staff Members," *The Clarion* [Lincoln University student newspaper], 15 May 1970, 1; 3 November 1972, 1.

36. Pawley interview, 13 December 1990.

Chapter 12
"Lake Placid: 'A Recreational Center for Colored People' in the Missouri Ozarks"

1. This essay originally appeared in the October 2000 issue of the *Missouri Historical Review* and is reprinted with the permission of the State Historical Society of Missouri. It was coauthored with Evan P. Orr, then an undergraduate student working with Gary R. Kremer in the William Woods University honors program.

2. "Contract for sale of land," in Case File No. 2479, Morgan County Circuit Court Records, April 1942 term, Morgan County Courthouse, Versailles, Missouri. This parcel of land included 271 acres in Morgan County and 75 acres in adjoining Benton County.

3. The story of segregation in Kansas City during this era is well told by Sherry Lamb Schirmer, "Landscape of Denial: Space, Status, and Gender in the Construction of Racial Perceptions, 1900–1958" (PhD diss., University of Kansas, Lawrence, 1995).

4. For more on the City Beautiful Movement, see William H. Wilson, *The City Beautiful Movement in Kansas City* (Columbia: University of Missouri Press, 1964), and William S. Worley, *J. C. Nichols and the Shaping of Kansas City: Innovation in Planned Residential Communities* (Columbia: University of Missouri Press, 1990).

5. For more on P. C. Turner, see Young and Young, *Your Kansas City and Mine* (Kansas City: privately published, 1950). Also helpful is a late-in-life interview with Turner in the *Kansas City Call*, 6 December 1963.

6. Young and Young, *Your Kansas City and Mine*, 58.

7. "Contract for sale of land."

8. Ibid.

9. Emma Jean Clark, interview by Gary Kremer and John Viessman, tape recording, 10 November 1999.

10. Regina Akers, "Welcoming Waters," *Kansas City Star Magazine*, 26 July 1992; Leonard Pryor, interviews by Kremer and Viessman, tape recordings, 3, 17 August, 1 September, 1 December 1999.

11. Robert H. Ferrell, *Truman and Pendergast* (Columbia: University of Missouri Press, 1999), 30.

12. Lawrence H. Larsen and Nancy J. Hulston, *Pendergast!* (Columbia: University of Missouri Press, 1997), 105. According to Dr. Carl Peterson, when Pendergast wanted to hide an associate who was having trouble with the law, he would ask Turn-

er to admit him as a patient to General Hospital No. 2. Carl Peterson, interview by Kremer and Viessman, tape recording, 17 August 1999. Pryor, interviews, 3, 17 August, 1 September 1999.

13. William J. Thompkins obituary, *Kansas City Call*, 11 August 1944.

14. Girard T. Bryant to Keith Turner, 23 June 1988, copy in possession of authors.

15. Young and Young, *Your Kansas City and Mine*, 104; *Kansas City Call*, 6 June 1941.

16. Pryor, interviews, 3, 17 August, 1 September, 1 December 1999.

17. Gary R. Kremer and Donald H. Ewalt, Jr., *Missouri's Black Historic Sites: A Preliminary Survey of the State* (Jefferson City: Missouri Department of Natural Resources, 1980), 18, 26.

18. Betty Wray Curnutt and Alice Wray Jones, interview by Kremer and Viessman, tape recording, 17 December 1999.

19. *Stover Tri-County Republican*, 21 May 1937.

20. Clark, interview. See also work papers filed with the WPA in Record Group 69.5, Records of WPA Projects, Morgan County, roll 856, National Archives, Washington, DC.

21. Young and Young, *Your Kansas City and Mine*, 97.

22. Bryant to Turner.

23. Mayme Hughes Rodgers, interviews by Kremer and Viessman, tape recordings, 12 December 1997, 22 September 1999; Pryor, interview, 17 August 1999.

24. William Henry Houston death certificate, Missouri Department of Health, Division of Vital Records, Jefferson City; *Kansas City Call*, 23 May 1941.

25. Barbara Pullam Thompson, interviews by Kremer and Viessman, tape recordings, 5 May, 11 June 1998.

26. Lake Placid Resort, Inc., incorporation papers, File No. 62981, Corporations Division, Office of the Secretary of State of Missouri, State Information Center, Jefferson City.

27. H. O. Cook, financial secretary, Lake Placid Lot Owners' Association, to Lake Placid Lot Owners, 30 September 1941; *Kansas City Call*, 19 June 1942; Lake Placid guest register, copy in possession of authors.

28. Case File No. 2479, Morgan County Circuit Court Records, April 1942 term.

29. Pryor, interviews, 3, 17 August, 1 September, 1 December 1999.

30. Ibid., 1 September 1999.

31. Ibid.

32. Andrew "Papa Jack" Jackson obituary, *St. Louis Post-Dispatch*, 13 April 1993. For information about the Ville see Gary R. Kremer and Donald H. Ewalt, Jr., "The Historian as Preservationist: A Missouri Case Study," *Public Historian* 3 (Fall 1981): 5–22.

33. John and Clarice Davis, interview by Kremer and Viessman, tape recording, 22 August 1999.

34. Vivian DeShields Rasberry, interview by Kremer and Viessman, tape recording, 13 August 1998.

35. All of the interviewees talked about Fourth of July celebrations. The most elaborate descriptions came from multiple interviews with Leonard Pryor, "July 4, 1953, at Lake Placid" (copy in possession of authors).

36. Clark, interview.

37. Alta Wray, interview by Kremer and Viessman, tape recording, 17 December 1999.

38. Curnutt and Jones, interview.

39. Peterson, interview.

40. *Kansas City Call*, 28 January–3 February 1966; Dr. Percy C. Turner, obituary, memorial service program, 23 January 1966 (copy in possession of authors).

41. Rodgers, interviews, 12 December 1997, 22 September 1999.

42. Evelyn Cooper, interview by Kremer and Viessman, tape recording, 19 January 2000.

43. Robert Wilson to Gary Kremer, e-mail, 17 January 2000.

44. Keith Turner and Miles Turner, interview by Kremer and Viessman, tape recording, 22 August 1999.

45. Craig Pryor, interview by Kremer and Viessman, tape recording, 18 January 2000.

46. Renee Pryor Newton, interview by Kremer and Viessman, tape recording, 12 January 2000.

Chapter 13
"William J. Thompkins: African American
Physician, Politician, and Publisher"

1. This essay originally appeared in the April 2007 issue of the *Missouri Historical Review* and is reprinted with the permission of the State Historical Society of Missouri.

2. Frank P. Walsh to Franklin D. Roosevelt, 22 September 1931, William J. Thompkins file, Collection PPF 8751, Franklin D. Roosevelt Papers, Franklin D. Roosevelt Library, Hyde Park, New York (hereafter cited as FDR Papers).

3. Ibid.; Franklin D. Mitchell, *Embattled Democracy: Missouri Democratic Politics, 1919–1932* (Columbia: University of Missouri Press, 1968), 191n8.

4. Helpful studies documenting the movement of African Americans from the Republican to the Democratic Party during the decades of the 1920s and 1930s include Larry H. Grothaus, "The Negro in Missouri Politics, 1890–1941" (PhD diss., University of Missouri–Columbia, 1970); Nancy J. Weiss, *Farewell to the Party of Lincoln: Black Politics in the Age of FDR* (Princeton, NJ: Princeton University Press, 1983); Dennis S. Nordin, *The New Deal's Black Congressman: A Life of Arthur Wergs Mitchell* (Columbia: University of Missouri Press, 1997).

5. *Tenth Census of the United States, 1880, Population Schedule*, "Cole County" (National Archives Microfilm Publication T9, roll 682), 40A.

6. *Beasley's Jefferson City Directory, for 1877–8* (Jefferson City, MO: Regan & Carter, 1877), 110, 112; *Sanborn Fire Insurance Maps of Missouri: Jefferson City* (New York: Sanborn, n.d.), 6–8.

7. William Rufus Jackson, *Missouri Democracy: A History of the Party and Its Representative Members, Past and Present* (Chicago: S. J. Clarke, 1935), 3:846.

8. "Lincoln Institute, Register for the Year Commencing Sept. 5, 1892 and ending June 1893, Inman E. Page, President," 124–25 (Ethnic Studies Center, Inman E. Page Library, Lincoln University, Jefferson City, MO). Curiously, this register identifies Thompkins's mother as being "Marion Thompkins," who, in reality, was the young man's father. *Thirtieth Annual Catalogue of Lincoln Institute*, 1900–1901 (Jefferson City, MO: Tribune, 1901), 37; Savage, *The History of Lincoln University*. The *Twelfth Census of the United States, 1900, Population Schedule*, "Cole County" (National Archives Microfilm Publication T623, roll 850), 99A, indicates that Thompkins was a "student" that year, living in the home of his grandmother Matilda Nelson.

9. *Thirty-first Annual Catalogue of Lincoln Institute, 1902–1903* (Jefferson City, MO: Republican, 1902), 32.

10. Jackson, *Missouri Democracy*, 3:846.

11. Thomas J. Ward, *Black Physicians in the Jim Crow South* (Fayetteville: University of Arkansas Press, 2003), 4–5, 18–19.

12. Marion Thompkins Ross, telephone interview by author, 10 March 2004; Ward, *Black Physicians*, 15.

13. Register of Physicians, vol. 2, State Board of Health Collection, Missouri State Archives, Jefferson City.

14. J. Edward Perry, *Forty Cords of Wood: Memoirs of a Medical Doctor* (Jefferson City, MO: Lincoln University, 1947), 140–41. Another reason that Thompkins may have gone to Kansas City is that his father, Marion, was living there by about 1890. He appears in Kansas City directories over the next two decades. Although Eliza Thompkins appears as a widow in the 1880 federal census, her husband, William's father, did not die until 26 November 1910. Marion's death certificate was signed by William (Marion Thompkins, death certificate, File No. 34432, Death Records, Missouri State Archives). Unfortunately, Marion Thompkins Ross was unable to shed any light on the apparent estrangement between her father's parents.

15. Walsh to Lane, 3 September 1913; Thompkins to Walsh, 6 October 1913, both in Frank P. Walsh Papers, Archives and Manuscript Division, The New York Public Library. The author is grateful to John McKerley for bringing these letters to his attention.

16. Charles E. Coulter, *"Take Up the Black Man's Burden": Kansas City's African American Communities, 1865–1939* (Columbia: University of Missouri Press, 2006), 210.

17. Ibid.; Perry, *Forty Cords of Wood*, 374.

18. R. E. L. Morris and Drake Watson to Woodrow Wilson, 18 January 1917, folder 1, William J. Thompkins Collection, Historical Society of Washington, DC.

19. Marion Thompkins Ross interview; Sherry Lamb Schirmer, *A City Divided: The Racial Landscape of Kansas City, 1900–1960* (Columbia: University of Missouri Press, 2002), 65; Grothaus, "Negro in Missouri Politics," 97.

20. *Kansas City Sun*, 22 February 1919.

21. Ibid., 1 March 1919.

22. Schirmer, *City Divided*, 163–64.

23. Ibid., 163; Thompkins to Lavan, n.d., Lincoln Collection, Missouri Valley Special Collections, Kansas City (MO) Public Library. This report is undated; articles about it appeared in the *Kansas City Times* and the *Kansas City Star* on 10 June 1926.

24. Thompkins to Lavan; *Fourteenth Census of the United States Taken in the Year 1920: Population* (Washington, DC: GPO, 1922), 2:53; *Fifteenth Census of the United States, 1930* (Washington, DC: GPO, 1931), vol. 3, pt. 1, p. 61.

25. Thompkins to Lavan; *Kansas City Call*, 10 June, 9 September 1927.

26. Coulter, *"Take Up the Black Man's Burden,"* 114; Schirmer, *City Divided*, 163.

27. Samuel O'Dell, "Blacks, the Democratic Party, and the Presidential Election of 1928: A Mild Rejoinder," *Phylon* 48 (Spring 1987): 6–7. See also Grothaus, "Negro in Missouri Politics," 121. In 1941 former Missouri legislator, congressman, and US senator Harry B. Hawes confirmed Thompkins's role on behalf of Democrats in the 1928 election when he wrote a letter to the doctor, commenting, "The only thing that interests me are recollections of the old days when you had charge of the Negro Division in the Smith campaign and I formed a high opinion of your ability." Hawes to Thompkins, 31 March 1941, folder 1, Thompkins Collection.

28. Unsigned letter (probably from Wilson's campaign manager, C. A. Leedy Jr.) to Thompkins, 20 June 1932, folder 573, Francis M. Wilson Papers, Western Historical

Manuscript Collection, University of Missouri–Columbia (hereafter cited as WHMC-Columbia).

29. Thompkins to Eleanor Roosevelt, 6 April 1935, Eleanor Roosevelt Collection, Series 70, FDR Papers.

30. *Kansas City American*, 14 July 1932.

31. Grothaus, "Negro in Missouri Politics," 135.

32. Thompkins to Howe, 19 November 1932, Series PPF 3634, FDR Papers; Nordin, *New Deal's Black Congressman*, 43. In 1934, Mitchell became the first African American to be elected to the US Congress as a Democrat.

33. Thompkins to Ralph F. Lozier, 8 May 1933, folder 1766, Ralph F. Lozier Papers, WHMC-Columbia.

34. Shannon to Farley, 8 May 1933; Cochran to Farley, 12 May 1933, both in Eleanor Roosevelt Collection, Series 100, FDR Papers.

35. Thompkins to Eleanor Roosevelt, 15 May 1933, ibid.

36. Dennis Nordin writes that African Americans who sought patronage positions in the wake of the 1932 Democratic victory were stymied by party leaders who refused to make any promises because they feared "a Southern backlash." Nordin concludes, "Making matters worse, nobody close to Roosevelt had even been courageous enough to thank the faithful minority workers properly." Nordin, *New Deal's Black Congressman*, 42.

37. Farley to Marvin H. Mcintyre, 14 March 1934; Jefferson S. Coage to FDR, 24 April 1934; Thompkins to FDR, 27 September 1934; Thompkins to Howe, 25 August 1934, all in Official File Collection (hereafter cited as OF), Series 51-c, FDR Papers.

38. Marion Thompkins Ross, interview by author, 14 February 2006.

39. Ibid.; William F. Dancy, interview by John Viessman and author, 17 October 2001.

40. Thompkins continued to serve on the Lincoln University board until 14 March 1939. Lloyd C. Stark to Thompkins, 14 March 1939, folder 1742, Lloyd Crow Stark Papers, WHMC-Columbia.

41. Thompkins to McIntyre, 16 November 1934, OF Collection, Series 51-c.

42. Harry H. Vaughan Oral History, 14, 16 January 1963, at www.trumanlibrary.org/oralhist/vaughanl.htm. See also Robert L. Sweeney Oral History, 12 December 1977, at www.trumanlibrary.org/oralhist/sweeneyr.htm.

43. Thompkins to McIntyre, 16 November, 25 September 1934, and Thompkins to Howe, 28 October 1934, OF Collection, Series 51-c.

44. Eleanor Roosevelt to Thompkins, 22 January 1935, Eleanor Roosevelt Collection, Series 100.

45. William J. Thompkins, "Goodwill Tour of Dr. William J. Thompkins through the Heart of the South Preaching the Doctrine of the New Deal," unpublished manuscript, 1935, OF Collection, Series 51-c.

46. Ibid. Thompkins included in his report on his trip what he referred to as "Extracts from the Southern Press" about his travels. According to Thompkins, this comment was reported in the *Mobile (AL) Press* on 1 March 1935.

47. Ibid.

48. Thompkins to FDR, 5 November 1935, OF Collection, Series 51-c.

49. Thompkins to Democratic National Committee, telegram, 22 February 1936, ibid.

50. H. C. McConnick to Jack Nichols, 25 February 1936, ibid.

51. Sam Battles to FDR, 29 February 1936, ibid.

52. Robert H. Ferrell, *Truman and Pendergast* (Columbia: University of Missouri Press, 1999), 86, 95–96.

53. Thompkins to FDR, Attention: General Watson, 23, 28, 29 October 1940, OF Collection, Series 51-c.

54. Thompkins to FDR, 5 November 1940, ibid.

55. Thompkins to Mcintyre, 26 June 1941, ibid.

56. Thomas Lee Green, "Black Cabinet Members in the Franklin Delano Roosevelt Administration" (PhD diss., University of Colorado, 1971), 207.

57. *Chicago (IL) Defender*, 12 June 1943.

58. Thompkins to Houghteling, 11 August 1943, C. Jasper Bell Papers, WHMC-Columbia.

59. FDR to Thompkins, 5 August 1944, OF Collection, Series 51-c; Marion Thompkins Ross interviews, 10 March 2004, 14 February 2006.

Chapter 14
"The Abraham Lincoln Legacy in Missouri"

1. This essay originally appeared in the January 2009 issue of the *Missouri Historical Review* and is reprinted with the permission of the State Historical Society of Missouri.

2. *Lincoln Clarion*, 20 May 1955, 1, 6.

3. William E. Parrish, *Turbulent Partnership: Missouri and the Union, 1861–1865* (Columbia: University of Missouri Press, 1963), 5–6; *Liberty Tribune*, 14 December 1860, 4; *Columbia Statesman*, 25 January 1861, 2.

4. The *Columbia Statesman* carried an extensive article on President Lincoln's effort to appeal to the border states on 8 August 1862, 1.

5. Parrish, *Turbulent Partnership*, 60–62.

6. *Jefferson City Missouri State Times*, 14 January 1865, 1.

7. Examples of different dates for emancipation celebrations can be gleaned from a variety of newspapers, including the *Columbia Missouri Statesman*, 30 December 1881, 3; *Jefferson City Daily Tribune*, 11 September 1892, 4; *Columbia Missourian*, 4 August 1926, 6; Sehon Williams, interview with author, 2 August 2006, Western Historical Manuscript Collection–Columbia (hereafter cited as WHMC-Columbia); Fielding Draffen, interview with author, 19 June 1997, Friends of Arrow Rock Archives, Arrow Rock, MO.

8. Fisk to Rosecrans, 31 May 1864, *The War of the Rebellion: A Compilation of the Official Records of the Union and Confederate Armies* (Washington, DC: GPO, 1880–1901), ser. 1, vol. 34, pt. 4, p. 193, http://cdl.library.cornell.edu/moa/moa_browse.html; Fisk to Saunders, 3 March 1865, ibid., vol. 48, pt. 1, p. 1078 (hereafter cited as *OR;* all references to series 1, giving volume number, part number, and page).

9. *Fayette Howard County Advertiser*, 15 January 1864, 2.

10. James M. McPherson, *The Negro's Civil War: How American Negroes Felt and Acted during the War for the Union* (New York: Pantheon Books, 1965), 169. The classic work on African American soldiers during the Civil War remains Dudley Taylor Cornish, *The Sable Arm: Negro Troops in the Union Army, 1861–1865* (New York: Longmans, Green, 1956).

11. "General Order for Colored Troops," *Fayette Howard County Advertiser*, 25 December 1863, 4. For an advertisement recruiting African American soldiers for "$100 Bounty and Pay Not Exceeding $300 to Loyal Owners," see *Columbia Missouri States-*

man, 29 July 1864, 4.

12. John W. Blassingame, "The Recruitment of Negro Troops in Missouri during the Civil War," *Missouri Historical Review* 58 (April 1964): 336.

13. Fisk to Barnes, 22 March 1865, *OR* 48.1.1239.

14. Minutes of meeting of Board of Aldermen, 18 August 1864, *Journal of Jefferson City City Council/Board of Aldermen Proceedings,* Record Book 2, 1859–1872, City of Jefferson, City Hall, Jefferson City, MO.

15. *Jefferson City Missouri State Times,* 14 January 1865.

16. Fisk to Yeatman, 25 March 1865, *OR* 48.1.1257.

17. *Ninth Census* (1870) (Washington, DC: GPO, 1872), 1:187, 188, 190, 193; *Tenth Census* (1880) (Washington, DC: GPO, 1883), 1:388–89. Lawrence O. Christensen makes this same point about Howard County in a recent essay, "Carr W. Pritchett and the Civil War Era in Glasgow and Fayette," *Missouri Historical Review* 103 (October 2008): 49.

18. Gary R. Kremer and Antonio F. Holland, *Missouri's Black Heritage,* rev. ed. (Columbia: University of Missouri Press, 1993), 112–13.

19. Data in this and the subsequent paragraph are compiled from an analysis of census figures available through Ancestry.com. *Eleventh Census* (1890) (Washington, DC: GPO, 1895), 1:539–40.

20. Ibid.

21. Gary R. Kremer and Cindy M. Mackey, "'Yours for the Race': The Life and Work of Josephine Silone Yates," *Missouri Historical Review* 90 (January 1996): 205, 211.

22. Gary R. Kremer and Lynn Morrow, "Pennytown: A Freedmen's Hamlet, 1871–1945," *Missouri Folklore Society Journal* 11–12 (1989–1990): 78.

23. Ibid.

24. W. E. B. DuBois, *Black Reconstruction in America* (New York: Atheneum, 1969), 234.

25. John Opie, "Homestead Act," in *The Oxford Companion to United States History,* ed. Paul S. Boyer (New York: Oxford University Press, 2001), 344.

26. The term "Exoduster" was used contemporaneously to refer to African Americans fleeing the South for Missouri and Kansas in the wake of the end of Reconstruction. These migrants identified with the ancient Jews who fled their captivity in Egypt for freedom in Israel.

27. Gary R. Kremer, "African Americans in the Rural Missouri Ozarks" (unpublished paper); Gary R. Kremer and Trina Philpot, "The Whitley Sisters Remember: Living with Segregation in Kansas City, Missouri," *Kawsmouth: A Journal of Regional History* 2 (Autumn 1999): 50–63.

28. Kremer, "African Americans in the Rural Missouri Ozarks."

29. Ibid.; *Lebanon Laclede County Sentinel,* 28 July 1905, 4.

30. Gary R. Kremer, "The Emergence of 'Morocco,' a Southeast Missouri Labor Village" (unpublished paper).

31. DuBois, *Black Reconstruction,* 234.

32. Kremer and Holland, *Missouri's Black Heritage,* 38.

33. W. Sherman Savage, "The Legal Provisions for Negro Schools in Missouri from 1865 to 1890," *Journal of Negro History* 16 (July 1931): 309–21.

34. Unless otherwise indicated, information on Lincoln schools in this essay was compiled by the author and historian Brett Rogers in a study completed over a four-year period for the Missouri State Office of Historic Preservation. This list of schools is more illustrative than exhaustive. Gary R. Kremer and Brett Rogers, "African

American Schools in Rural and Small Town Missouri," State Historic Preservation Office, Missouri Department of Natural Resources, Jefferson City, 1999–2003.

35. Fannie Marie Tolson, interview with author, 17 May 2000, Gary R. Kremer Papers, the State Historical Society of Missouri.

36. Susan Curtis, *Dancing to a Black Man's Tune: A Life of Scott Joplin* (Columbia: University of Missouri Press, 1994), 72.

37. Young and Young, *Your Kansas City and Mine, 1850–1950* (Kansas City: 1950), 21, 156.

38. Savage, *The History of Lincoln University*, 1–2.

39. Ibid., 2–3.

40. Larry H. Grothaus, "The Negro in Missouri Politics, 1890–1941" (PhD diss., University of Missouri–Columbia, 1970); Gary R. Kremer, "William J. Thompkins: African American Physician, Politician, and Publisher," *Missouri Historical Review* 101 (April 2007): 168–82.

41. Gary R. Kremer, "Lincoln University: Black Culture Mecca of the Midwest, 1921–1955," in *Black Heartland: African American Life, the Middle West, and the Meaning of American Regionalism,* ed. Gerald Early, African and Afro-American Studies Occasional Papers Series, vol. 1, no. 2 (St. Louis, MO: Washington University, 1997), 37–49; Savage, *The History of Lincoln University,* 168–69.

42. Daniel T. Kelleher, "The Case of Lloyd Lionel Gaines: The Demise of the Separate but Equal Doctrine," *Journal of Negro History* 56 (October 1971): 262–71; Robert McLaren Sawyer, "The Gaines Case: Its Background and Influence on the University of Missouri and Lincoln University, 1936–1950" (PhD diss., University of Missouri–Columbia, 1966).

43. Thomas D. Pawley III, interview with author, 11 January 2006, WHMC-Columbia.

Index

IAbbott, Flora, 79
Adams, Mary Ann, 35
Adams, Pearl, 111
African American exodus, 80, 205, 206
African American population, 77, 96,
    98, 131, 175, 202, 204
African Methodist Episcopal Church,
    Arrow Rock, Missouri, 101
African Methodist Episcopal Church,
    Neosho, Missouri, 79
Afro-American Council, Chicago,
    Illinois, 52
Allen, Benjamin F., 50, 51
Ancient Free and Accepted Prince
    Hall Masons, 102
Anthony, Oscar, 1
Arrow Rock, Missouri, 12, 95–112
Atlanta Exposition, 1895, 83

Banks, John T., 109
Baptist Youth Training Union
    (BYTU), 120
Barnes, J. W., 203
Bartlett, Herschel, 84
Bartlett Agricultural and Industrial
    School, 83–90. See also Dalton
    Vocational School
Bassett, Ebenezer Don Carlos, 22
Bate, Langston Fairchild, 160
Battle, Eliot F., 93
Battle of Newtonia, 71, 72
Battles, Sam, 197
Beal, Rev. C. R., 25
Bell, Senator John, 200
Benton, Thomas Hart, 200, 207, 212

Berlin, Ira, 12, 112
Bethel African Methodist Episcopal
    Church, Kansas City, Missouri,
    133, 137
Billingsley, Andrew, 12, 110
Birks, Lella Jo, 119
Black families, 32, 63
Black Folks Day, 38
Black Independence Day, 39
Blackman, Reed J., 171, 173, 179
Blackwater Lodge of the United
    Brothers of Friendship, Napton,
    Missouri, 36
Blackwater River, 34
Blantyre, Steve, 177, 178
Blue, Cecil Archibald, 160–64, 167,
    170
Blue River, Kansas City, Missouri,
    114, 115, 118, 128
Bluford, Lucile, 164, 167
Blumer, Herbert, 104
Blyden, Edward W., 45
Boonslick, 97, 201
Boston Woman's Era Club, 46
Bowles, Ethel, 144, 146–56
Breckenridge, John C., 71, 201
Bingham's Grove, 103
Briscoe, Sherman, 198
Brooks, W. P., 59
Brotherhood of Sleeping Car Porters,
    198
Brown, Dwight H., 178
Brown, Forbes, 72
Brown, Frank, 38
Brown, John, 101

Brown, John, abolitionist, 18;
  raid of, 18
Brown, Rena, 108
Brown, Sterling, 160, 163, 170
Brown, Thomas, 101
Brown, William, 33, 37
Brown Lodge No. 22, 102
Bruce, Blanche K., 48, 175
Bruce, Josephine, 48
Bruce, Nathaniel C., 8, 82–94
Bruce Watkins Memorial Highway,
  141
Bryant, Girard T., 175, 177, 178, 180
Bryant School, Kansas City, Missouri,
  134
Bullock, Henry, 18
Bullock, Yvonne Brooks, 128, 129
Burge, Mary, 111
Busch, Adolphus I, 84
Butler, Evaline, 30
Butler, John W., 91

C. W. Wright Lodge No. 29, 36
Call, The (Kansas City), 15, 120, 123,
  192
Capital City Lodge No. 9, 61
Carrion, W. S., 65
Carroll, Jackson, 70
Carter, Eva, 195
Carver, George Washington, 8, 9,
  68–81, 135, 196
Carver, James, 69, 70, 72, 74–76
Carver, Mary, 69, 70, 72
Carver, Moses, 69, 70, 72, 75, 78
Carver, Susan, 69, 70, 72, 75, 78
Case, John F., 87, 89
Cherokee freedmen, 62
Chicago Women's Club, 48
Chillicothe Home for White Girls, 145
Christianization, 57
City Beautiful Movement, 171
City Hospital Number 2, Kansas City,
  Missouri, 140, 196
Clapp, Dr. Phillip Greely, 165
Clark, Bennett Champ, 174, 194

Clark, Emma Jean, 176, 181
Clark-Lewis, Elizabeth, 99
Clay, Andrew, 89
Cochran, John J., 193
Coleman, Ione, 183
Colored Farm Bureau, 89
Colored Women's League, 42
Community Committee for Social
  Action of Greater Kansas City, 141
Compromise of 1877, 80
Conway, Thelma Van Buren, 109
Cook, H. O. and Myrtle, 175
Cooper, Anna Julia, 52
Cooper, Evelyn, 183
Cooper, Warren, 181
Cooper's Store, Stover, Missouri, 181,
  183
Coppin, Fannie Jackson, 43
Couch, J. W. and Laura, 114
Cox, Henry L., 134
Cox, Oliver Cromwell, 169
Craven, Dora Horn, 127
Crispus Attucks School, Kansas City,
  Missouri, 114
Crogman, Elizabeth Bruce, 136
Crossland, J. R. A., 65

Dalton, George D., 84
Dalton Vocational School, 8, 83–85,
  89, 91–94. *See also* Bartlett
  Agricultural and Industrial School
Dancy, William, 195
Daniel, Walter, 170
Daniel's lumberyard, Marshall,
  Missouri, 36
Daughters of Bethel, The, 134
Davis, Arthur P., 163
Davis, Clarice Dreer, 180
Del Ray Gardens, 124
Denton, John and Sallie, 131, 137, 140
Dickey, Michael, 95
Douglas, Stephen A., 71, 200
Douglas, T. R., 84
Douglass, Frederick, 49, 63, 70, 175,
  194

Douglass, Joseph, 49
Dowdy, William, 160
Draffen, Fielding, 107, 202
Dreer, Herman, 180
Drew, H. L., 90
DuBois, W. E. B., 1, 16, 47, 49, 77, 83, 99, 159, 167, 169, 190, 205, 206
Dunbar, Paul Lawrence, 121
Dunbar High School, Washington, D.C., 160, 163, 164
Dunbar School, Kansas City, Missouri, 122, 126
Duncanson, Robert S., 162
Dyer, Leonidas C., 195

Education, African American, 19–27, 45, 76–80, 82, 83, 100, 146, 159, 207
Educators, African American, 19–27, 45, 54–67, 83, 100
Edwards, Carl, 109
Edwards, Lewis, 103
1860 Presidential Election, 200
Eldridge, Alfred, 206
Eldridge, Missouri, 206
Elliff, Joseph D., 84
Emancipation Proclamation, 18, 97, 98, 100, 201, 202, 206
Evans, Carlis, 177
Evans, Mary, 127
Ewing, John, 84

Fairview Colored Baptist Church, Arrow Rock, Missouri, 100
Falls, Robert, 101
Farley, James A., 193, 194
Finley, Betty Banks, 109
Finley, Mrs. J. B., 37
Finnel, Isaac, 103
First Nebraska Regiment, 18
Fisk, General Clinton B., 97, 202, 203
Fletcher, Governor Thomas C., 21, 210
Florence Home for Negro Girls, Kansas City, Missouri, 136

Florida Special, The, 196
Foster, Beverly R., 91, 92
Foster, Richard B., 7, 17–27, 210
Franklin, Chester, 16, 192
Fraternal organizations, 12, 36, 55, 101, 103, 111
Frazier, E. Franklin, 55, 56
Freeman, The, (Indianapolis), 50, 52
Freedmen, 29, 57, 58, 95, 98
Freedmen's Bureau, 19, 25
Freedmen's Hamlet, 30, 39
Free Will Baptist Church, Arrow Rock, Missouri, 110
Free Will Baptist Church, Pennytown, Missouri, 36, 38, 39
Fremont, General John C., 201
Frost, Stephen, 79, 80
Fuller, O. Anderson, 165

Gaines, Lloyd, 164, 167
Gaines v. Missouri, 211
Gardner, Frederick D., 88, 217
Garth, Mary, 116, 117, 127
Gatewood, Willard, 42
Gays, The, 125
General Hospital No. 2, Kansas City, Missouri, 171, 174, 182, 188
Gilbert, Rev. A. A., 120
Gilbert Memorial AME Church, Kansas City, Missouri, 120
Gillespie, Rosa Mae, 117, 123
Gillum, Gertrude, 115, 118, 123, 126, 127
Girl Reserves, 135, 136
Goins, Annie C., 121
Goodwin, Eva, 75
Gorman, Lee, 101
Grand United Order of Odd Fellows of America Lodge No. 3201, 103, 104
Grant, James, 70
Great Depression, 138, 139, 171, 192
Great Migration, 130, 131, 136, 191
Green, Dick, 31
Green, Harrison, 100, 103

Greene, Dr. Lorenzo Johnston, 2–7, 163, 164, 167, 168, 170
Green Grove Baptist Church, Kansas City, Missouri, 120
Green Grove School, Leeds, Missouri, 121
Green Valley Methodist Church, Pennytown, Missouri, 36–38
Grotjan, Donald, 94
Gutman, Herbert, 32
Guy, G. W., 59, 60

Habernal, Teresa, 112
Haggin, John, 30
Hall, Sue, 112
Hall, Dr. Tom, 35, 37
Hall Ground, 37
Hardee, Cary, 159
Hartville, Missouri, 131
Hayes, Rutherford B., 80
Heariold, F. C., 91
Hennings Jr., Thomas C., 195
Herriford, Joe E., 60
Hickman, James I., 202
Hill, Newton, 101
Holman, M. Carl, 167, 170
Holmes, Rev. D. A., 141
Holt, Nicholas, 76
Holt, Rackham, 74
Home remedies, 35, 78
Homestead Act, 206
Hoover, Herbert, 186, 192, 193
Houghteling, James L., 199
Household of Ruth, 104
Houston, William, 177
Howard, Clarence H., 86
Howard Freedmen's Hospital, 187
Howard Medical School, 187
Howe, Louis M., 193, 194
Hubley, Easter, 117
Hughes, Langston, 166, 170
Hughes, Leonard and Eva, 177
Hughes, Roland L., 94
Hughes, Rosia, 94
Hurt, R. Douglas, 95

Huston Tavern, Arrow Rock, Missouri, 107
Hutchinson, Liza, 104

Industrialization, 142
Influenza Epidemic, 1918–1919, 35
Institute for Colored Youth, 43
Ittner, William B., 84

Jacks, John W., 47
Jackson, Andrew S., 180
Jackson, Claiborne Fox, 70, 71, 207
Jackson, J. B., 30
Jackson, James, 32
Jackson, Jim, 203
Jackson, Lawrence, 127
Jackson, Nellie, 37, 38
James, W. K., 84, 89
Jason, W. B., 92, 139
Jett, Jeffry, 139
Jim Crow Era, 111, 113, 179, 184, 190, 206, 211
Johnson, Carl, 179
Johnson, Dorothy, 136
Jones, Alice Wray, 176
Jones, Charles, 117
Jones, Victoria, 93
Joplin, Scott, 50
Josephine Silone Yates Art Club, Sedalia, Missouri, 49
Josephine Silone Yates Club, Clayton, Missouri, 49
Journal of Negro History, 167
Juvenile Justice System, Missouri, 143

Kahler, Denzil, 94
Kansas City American, 15, 174, 192, 196
Kansas City Health Department, 190
Kansas City Monarchs, 138
Kansas City Municipal Farm, 126
Kansas City Urban League, 136
Kansas City Women's League, 46
Kearns, Bill, 109
Kelley, Robin D. G., 101

Kemper, W. T., 192, 194
Kessler, George, 171
Krekel, Arnold, 210

Lake City Arsenal, 128
Lake Placid, Missouri, 14, 171–84
Lake Placid Dam, 175, 176
Lake Placid Lot Owners' Association, 178, 181, 183
Lake Placid Resort, 178, 179
Lane, Franklin K., 188
Lavan, Dr. John, 191
Lawrence, C. L. , Sr., 32
Lawrence, Stanley, 37
Lee, Charles A., 90
Lee, Ulysses S., 163
Leeds, Missouri, 13, 113–29
Leeds Farm, 126
Lewis, Daniel, 30
Lewis, Edward S., 104
Lewis, Dr. Joe Houston, 177
Lewis, Penelope, 39
Lewis, Rev. Richard, 36
Lewis, William E., 32
Liberty Park, Kansas City, Missouri, 122, 123
Liberty Tavern, Kansas City, Missouri, 123, 127
Lincoln, Abraham, 70, 186, 200–212
Lincoln, C. Eric, 110
Lincoln High School, Kansas City, Missouri, 126, 134
Lincoln Theatre, Kansas City, Missouri, 120, 137
Lincoln University, Jefferson City, Missouri , 11, 15, 18, 23, 25, 26, 42–44, 50, 139, 145, 158–70, 174, 187, 210
Little Dixie, 95, 110
Littrell, Felby, 89
Litwack, Leon, 9, 29
Logan, Rayford W., 28
Louis, Joe, 125, 197
Lyon, Nathaniel, 71

M Street High School, Washington, D.C., 52
M. W. Grand Lodge, 62
Madison, Dr. W. H., 35
Malone, Dolly Mosby, 115, 121, 125–27
Maple, Denzil, 118
Martin, Thomas and Mariah, 101
Masonic Home, 60–62, 64, 65
Matthews, Col. J. E., 150
McCormick, Rev. Thomas, 117, 127
McGilton, Rachel, 99
McIntyre, Marvin Hunter, 195, 198
Merry, David, 35
Midwest Journal, 167, 168
Military Institute, Lexington, Missouri, 26
Minister Resident and Consul General, Liberia, 57
Missouri Corn Growers' Association, 84
Missouri Equal Rights League, 58
Missouri Farmers' Association, 40
Missouri Industrial Home for Negro Girls, Tipton, Missouri, 10, 11, 142–57
Missouri-Mid-Western States Negro Farmers' and Farm Women's Conference, 86-87
Missouri Negro Industrial Commission, 88, 90
Missouri Ozarks, 131, 172, 178, 184, 205, 206
Missouri Valley College, 110
Mitchell, Arthur Wergs, 193
Moberly School Board, 90
Monrovia, Liberia, 58
Morocco, Missouri, 206
Morris, R. E. L., 189
Mosely, W. G., 92
Most Worshipful Grand Lodge of Missouri, 59, 60, 62, 67, 104
Mountain, Elsie, 135
Muehlebach Stadium, Kansas City, Missouri, 138

Mumford, Frederick B., 89
Muraskin, William A., 55, 59, 102
Murray, Matthew S., 174

NAACP, Marshall, Missouri, 38
Nagel, Charles, 84
Napier, Jess, 109
Napton, William Barclay, 96, 98
Natchez Seminary, Natchez,
    Mississippi, 43
National Association of Colored
    Women, 42, 47, 175
National Colored Democratic
    Association, 175, 192
National Federation of Afro-
    American Women, 42
National Negro Constitution League
    of America, 190
National Youth Administration, 139
Negro Central League, 190
Negro Democratic Organization, The,
    144
Nelson, W. L., 89
Neosho, Missouri, 77, 78
New Deal Program, 163, 194, 196, 211
Newton, Renee Pryor, 184
Newton County, Missouri, 70–72
Nichols, Hortense, 110
Nicholson, Hazel, 120, 124

Oberlin College, 55, 56
Ogden, Peter, 103
Oklahoma Territory, 57
Olive Branch, 51, 52
Over East restaurant, Arrow Rock,
    Missouri, 109
Owens, Jessie, 198

Page, Inman E., 43, 44, 188
Panama-Pacific International
    Exposition, San Francisco, 86
Park, Guy E., 144
Parker, Earl, 109
Parker, Lester, 109
Parker, Minnie J., 109

Parker, Thomas A., 210
Parks, James Dallas, 162
Parrish, E. M., 91, 93
Paseo Baptist Church, Kansas City,
    Missouri, 141
Payne, Felix, Jr., 195
Payne, Felix, Sr., 141, 191, 195
Payne, W. H., 25
Pawley III, Thomas D., 164, 165, 169,
    170
Pearson, Elizabeth, 100
Pearson, Mary Lou, 110
Pearson, William, 65
Pelham, J. H., 61
Pendergast, Tom, 15, 127, 128, 174,
    175, 191–93
Penny, Joseph, 29, 30, 205
Pennytown, Missouri, 28–40, 205
People's Finance Company, 178
Perry, Dr. J. Edward, 181, 188, 189
Perry, Ruth Wilson Banks, 111
Peterson, Dr. Carl, 182
Phoenix Lodge No. 78, St. Louis, 66
Phyllis Wheatley Club, Buffalo, New
    York, 48
Pilgrim's Rest Church, Kansas City,
    Missouri, 120
Populism, 142
Pratt and Whitney, 128
Price, Sterling, 71
Price, William L., 97
Pride, Armistead S., 164
Prince Hall Freemasonry, 55, 58–60,
    102
Progressives, 142
Pryor, Craig, 184
Pryor, Eulah, 133, 140
Pryor, Leonard, 179
Pullam, Arthur "Chic," 177, 178
Pullam, Richard, 178

R. T. Coles Junior Vocational High
    School, 134
Radical Republicans, 56, 57, 100, 201
Railey, Edward, 30

Rainey, T. C., 98, 111
Randolph, A. Philip, 198
Rasberry, Vivian DeShields, 180
Ray, Rev. Kenneth E., 115, 120, 122
Reconstruction (1865–1877), 18–27
Rector, Sarah, 124
Reedy, Sidney J., 167
Reeve, John Bunyan, 43
Richardson, Clement, 90
Richardson, Darie and Myrtle, 127
Richardson, Isola, 127
Ritter, Archbishop Joseph, 2
Robinson, Charles L., 44
Robinson, Nelson, 101
Robinson, Reginald S., 93
Robinson, Ruby, 119
Rodgers, Mayme Hughes, 177, 182
Rogers High School, Newport, Rhode
    Island, 43
Roosevelt, Eleanor, 192, 194, 196
Roosevelt, Franklin Delano, 139, 171,
    173, 175, 186, 192, 193, 195–99,
    211
Rosecrans, Major General William,
    202
Ross, Marion Thompkins, 187, 189,
    199
Ross, Whitfield, 121
Rothman, David, 151
Ruffin, Josephine St. Pierre, 42, 47

Sable Arm, The, 202
Salem, Dorothy, 47
Saline County, Missouri, 12, 28, 29,
    31, 36, 38, 96, 97
Salt Fork Township, Saline County,
    Missouri, 31
Sandburg, Carl, 166
Sanders, Thomas, 65
Sappington, William B., 101
Savage, Roena, 166
Savage, W. Sherman, 44, 160, 166
Schools, African American, 19–27, 79,
    114, 159, 207, 208

Separate but equal doctrine, 164
Shannon, Elias D., 36
Shannon, Joseph B., 193
Shannon's Woods, 34, 37
Shelby, Elizabeth, 144
Silone, Alexander, 42
Silone, Parthenia Reeve, 42
Simmons, Dr. S. P., 35
Simpson College, 68
Sisters of Mysterious Ten, 33, 36
Sixty-fifth United States Colored
    Infantry, 18, 210
Sixty-second United States Colored
    Infantry, 18, 24, 210
Slavery: in Newton County, Missouri,
    69–72; in Saline County, Missouri,
    96–98
Smith, Al, 192
Smith, Henry M., 44
Smith, Vivienne Starks, 118
Smith-for-President Colored League,
    192
Snell, Ketchum E., 175, 176, 178, 181,
    182
Sojourner, J. M., 171–74, 178, 179, 184
Sojourner, Josephine Abbie, 178
Sojourner Press, 171
Soldiers, African American, 136, 203,
    211
Spears, Albert, 100
Spears, Francis, 34, 37
Spears, Willa, 34
St. Pierre Ruffin, Josephine, 42
Stark, Lloyd C., 197
State Inspector of Negro Schools,
    90–92
State Superintendent of Schools, 19
State Teachers' Association, St. Louis,
    19
Steward, Stephen, 101
Sumner High School, 180
Switzler, Frank, 99
Swope, Thomas Hunton, 171
Swope Park, Kansas City, Missouri,
    171, 172

Tandy, Charleton H., 55
Taylor, Bessie, 121
Taylor, Elizabeth, 104
Teabeau, Hazel McDaniel, 165
Terrell, Mary Church, 42, 47
Thomlea School, Pennytown, Missouri, 38
Thompkins, Helen, 194
Thompkins, Jessie, 194
Thompkins, Marion and Eliza, 186
Thompkins, Dr. William J., 15, 92, 174, 175, 185–99
Thompson, Barbara Pullam, 137, 138, 177, 178
Tippen, James, 99
Tippen, Mollie, 99
Todd, Reverend Will, 107
Travelers, The, 180
Trigg, Cyrus, 27
Trigg, John Thomas, 100
Trotter, Monroe, 175
True Blue Lodge, St. Louis, Missouri, 65
Truman, Harry S., 174, 175, 195, 197, 199
Tuberculosis, 190
Turner, Dr. Keith, 183
Turner, James Milton, 7, 8, 22, 54–67, 99, 100, 210
Turner, Maxine, 179
Turner, Mayme, 178, 182
Turner, Dr. Percy C., 15, 140, 171–74, 178–84
Tuskegee Institute, 44, 45, 78, 82, 83
Twin Citian Club, 140
Tyre, James, 101
Tyrus, John, 102

United Brothers of Friendship, 36

Van Buren, William Huston, 109
Vaughan, Harry H., 195
Vaughn, George L., 67
Vine Street Corridor, 114
Vocational training, 135, 146, 159

Walker, Clara Horne, 129
Walsh, Frank P., 186, 188
Washington, Booker T., 9, 45, 63, 82, 146
Washington, Margaret Murray, 48, 49
Watermelon Hill, 172
Watkins, Andrew, 77
Watkins, Mariah, 77–79
Watson, Drake, 189
Watson, General Edwin M., 197
Watson, Percy, 36
Weaver, Frederick S., 198
Webb, Dr., 35
Webster, Dr. Thomas A., 136
Wells-Barnett, Ida B., 42, 48
Wendell Phillips School, Kansas City, Missouri, 45, 134
Western Exchange Bank, 95
Wheatley-Provident Hospital, Kansas City, Missouri, 140, 181, 182
Wheeler, Ada, 37
Whiskers Band, 181
White, Robert, 129
White, W. T., 121
Whitley, Frank and Opal, 131, 132
Whitley, Geneva, 13, 130–41
Whitley, Gertrude, 13, 130–41
Whitley, Irene, 13, 130–41
Whittie's restaurant, Arrow Rock, Missouri, 109
Widow's Son Lodge, St. Louis, Missouri, 59–62, 65
Wiest, Dr. C. A., 171, 173, 179
Wiggins, Roland, 92
Wilhelm, Henry S., 100
Wilkerson Lodge, 65
Wilkins, Roy, 90
William Henry Lodge No. 45, Platte City, Missouri, 65
Williams, Bishop Marvin H., 106–8
Willkie, Wendell, 197
Wilson, Francis M., 192
Wilson, Paul L. and Dorris D., 183
Wilson, Robert, 183
Wilson, Woodrow, 189

Wilson, Yvonne Starks, 125
Winfrey, Eunice Kenoly, 206
Wolters, Raymond, 160
Women's Congress, Chicago, Illinois, 52
Women's Era, 46
Women's League of Kansas City, 46
Woods, Mary, 126
Woodson, Carter G., 17, 18, 163
Woodward, Dr. Calvin N., 84
Works Progress Administration , 128, 173–76
World War I (1914–1918), 190
Wray, Alice and Betty, 181, 182

Wray, Alta, 181
Wray, Jodie , 176, 181
Wright, Charley, 103
Wyatt, William, 180
Wyeth, Huston, 86

Yates, Josephine Silone, 11, 41–53
Yates, Josephine Silone, Jr. , 45
Yates, William Blyden, 45
Yates, William W., 45
Yates Literary and Art Club, Louisiana, Missouri, 49
Young, Nathan B., 11, 89, 159, 160
YWCA, Kansas City, Missouri, 135